The
GODFATHER
was a
GIRL

EAMON EVANS

hardie grant books

MELBOURNE • LONDON

Published in 2011 by Hardie Grant Books

Hardie Grant Books (Australia)
Ground Floor, Building 1
658 Church St
Richmind, Victoria 3121
www.hardiegrant.com.au

Hardie Grant Books (UK)
Dudley House, North Suite
34–35 Southampton Street
London WC2E 7HF
www.hardiegrant.co.uk

National Library of Australia Cataloguing-in-Publication entry

Evans, Eamon.
  The godfather was a girl : the real-life people who inspired
  famous characters / Eamon Evans.
  ISBN: 9781740669894 (pbk.)
  Subjects: Influence (Literary, artistic, etc.)
821.7

Cover and text design by Josh Durham, Design by Committee
Typesetting by Kirby Jones
Typeset in Sabon 11.5/16pt
Colour reproduction by Splitting Image Colour Studio

Printed and bound in Australia by Griffin Press

To Henry and Eliza

INTRODUCTION

'Originality,' says Voltaire, 'is nothing but judicious imitation'. Something old dressed up as something new, with a different backstory and more modish name.

'That is correct,' says Eamon Evans (no doubt to Voltaire's relief). When a would-be writer sits down at their desk, inspiration so often simply fails to strike. They might scratch their head for a bit: nothing. Then stare at the wall for a while … even less. Whether they've worked with a stone and a chisel, a quill and a parchment, or the very latest in fancy-pants iPads, anyone who has ever tried to write fiction has known what it is to write nothing at all.

Inspiration, however, might just be *behind* the wall. On the toilet, perhaps, or mowing the lawn. It could be hiding in a history book, nestling in a newspaper or teaching chemistry at your children's school.

Whether or not life imitates art, art very often imitates life. Behind many a fictional character lurks a person who really lived – someone who, simply by existing, inspired a writer to create that character, equipped them with a certain quality or placed them in a particular plight.

We all know that *Seinfield*'s Kramer and George were drawn from real people, but so too were Sherlock Holmes and Jughead Jones, Ali G and Mick Dundee. There's a real Mr Burns and a real Mr Big. Harry really did meet Sally and Will really does know Grace. Even Jaws, Moby Dick and Winnie the Pooh were based on an actual shark, an authentic whale and, you guessed it, a real live bear.

To take almost 400 examples, you first need to buy this book. The real Godfather, you will discover, was actually a mother, the real Lady Macbeth actually quite nice. Anne of Green Gables was inspired by a chorus girl and Big Brother was based on a businessman. King Kong started out a lizard and Chewbacca began life as a dog.

In short, you're in for some nasty shocks. Find a comfy chair to feel faint in, and say farewell to your inner child. This is real life.

(the real) Eamon Evans

ACKNOWLEDGEMENTS

Many thanks to Sharon Mullins, Rose Michael and Brooke Clark for their eagle-eyed editing and Cheryl McGrath for her patient picture hunting.

Thank you to Jenny, Mum, Dad and Caitlin for everything else.

FOREWORD

I love this book.

That was the initial foreword I wrote and submitted for Eamon Evans's enlightening new book, *The Godfather Was a Girl and Blanche DuBois was a Guy*. After the publisher wrote back a rather strongly worded email requesting something more substantial from me, I quickly realised they wanted a foreword and not simply four words.

Having never been afforded the privilege of such a task, I initially struggled. After much deliberation and soul-searching, I finally dismissed the idea of getting someone to ghostwrite it, and found a helping hand in Eamon's introduction, where he reminds us that inspiration can come from anywhere. I read on.

Upon completion of the book, I quickly found the motivation to write the foreword. The driving force behind a foreword coming from the book itself? Who knew?!

And so here is my foreword: skip this silly little page and GET STRAIGHT TO READING THE BOOK. Why waste time with this insignificant and irrelevant part of the book when you could be discovering the story of who JD from Scrubs was based on?

If only we had more crusaders like Eamon Evans out there discovering and collecting the 'real-life tales of fictional characters' instead of being forced to endure our daily dose of 'fictional tales of real-life characters'. Quite simply, I wish I were more like Eamon. He has produced a book that enlightens and entertains. I have delivered a foreword that does nothing but delay the enjoyment of the fascinating and interesting stories Eamon has compiled.

Eamon Evans makes me want to be a better man. Not just a better man, a man with an intriguing and amazing real-life story that could be the inspiration for a hugely famous fictional character. This book makes me realise I am not.

From Keyser Soze to Little Jack Horner, from Don Draper to Nacho Libre – the true characters and stories of these icons of popular culture are yours to delightfully discover.

If it weren't for this book, the true stories of Radar O'Reilly, Krusty the Clown, Dirk Diggler, Indiana Jones, Andy Dufresne and Ron Burgundy would go forever untold.

To Eamon I say congratulations. To you the reader I say enjoy. This is the book I wish was around when I was growing up because then I would have read at least one.

I love this book.

Sam Pang

P.S. The author quite humbly failed to include his own extraordinary and compelling tale so I give it to you now: Eamon Evans, with his trademark blend of youthful authority, alliterative name and elderly naivety, was the inspiration for the character of Benjamin Button.

CONTENTS

Chapter 1
Alpha males

ROCKY BALBOA

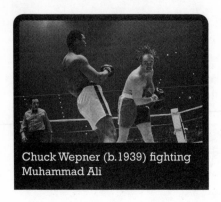

Chuck Wepner (b.1939) fighting Muhammad Ali

There's a lot to be said for never giving up – but none of it is positive.

Nicknamed 'the Bayonne bleeder' because of his tendency to bleed on spectators, Chuck Wepner clocked up fourteen losses and 300 stitches throughout a less-than-stellar boxing career. 'I was always too stubborn to give up the fight,' says the self-proclaimed 'tough guy with a big heart'.

In 1975, Mr Never-Say-Die got his reward: a great opportunity to die at the hands of Muhammad Ali. Just like Apollo Creed in *Rocky*, the champ was looking for an easy match but, remarkably, didn't get one. Instead, the balding, thirty-five-year-old journeyman lasted fifteen painful rounds (before staggering off with a broken nose to receive another twenty-three stitches). 'There's not another human being in the world that can go fifteen rounds like that,' commented an admiring Ali.

He was wrong, of course. Rocky Balboa went many rounds like that – defeating many big men with the help of a big heart, some 80s hits and a few inspirational training montages. The character's career began the night of the Wepner fight, which *Rocky*'s creator Sylvester Stallone watched on TV. 'It wasn't at all regarded as a serious battle. But as the fight progressed, this miracle unfolded. He hung in there. People went absolutely crazy … We had witnessed an incredible triumph of the human spirit and we loved it. That night, Rocky Balboa was born.'

The real Rocky's later career was marginally less triumphant. Retiring a few years after the fight, Wepner went on to try his hand at wrestling (losing to Andre the Giant), memoir writing (the still-unpublished 'Toe to toe with any foe'), and cocaine snorting (he was jailed 1986–88). These days he works at a bottle shop.

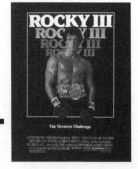

Rocky premiered in 1976. The movie and its five sequels were written by, and starred, Sylvester Stallone

BULL DURHAM'S NUKE LALOOSH

Steve Dalkowski (b.1939)

Strange but true: there's baseball in Jane Austen. Catherine, the heroine of *Northanger Abbey*, likes 'cricket, baseball and riding on horseback' – proving that the game was played in England long before being 'invented' in the States.

Less strange but also true: there's baseball in *Bull Durham*. Kevin Costner's breakout movie (was there ever a sadder phrase?) sees him play a mediocre veteran of the minor leagues – a player blessed with wisdom but not much in the way of talent. In stark contrast to Kevin's Bull Durham is Tim Robbins's Nuke LaLoosh, a wayward young pitcher with a golden arm and a brain mostly made of brick. The film sees Bull take Nuke under his wing, teaching the hard-partying hot shot to revere the game and the rest of us to not rent baseball movies.

Writer/director Ron Shelton can be forgiven for making them, though: he played the game for many years. His manager was one Joe Altobelli, a former mentor of a minor league legend named Steve Dalkowski. 'Joe … would always tell me "Dalko" stories,' says Shelton.

'Dalko' stories generally involved a lot of alcohol. Thought to be the fastest pitcher in baseball history, Dalkowski was called 'White Lightning' on the pitch, and 'a hopeless alcoholic' off it. Averaging something like fourteen strikeouts and fourteen walks a game, the cocky star's endless partying meant that he ultimately didn't make it into the major league. Thanks to alcohol-induced dementia, he ended up in a nursing home instead.

Bull Durham premiered in 1988. Written and directed by Ron Shelton, the movie starred Kevin Costner and Tim Robbins

3

NACHO LIBRE'S IGNACIO

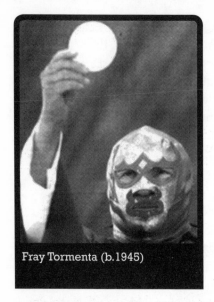

Fray Tormenta (b.1945)

Death comes to us all, with a slow, relentless tread. Philosophical reflection is the only real way to deal with this. For example: 'Oh well. At least I'll no longer be in a world where millions of people watch *Nacho Libre*.'

To be fair, actor Jack Black isn't entirely to blame for this so-called comedy about an overweight Mexican priest who moonlights as an overweight Mexican wrestler. It turns out that a real-life Mexican churchman *did* actually don a mask and wrestling tights in an attempt to make money for orphans, just like the well-meaning Ignacio.

A Dominican do-gooder in the Diocese of Texcoco, Father Sergio Benítez led a double life for years. After putting on a mask he became 'Fray Tormenta' ('Father Storm'), the tubby terror of the ring.

Father Sergio is now retired from wrestling, but his legend lives on. One of the bigger little ones in his orphanage has inherited the red-and-yellow mask. Hopefully this won't lead to a sequel.

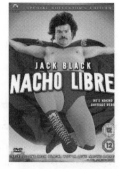

Nacho Libre premiered in 2006. The movie starred Jack Black

HAPPY GILMORE

Kyle McDonough (b.1966)

Golf, as they say, is a good excuse for a walk.

There is, however, no excuse for *Happy Gilmore*. The tale of a bad (and annoying) ice-hockey player who becomes a good (and annoying) golf pro, Adam Sandler's lamest movie in a long career of lame movies was inspired by a childhood friend.

Sandler's schoolmate in the New Hampshire town of Manchester, Kyle McDonough plays golf with the actor to this day. His real love, however, is ice hockey. Judged too small for the NHL, the real 'Happy Gilmore' was a star at the University of Vermont and spent thirteen years playing professionally in Scandinavia and Scotland.

These days McDonough is back in Manchester, working as the high-school team's head coach. Adam Sandler spends his time in New York and LA, counting up all his cash.

Happy Gilmore premiered in 1996. The movie was written by, and starred, Adam Sandler

DAYS OF THUNDER'S COLE TRICKLE

Tim Richmond (1955–89)

Have you seen *Top Gun*? If so, let's pretend for a moment that it contained not planes but cars. Next – and this will be a little more difficult – try to picture Nicole Kidman as a brain surgeon. If you can manage that, congratulations. You've now seen *Days of Thunder*.

NASCAR fans in the 80s essentially saw the movie too. Tom Cruise's flashy stock-car driver Cole Trickle was based on one Tim Richmond – a highly sexed hot shot described by some as 'a James Dean–like character'. Other people said he was 'an arrogant, cocky son of a bitch who thought he was better than anyone in the world'.

Like Cole, Richmond transferred from Indy-style cars to stock cars – ruffling a lot of feathers and causing a lot of accidents – before being mentored by a wise old crew chief ('Rubbin's racin', 'Tires is what wins races', etc.) and winning a race or two. The scene where the character's ordered back out on the track to hit the pace car (because 'You've hit everything else and I want you to be perfect') really happened. And, like Cole, Richmond really did shag a doctor.

He also shagged everyone else. Impossibly good looking and glamorous, the driver liked to hang a banner out of his hotel window so female fans would know where to find him. In the end, they could have found him in a hospital. Sadly, Richmond ended up dying of AIDS aged just thirty-four.

Days of Thunder premiered in 1990. The movie starred Tom Cruise, Nicole Kidman and Robert Duvall

THE FAST AND THE FURIOUS'S DOMINIC TORRETTO

Can Vin Diesel out-act a car? Watch *The Fast and the Furious* if you want to find out. There is essentially no other reason to.

Actually, no. Ralphy Estevez, at least, has a second reason to watch the movie, because it's on him that the Vin Diesel character was based. A petrolhead from New York, Ralphy was the anonymous subject of a movie-inspiring magazine article about illegal street racers and their tricked-out cars. It was from him that the character borrowed the line, 'I live my life a quarter-mile at a time'.

'When I heard that in the theatre I laughed hard,' says Ralphy, who 'ran a Mitsubishi Starion and a wild 1990 Nissan 33ZX twin turbo' in his racing days and now runs a shop called Drag Race Technology.

'Also, the scene where they chase Vin Diesel and he parks in a garage and walks out, that actually happened to me. I told [the writer] that story. There are a lot of things that only he and I knew about that made it into the movie; things that happened to me in real life.'

The Fast and the Furious premiered in 2001 and spawned many sequels. Based on a *Vibe Magazine* article by Ken Li, the movie starred Vin Diesel and Paul Walker

A STREETCAR NAMED DESIRE'S STANLEY KOWALSKI

Tennessee Williams (1911–83)

The key to being a good actor, says the Stanislavsky method, is to scratch, burp, mumble and fart.

Of course, this sort of raw, gritty realism requires the right role. (Ophelia wouldn't work, for example.) In *A Streetcar Named Desire*, Marlon Brando found the right role. Brutish, sensual, rude and crude, the movie's thuggish working-class character, Stanley Kowalski, is like a gorilla whose mother neglected him and let him watch too many violent movies.

He was also like Pancho Gonzales. Not the former tennis player of that name, but a short-tempered, super-butch Mexican boxer who was sleeping with *Streetcar*'s creator, Tennessee Williams. The character had 'a tinge of "rough trade"' about him, says one commentator. He can be seen as that 'gay male staple – the street hustler, hot and dangerous'.

Tennessee Williams, on the other hand, was a 'small, effeminate gay man' – the kind of guy who got 'called "sissy" by neighbourhood boys'. Some even say he used himself as the model for one of the play's decidedly female characters, the Southern belle Blanche duBois.

Like Blanche, they point out, Tennessee was an itinerant, sexually adventurous alcoholic who enjoyed the occasional lie. 'If he would tell you something it wouldn't be necessarily true,' recalled the playwright's brother. 'And Blanche says in *Streetcar*, "I don't tell what's true, I tell what ought to be true".'

A Streetcar Named Desire, a play by Tennessee Williams, was first staged in 1947. The movie with Marlon Brando premiered in 1951

POPEYE THE SAILOR MAN

Spinach isn't actually *that* good for you. The idea that it's rich in iron began with a medical table published in 1870 – which misplaced a decimal point.

Annoying Frank Fiegel also wouldn't be that good for you. This one-eyed, pipe-smoking farm labourer didn't get superhuman strength from cans of spinach, but he could get quite lively after a bottle of bourbon. With a small, wiry frame and big, jutting chin, 'Rocky' Fiegel was often between jobs, so he kept busy by getting into fights. So notorious was the childless bachelor (who shared a dilapidated house with his mum), that relatives living sixty miles away were driven to change their name.

Someone also changed Frank's name. Thanks to a cartoonist born in his home town, he's also known as 'Popeye'. Go to Chester, Illinois these days and you'll actually see a statue of the street-fighting wino (though some citizens didn't want it, saying town money shouldn't be spent to 'immortalise a bum').

You can also see what remains of Paskel's General Store. Its tall, skinny owner, Dora Paskel, wore a tight bun at the nape of her neck, just like Popeye's goil, Olive Oyl.

And a little further down the road you can see what remains of Chester's opera house. *Its* former owner is said to have been the model for the hamburger-mooching J Wellington Wimpy. Bill 'Wimpy' Schubert supposedly loved burgers so much that he would send employees out to fetch them during a show.

Popeye the Sailor Man first appeared in a 1929 comic strip by Elzie Segar and the character has gone on to have many adventures

THE MAN FROM SNOWY RIVER

Jack Riley (1838–1914)

Casanova died from syphilis and one of the Beach Boys drowned.

To this list of life's little ironies now comes another entry. 'The man from Snowy River' died above a snowy river, after his horse slipped on an ice-covered bridge. Charles McKeahnie had found fame for some rather more skilful riding ten years earlier, when he chased a wild brumby across jagged mountain country until it crashed into a boulder and died. A local poet wrote about the ride and a rather better-known poet took it from there.

Or did Banjo Paterson take it from elsewhere? Tourism officials in Corryong, Victoria argue that an entirely different man from Snowy River was the real inspiration for the poem. Stockman Jack Riley lived alone on Mt Kosciuszko for twenty years, eating damper, harassing cows and growing an impressive beard. While he never did anything especially dramatic, he did meet Banjo at least twice.

The Man from Snowy River, a poem by Banjo Paterson, was published in 1890. The movie starring Tom Burlinson and Sigrid Thornton premiered in 1982

CROCODILE DUNDEE

Rodney Ansell
(1953–99)

For a movie to be seen by boys, it needs at least one character who's all man. Someone powerful of jaw and leathery of skin, smelly of armpit and right of wing.

Someone, that is, like Rod Ansell. In 1977, this buff, blond buffalo hunter survived two months in the Australian outback after an animal overturned his small boat. Flown to the big smoke for a chat with BBC TV interviewer Michael Parkinson, the real man kept it real – confessing that he'd been baffled by his hotel room's bidet and slept in a swag on the floor. Paul Hogan's producer saw the show, thought 'fish out of water' vehicle and threw in some crocs for good measure.

As a franchise, *Crocodile Dundee* died with a whimper. (If you missed the third movie, you are not alone.)

As a man, he went with a bang. Refused any royalties from the movies, Ansell started growing marijuana for a career and taking speed in his spare time. After a few years of this, the rugged outdoorsman naturally came to believe that a cult of homicidal Freemasons had kidnapped his children, and so, rugged-outdoorsman-like, reached for his guns. Our drug-addled action hero shot four innocent strangers, killing one, before finally being shot by police.

Crocodile Dundee premiered in 1986. The movie and its two sequels starred Paul Hogan

WALTZING MATILDA'S JOLLY SWAGMAN

What do you get when you combine stagnant water with a suicidal German immigrant, some unsuccessful industrial action and 140 murdered sheep? Australia's national song.

Waltzing Matilda is said to have been written in the summer of 1895 when Banjo Paterson took a holiday at Dagworth Homestead, a sheep station in sunny Queensland. The poet was told about an incident that had happened at the station a few months earlier, when the great shearers' strike was in full swing. One of Dagworth's not-so-jolly swagmen, striking union shearer Samuel Hoffmeister, had shot his gun in the air, set fire to the woolshed and made a break for the hills, figuring that this probably wouldn't get him a raise. Cornered by his irate boss and three troopers at Combo Waterhole, Hoffmeister killed himself to avoid being captured.

It is unclear whether his ghost may be heard as you pass by that billabong. Tourists certainly can be.

Waltzing Matilda, a song by Banjo Paterson, was first sung in 1895

THE MARLBORO MAN

Clarence Hailey Long (1910–78)

Think back to the 1950s, a time when men were men and women ironed their shirts. Now ask yourself how many of those men – shoe-shining, hair-parting, Red-hating Republicans – were likely to buy cigarettes that were supposed to be 'as fresh as the month of May'. Less than 1 per cent of males smoked Marlboros in 1953, so the company decided to butch up the brand.

Enter Clarence Hailey Long. Despite having a girl's middle name, the thirty-nine-year-old Texas cowboy was all testicles. 'A silent man ... with a face sunburned to the colour of saddle leather', Long spent his time roping steers, riding horses, gazing upon yonder prairies and breathing the clean air of freedom.

So he was a natural subject for a magazine series on life in the American West.

To cut a Long story short, an adman saw the photo, thought, 'Hey, that's macho,' and an advertising icon was born. Today Marlboros are America's number-one cigarette – and two Marlboro Men are dead from lung cancer.

The 'Marlboro Man' advertising campaign was launched in 1954

JAWS' CAPTAIN QUINT

Statistically speaking, you're more likely to be killed by furniture than in the jaws of a great white shark. True, we don't spend all that much time sitting on sharks – but if animals could sue for defamation, the author of *Jaws* would be in the dock.

Also keen to sue him – for royalties – was a Long Island shark hunter named Frank Mundus. Famous for once capturing a 2000-kilogram great white, Mundus was 'Quint'-like in every detail (apart from his painted toenails, shark-tooth necklace, jewel-handled dagger and akubra hat). This resemblance wasn't coincidental. When *Jaws'* author was researching the book, Mundus took him out shark hunting several times, showing off some of the techniques used by Quint in the book.

Notoriously bloodthirsty (he liked to decorate his boat with shark carcasses and use whales and cats for bait), Mundus didn't inspire Quint's grisly fate, however. He died peacefully in his bed at the age of eighty-six, proving once again that, for sharks, there's no justice at all.

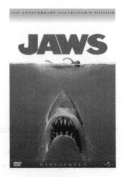

Jaws, a novel by Peter Benchley, was published in 1974. The Steven Spielberg movie premiered in 1975

UNFORGIVEN'S WILLIAM MUNNY

John Wesley Hardin (1853–95)

Things could get a little rough out in the Wild West. If somebody didn't hit you, it was probably because they were planning to shoot you instead.

In Clint Eastwood's *Unforgiven*, wrinkly-faced pig farmer William Munny is filled with regret about his blood-soaked youth, so naturally chooses to spend his dotage as a contract killer. 'I've always been lucky when it comes to killin' folks,' he muses, shortly after killin' some folks.

The story of the real William Munny, John Wesley Hardin, reveals that beneath a callous exterior you'll often find a callous heart. The inspiration for *The Shootist*, a novel about an ageing gunman which in turn inspired *Unforgiven*, Hardin had shot four men by the age of fifteen and stabbed at least one kid.

He went on to kill forty-two people in the next eight years – one of them for snoring – before having a change of heart (of sorts) and becoming a lawyer instead.

Unforgiven premiered in 1992. The movie starred, and was directed by, Clint Eastwood

THE OLD MAN AND THE SEA'S SANTIAGO

Gregorio Fuentes (1897–2002) onboard with Ernest Hemingway

The Old Man and the Sea is a book. About an old man. And the sea. It was written like this. In short, sharp sentences. Brisk, masculine prose.

Okay, done now. Ernest Hemingway always insisted that his novel's old man (an indomitable Cuban fisherman who battles sharks to reel in a giant marlin) was based on 'no-one in particular'.

Gregorio Fuentes disagreed. 'I was with Hemingway when he got the idea,' said the first mate of that author's fishing yacht, who died in 2002 aged 104. Out on the ocean, Gregorio and Hemingway saw a skiff surrounded by sharks – just the one elderly sailor on it, doing all he could to bring in a fish. 'We stopped and offered to help, but the old man shouted for us to get away. Later we heard the old man had died, which saddened [Hemingway] deeply. I know that is why he wrote the book.'

But could Gregorio have been a model as well? Described by Hemingway as a man who 'would rather fish than eat or sleep', he too was a craggy-faced Cuban born in the Canary Islands with eyes that were 'blue like the sea'. Gregorio certainly also knew how to sail, once surviving a storm with winds of 180 miles per hour.

He may have lacked the character's humble, spiritual side, however. Gregorio spent his retirement charging tourists $15 to see him. A photo cost $20 more.

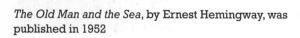

The Old Man and the Sea, by Ernest Hemingway, was published in 1952

THE DUKES OF HAZARD

If you've seen one high-speed car chase, you *haven't* seen 'em all. The Dukes of Hazzard County gave us thousands over the years, though it turns out that the pair weren't actually *that* good at driving. Producers needed around 300 cars to film the show – the broken pieces of which can be found in rubbish tips all over the South.

Jerry Rushing only needed one. This real-life good ole boy had a Chrysler nicknamed 'Traveler' (after General Robert Lee's favourite horse) that could go 225 kilometres per hour. This was easily faster than most police cars, which helps when you're smuggling illegal whisky.

Rushing's career hurtlin' along highways, buildin' up a gun collection and eatin' grits and beans had B-movie written all over it, so someone duly made one. The 1975 film, *Moonrunners*, was very much based on Rushing's life 'running' moonshine whisky for his bible-quotin' grandpaw.

And a subsequent TV series, *The Dukes of Hazzard*, was very much based on *Moonrunners*. (Though, instead of 'Traveler', the Hazzard brothers' car was called the 'General Lee'.)

Rushing himself made this point while suing for royalties. He received an undisclosed amount in compensation – and used it to open a wild boar hunting lodge. Yee-haw …

The TV show, *The Dukes of Hazzard*, screened 1979–85

CAPTAIN BLOOD

'Blood' just isn't a great name for a surgeon. Not as bad, perhaps, as 'Dr Tumour', but on the whole you'd rather see 'Dr Health'.

It is, however, a perfect name for a pirate. Which must have been one small consolation for Dr Thomas Blood when he was eventually forced to become one. *Captain Blood* sees this swashbuckling surgeon condemned to a life of slavery after he 'treasonously' tends to enemies of the king. Undeterred, our hero slips away from his owner in the Caribbean, steals a Spanish frigate, and does a bit of buccaneering upon the high seas.

All in all, a character custom-made for Errol Flynn – and for which he has one Dr Henry Pitman to thank. Like the character, this real-life seventeenth-century doctor was moved by 'pity and compassion' to care for his king's enemies, and received very little pity and compassion in return. As recorded in the snappily titled *A Relation of the Great Sufferings and Strange Adventures of Henry Pitman*, he too was banished to Barbados, but managed to make his escape.

Pitman went easy on the piracy, however. Unlike Dr/Captain Blood, he rather tamely sailed to New York, where he bided his time tending to the sick until a new king took the crown.

Boring. Which is why a film version of *A Relation of the Great Sufferings and Strange Adventures of Henry Pitman* isn't coming soon to a screen near you.

Captain Blood, by Rafael Sabatini, was published in 1922. The movie starring Errol Flynn premiered in 1935

ROBINSON CRUSOE

Alexander Selkirk (1676–1721)

The value of 'getting away from it all' really depends on being able to get back. Despite having acres of sun-kissed beaches and untouched rainforest, not to mention all the oysters he could ever eat, Robinson Crusoe didn't much like his twenty-eight-year holiday on 'The Island of Despair'. (Though in fairness, it also came with cannibals.)

The real-life Robinson had no cannibals to keep him company – just a Bible, a musket, and one or two regrets. In 1704, a sailor got into an argument with his ship's captain, which it seems safe to say that he lost. Alexander Selkirk was dumped on an uninhabited island 674 kilometres west of Chile and was marooned there for four long years.

Returning to Scotland after a passing ship picked him up, the sailor wrote a famous, if not especially action-packed, autobiography. (While Robinson Crusoe built a house, grew crops, fought cannibals and spread civilisation, Selkirk mostly hunted goats.) A reviewer noted philosophically that 'This plain Man's Story is a memorable Example, that he is happiest who confines his Wants to natural Necessities; and he that goes further in his Desires, increases his Wants in Proportion to his Acquisitions'.

Meanwhile the forty-one-year-old plain Man was still busy tending to his natural Necessities, having shacked up with a sixteen-year-old dairymaid.

Robinson Crusoe, by Daniel Defoe, was published in 1719

Chapter 2
Children

SOUTH PARK CHARACTERS

'Face it, fart jokes are funny.' So, at least, says Matt Stone, co-creator of 'An Elephant Makes Love to a Pig', 'Cartman Gets an Anal Probe', 'Eeek, a Penis' and every other episode of the cartoon series *South Park*.

He's also the co-star. The character of Kyle (one of four foul-mouthed third-graders living in the 'pissant, white-bread mountain town' of South Park) is based on this subtle satirist. Like Stone, Kyle has to put up with being more or less the only Jew in town, apart from his parents, Gerald and Sheila.

Stone's co-writer Trey Parker also gets a gig. In the show, he's Kyle's friend Stan. Like Parker, this well-meaning everykid has a geologist father named Randy, a mother named Sharon and a sister named Shelley. 'Even Stan's last name, Marsh, was my dad's stepfather's name.'

While growing up in South Park (a grassland basin in the Rocky Mountains), Parker also had a friend called Kenny. Just like the Kenny on the TV show (a brightly dressed character who somehow manages to die in every episode), 'he had this orange coat and would always say things that we couldn't understand'.

'And he was the poorest kid in the neighbourhood [so] we were always, like, "What happened to Kenny? Is he dead?"'

South Park first screened in 1997. The TV series was created by Matt Stone and Trey Parkes

BRIDGE TO TERABITHIA'S LESLIE

The inspiration for the bridge to Terabithia, Silo Creek, Washinton

Adults keep a lot of secrets from children – Mum's money issues, Dad's drinking problem, Uncle Steve's sordid sex crime – but the main one is that life is quite dull. Cars, balloons and bunnies aren't actually *that* interesting when you've seen them a thousand times before. There aren't actually any fairies or dragons, or a Santa Claus or a man on the moon.

There also isn't a magical kingdom in suburban Washington. *Bridge to Terabithia* was inspired by the real-life friendship between the author's eight-year-old son David Paterson and seven-year-old Lisa Hill. Like the novel's Jess and Leslie, they played games in the woods near their homes: the make-believe realm of 'Terabithia' is really Washington's Sligo Creek. And, like Leslie, Lisa died young in a tragic accident, struck by lightning at the age of eight.

'I met her on my first day at a new school,' recalls David, who later wrote the movie based on the book for Disney. 'We became the best of friends, right from the start – neither of us had any other friends. At that time, it was very unusual for a boy and girl to be friends, but we never even thought of it that way.'

'My mom wrote the book as a way of trying to make sense of a senseless event ... She asked my permission to have it published – imagine that, being an adult who's written a book, and relying on the whim of an eight-year-old – and I said okay, as long as the book is dedicated to Lisa and to me, because it was really our story.'

Bridge to Terabithia, by Katherine Paterson, was published in 1977. The movie version premiered in 2007

THE LION, THE WITCH AND THE WARDROBE'S LUCY

CS Lewis's fateful wardrobe

To really go to Narnia, you don't need a wardrobe so much as a boat. Both England's Malvern Hills, where author CS Lewis liked to go hiking, and Ireland's County Down, where he grew up, claim to have inspired the magical land.

Bolstering the Irish claim is Dunluce Castle, an ancient fortress atop a hill by the sea, which much resembles Narnia's castle, Cair Paravel. On the other hand, the Malvern Hills are where Lewis supposedly saw a snow-covered lamppost and said it 'would make a very nice opening to a book'. Nearby, you can also find Arthur's Stone, a Neolithic tomb that looks very like the Stone Table where Aslan nobly sacrifices his life in the first book.

If you can't decide between the rival claims, don't worry. There may be two Lucys too. *The Lion, the Witch and the Wardrobe* is dedicated to Lucy Barfield, CS Lewis's godchild and the daughter of his lifelong friend. However, it's uncertain whether she gave anything more than her name to the youngest and kindest of the Pevensie children, as Lewis didn't see much of her before the book was written. (Afterwards, tragically, she developed multiple sclerosis, spending thirty-eight years in 'a slow, remorseless decline').

A more probable Lucy is June Freud, who later became a well-known West End star. Like the refugee Pevensie children in the book, she and her siblings were sent to live with a strange professor during WWII so as to be safe from the London blitz. That professor was, of course, CS Lewis. He once said, 'I never appreciated children until the war brought them to me.'

He also had a bit to say when one of them asked him what lay behind his dusty old wardrobe.

The Lion, the Witch and the Wardrobe, by CS Lewis, was published in 1950

ALICE (OF WONDERLAND)

Lorina, Edith and Alice Liddell (1852–1934)

The real Alice never went to Wonderland. She did, however, go on a grand tour of Europe, become a high-society hostess, and quite possibly shag a prince. (The evidence for this supposed affair is a little thin. But her good friend, Queen Victoria's son Leopold, *did* name his daughter after her, and serve as godfather to her son, also Leopold.)

But let's go back to the beginning. *Alice in Wonderland*, as many know, was created by an Oxford don named Charles Dodgson (better known as Lewis Carroll) to entertain Alice Liddell, the young daughter of a colleague, on a boat trip down the Thames.

What many don't know is that this trip is reproduced in chapter three: the Lory was Alice's sister Lorina Liddell, the Eaglet was Edith Liddell, and the Duck was one Reverend Duckwort. Dodgson himself is represented by the Dodo. (A confirmed stammerer, he sometimes stumbled over his surname: 'Do ... Do ... Dodgson'.)

As to Wonderland's other characters, the Cheshire Cat and the White Rabbit may have been inspired by carvings at Croft Church and Ripon Cathedral, where Dodgson's clergyman father had worked. Tweedledum and Tweedledee are thought to be Chang and Eng Bunker, the then–hugely famous conjoined twins from Siam who also gave us the term 'Siamese twins'. The Mad Hatter was most likely Theophilus Carter, an eccentric furniture maker famous for standing outside his Oxford shop every day wearing an apron and top hat. One of those mad-inventor types, his best-known invention was an 'alarm clock bed' that tipped the sleeper into cold water.

Alice's Adventures in Wonderland, by Charles Dodgson (aka Lewis Carroll), was published in 1865

ANNE OF GREEN GABLES

Evelyn Nesbit (1884–1967)

You can't judge a book by its content. Freckle-faced orphan Anne Shirley may *seem* like a wholesome dollop of sweet, syrupy goodness but she was modelled on an accessory to murder. Author Lucy Montgomery based Anne's red hair and pale, slender beauty on a chorus girl named Evelyn Nesbit – a morphine addict famous for watching her current boyfriend kill her (arguable abusive) ex and sporadically attempting suicide thereafter.

Anne's incessant joyfulness also comes with a caveat. Montgomery eventually committed suicide herself after a life 'filled with worry and dread'.

It's nice, then, to note that Green Gables does, in fact, have green gables. Visit Canada's Prince Edward Island and you'll find a charming nineteenth-century farmhouse of that name once owned by Montgomery's cousins. Wander a little further and you'll come across the models for the book's Haunted Woods, Lovers' Lane and Balsam Hollow – as well as, less enchantingly, a golf course.

Anne of Green Gables, by Lucy Maud Montgomery, was published in 1908

TOM BROWN

Thomas Hughes (1822–96)

When it comes to clinging to your schooldays, Thomas Hughes was an example to us all. This former Rugby School student wasn't content to just attend the occasional function, or strut about in an old school tie. No sir! Instead, he went to the wilds of Tennessee to found a utopian settlement called Rugby. It collapsed after a couple of years.

Tom Brown's Schooldays was more successful. The first hugely popular school novel, Hughes's tale of a kind, brave and sporty Rugby student being sporty, brave and kind owed a few plot lines to his brother, George. Mostly, however, it was about the author himself.

'Very like Tom Brown, only not so intellectual', Hughes was 'always cheerful and gay' and 'one of the best runners in the school', according to contemporaries. 'All the small boys liked him because he was kind and friendly to them.' Later, when Hughes ran for parliament, his election handbills even said 'Vote for Tom Brown'.

George Arthur, the weedy intellectual character Tom does his best to defend from bullies in the book, is said to have been based on Hughes's fellow Rugby student, Arthur Penrhyn Stanley. An ever-so-pious theologian, he ended up Dean of Westminster.

Tom Brown's Schooldays, by Thomas Hughes, was published in 1857

TO KILL A MOCKINGBIRD'S SCOUT FINCH

Harper's father AC Lee
(1880–1962)

America's favourite novel is very nearly an autobiography.

A 'rough 'n' tough tomboy' like her narrator, Scout Finch, *To Kill a Mockingbird* author Harper Lee had a father who was an attorney like Atticus and a mother with the maiden name Finch. Scout's fictional next-door-neighbour Dill was famously based on Lee's actual next-door-neighbour Truman Capote, and a real-life recluse like Boo Radley really did live down the street.

Less clear is where Lee found Tom Robinson. The black man wrongly convicted of raping a white woman by a jury of homicidal hicks could have had any number of models. The most likely is an actual trial that took place in Lee's home town of Monroeville (*Mockingbird*'s Maycomb) when she was six (Scout's age in the book). It saw a man named Walter Lett accused of raping a white girl and, being black, promptly sentenced to death.

The fact that he was almost certainly innocent was later noted, so the state changed his sentence to life imprisonment.

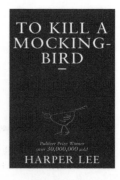

TO KILL A MOCKING-BIRD

Pulitzer Prize Winner
over 30,000,000 sold

HARPER LEE

To Kill a Mockingbird, by Harper Lee, was published in 1960

THE FAMOUS FIVE'S GEORGE

Enid Blyton (1897–1968)

'**You may look** like a boy and behave like a boy, but you're a girl all the same. And like it or not, girls have got to be taken care of.' So said Julian, the oldest member of Enid Blyton's Famous Five, who looked and behaved like a pompous git.

Far more popular with readers was the tomboy he was talking to. George ('Don't call me Georgina!') Kirrin was a short-haired, feisty pants-wearer determined to prove she was 'as good as any boy'. Once described as 'a very bad case of penis envy', she could climb trees, make fires and find smugglers with the best of them, and certainly knew how to say 'topping' and 'crumbs'. On the Five's jaunts around the countryside, it was always George who was dashed keen to tackle those horrid kidnappers, even if there was a beastly shortage of ginger beer.

The books never had a shortage of Enid Blyton, however. George is generally thought to have been based on the epically successful author, who was similarly temperamental and sporty. Like her character, Blyton loathed the constraints of Victorian femininity as a girl, while her mother tried her best to impose them. (Blyton ran away from home as a teenager and later refused to attend her mother's funeral.)

The author did, however, have a very close relationship with her own children's nanny. Some speculate that it was sexual.

The Famous Five first appeared in *Five on a Treasure Island*, by Enid Blyton, and later featured in many more books

CHARLIE BROWN

Charles M Schulz (1922–2000)

Childhood is too young an age to start feeling sad, hopeless and defeated by life. How will you fill your time as a teenager?

Rather recklessly, eight-year-old Charlie Brown went ahead and felt miserable anyway. This sad sack knew that people who look on the bright side of life are ignoring a hell of a lot. Named after one of cartoonist Charles Schulz's classmates, the loveable loser was largely based on Schulz himself. Like his creation, Schulz was a shy and isolated schoolboy with a housewife mother, a barber father, and a depressive streak six miles wide.

As to other Peanuts characters, Peppermint Patty was inspired by Schulz's sporty cousin, Patricia Swanson; Snoopy by his pet dog, Spike. Linus and Shermy were named after friends (Linus Maurer and Sherman Plepler) while the mother of another friend apparently inspired Shroeder. She played Beethoven incessantly in her living room.

Charlie Brown's unrequited love, the Little Red-Haired Girl, was based on an art school accountant, Donna Johnson. She went out with Schulz for a while but ended up rejecting his marriage proposal.

The real Lucy said 'yes'. Whether or not she was the 'world's greatest fussbudget' like that ever-assertive character, Schulz's first wife, Joyce, was certainly the dynamic one of the pair, forever building things on their property while he quietly pottered about in his den.

The *Peanuts* comic strip, by Charles M Schulz, first appeared in 1950

LITTLE MISS MUFFET

Little Miss Muffet, we are told, 'sat on a tuffet, eating her curds and whey'. But this doesn't actually tell us very much. A 'tuffet' could mean a mound of earth, a type of stool or something else altogether. 'Curds and whey' could be a kind of custard or a kind of cottage cheese. And 'Little Miss Muffet' could have been just about anyone.

The most plausible theory is that she was Prudence Muffet, the stepdaughter of a sixteenth-century medical researcher. Dr Thomas Muffet believed that sweet potatoes 'nourish mightily … engendering much flesh, blood and seed, but [without] increasing wind and lust'.

Rather more relevantly, he also believed that spiders were interesting. The author of at least one work of verse, Dr Muffet wrote the first scientific catalogue of British insects – a task that involved extensive study of our eight-legged friends. The theory goes that one of them might have slipped away, 'sat down beside' Miss Muffet and 'frightened her away', inspiring him to write a nursery rhyme as well.

In practice, we will never know.

The nursery rhyme, *Little Miss Muffet*, first appeared in print in 1805 but appears to date back to the sixteenth or seventeenth century

MARY (AND HER LITTLE LAMB)

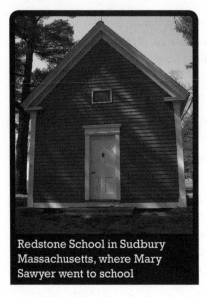

Redstone School in Sudbury Massachusetts, where Mary Sawyer went to school

Mary had a little lamb, until it was gored by a bull. The woolly star of the much-loved children's song came to an unhappy end one Thanksgiving morning after it was accidentally locked in a cowshed.

But let's go back to the start. In a small Massachusetts town in 1815, it's said, a farmer's daughter named Mary Sawyer sat up all night with a sickly lamb. By morning, it had decided that she was its mother, a role the little girl was happy to play.

'Its fleece was one of the finest and whitest, and I used to wash it regularly,' Mary later recalled. 'The lamb would hold down its head, shut its eyes and stand patiently as could be … It didn't take kindly to its own species, and when it was in the field it preferred to be with the cows and horses instead of with the other sheep.'

One day, of course, it decided it would prefer to be with Mary, and followed her to school. 'The teacher laughed outright and of course all the children giggled,' she later recalled. 'I was too embarrassed and ashamed to laugh or smile.'

And that would have been that, had not John Roulstone, the nephew of the local reverend, been inspired to write a poem.

The nursery rhyme, 'Mary Had a Little Lamb', was written by John Roulstone in the early nineteenth century

LITTLE JACK HORNER

Good staff are hard to find. Such may have been the Abbot of Glastonbury's final words as he was hanged, drawn and quartered in 1539. Though it's more likely that he said something like 'Aaargh!'

Either way, it's safe to assume that he wasn't too happy with his former steward, one Thomas Horner. Horner was one of the jury members who found his employer guilty – and he may have also helped send him to court in the first place.

Nobody quite knows why Henry VIII decided to execute the abbot, but a botched effort to keep on the king's good side probably didn't help his cause. In 1539, the story goes, the churchman sent the king the special gift of a big, fat Christmas pie. Inside that pie were the deeds to twelve enormous manor houses – a satisfying meal indeed.

Except there were only eleven deeds. The abbot had trusted young Thomas Horner to deliver the pie, but he didn't do his job very well. En route, some say he 'put in his thumb and pulled out a plum'. That is, stole one of the deeds.

After the abbot's death, let us note, Horner somehow managed to claim ownership of Mells Manor, which was home to some lucrative lead mines. *Plumbum*, let us also note, is Latin for 'lead' and 'Little Jack' is slang for 'young man'.

Horner's descendants still live in Mells Manor today.

An opportunistic, pie-loving character named 'Jacky Horner' first appeared in print in 'Namby Pamby', a 1725 ballad by Henry Carey, but he appears to predate the song by some years

HUCKLEBERRY FINN

Tom Blankenship's house in Hannibal

You can choose your friends but you can't choose your family. You also can't choose your family's friends. Mark Twain's parents, for example, were less than impressed with his good pal Tom Blankenship. The delinquent son of the town drunk, Blankenship was 'ignorant, unwashed, insufficiently fed; but he had as good a heart as ever any boy had,' Twain later wrote of his boyhood chum – and model for Huckleberry Finn.

'His liberties were totally unrestricted. He was the only really independent person – boy or man – in the community, and by consequence he was tranquilly and continuously happy and envied by the rest of us. And as his society was forbidden us by our parents the prohibition trebled and quadrupled its value, and therefore we sought and got more of his society than any other boy's.'

Blankenship (whose older brother helped hide a runaway slave, like Huck in the book) eventually became a reputable citizen, sad to say. He ended up a justice of the peace in Montana.

Elsewhere in Hannibal – the Mississippi River town that inspired St Petersberg in the book – lived Will Bowen, who became a river pilot, and John Briggs, who became a farmer. Together with Twain himself, they also became Tom Sawyer.

Tom's first love, Becky Thatcher, was based on Twain's first love, Laura Wright. And the much-feared Injun Joe is thought to have been inspired by an actually perfectly respectable citizen named Joe Douglas. Enormous, covered in smallpox scars and fond of wearing a red wig, this Native American reportedly lived to 102, when he got food poisoning from eating pickled pigs' feet.

The Adventures of Huckleberry Finn was first published in 1885

JUST WILLIAM

Richard Crompton's nephew
Tom Disher

Until the day you have children, happiness can be hard to find. 'Does that person like me?' you fret. 'Is my career going well?' To achieve pure peace of mind and contentment, so many variables must be simultaneously in place. For parents, however, bliss comes more easily. All you need is a break from the kids.

In the 'William Brown' books, Mr Brown knows the feeling. 'The human boy is given to us as a discipline,' says the scamp's long-suffering father. 'Though he is my own son I find it difficult to describe the atmosphere of peace and relief that pervades the house when he is out of it.'

Fortunately, the real William was also out of the house a lot. Growing up opposite fields and forests in Bury, the free-spirited John Lamburn wandered the countryside to his heart's content. As an adult, he wandered the world, working with the Rhodesian police, living for a time in China and flying with the real Biggles during WWII. Ending up a beekeeper, he also produced a fantasy novel plus a few books on natural history.

His more cerebral older sister produced several novels. Richmal Crompton Lamburn based the first of her 'William' stories on 'memories of my brother's boyhood'.

'When I'd exhausted those I had a nephew of eleven [Tom Disher], who was a real William. He was really useful – though less to his parents than to me.'

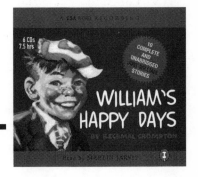

The first collection of Richmal Crompton *Just William* stories was published in 1922

PETER PAN

Michael Llewelyn Davies
(1900–21)

Peter Pan really was the boy who never grew up. He died at age twenty-one.

Partly modelled on Pan (a mischievous pagan god of the forest), Peter was directly inspired by the four-year-old Michael Llewelyn Davies and his four equally exuberant brothers. 'I made Peter by rubbing the five of you violently together, as savages with two sticks produce a flame,' wrote the playwright JM Barrie, who had befriended the boys while walking in Kensington Gardens, and ended up adopting them when their parents died.

Then they started dying too. George, the eldest, went in WWI. Michael, Barrie's favourite and the closest model for Peter Pan, drowned with his best friend at Oxford. Both non-swimmers, it's thought that they'd made a gay suicide pact but in reality we don't really know.

We *do* know that two other Davies brothers died natural deaths, but the same can't be said of the fifth. In 1960, Peter Llewelyn Davies walked out of a London pub and threw himself under a train. The sixty-three-year-old publisher was ill with emphysema, and his wife and three children were battling Huntington's disease – which at the time was generally fatal.

Peter Pan described death as 'an awfully big adventure'. But kids have been known to get things wrong.

Peter Pan first appeared in *The Little White Bird*, a 1902 novel by JM Barrie, and went on to be featured in many more

JCT JENNINGS

The real JCT Jennings may never have said 'Goodo!', let alone 'fossilised fishhooks'. We don't even know if he had any 'frantic bishes' or enjoyed eating 'oodles of tuck'.

What we *do* know is that, at least twice in his time at the Sussex public school Seaford College, the well-meaning-but-mischievous *Diarmaid* Jennings got his schoolmasters in a 'supersonic bate'. On one occasion, Diarmaid let a harmless spider loose in a dormitory, telling one and all it was poisonous. On another night, he snuck out of the dormitory to find a missing glove. He instead found a search party that had been sent out to locate him and quietly joined it at the back of the group.

We know about these incidents because of another student at the school, the future author, Anthony Buckeridge. Memories of Diarmaid's hijinks inspired him to create another well-meaning-but-mischievous schoolboy, the irrepressible JCT Jennings.

A jovial man with a big beard, Irish kilt and shoulder-length hair, Diarmaid continued his Jennings-like behaviour after school. He joined the army in WWII only to accidentally shoot himself in the foot.

Thereafter he settled in New Zealand, working first as a diesel engineer, and then as a farmer making parsnip wine.

Jennings first appeared in *Jennings Goes to School*, a 1950 novel by Anthony Buckeridge

LITTLE LORD FAUNTLEROY

Vivian Burnett (1876–1937)

In the mid 1880s a menace stalked American homes. Knee-length velvet pageboy suits became a major hit with mums. All over the nation, innocent boys were forced to wear floppy bows, fancy blouses and lace collars. Some even had to curl their hair.

Immediately to blame for all this was *Little Lord Fauntleroy* – a bestselling book about an American child who inherited ringlets and an English title, and ponced about in some lamentable clothes.

The ultimate responsibility, however, rests with Vivian Burnett, the boy on whom Fauntleroy was based. The eight-year-old son of author (and amateur clothes-maker) Frances Hodgson Burnett, Vivian inspired the little lord's refined dress sense, 'graceful, childish figure' and 'manly little face'.

The character's 'courtly manners' and stern principles came from Vivian too. Like Fauntleroy, he was good pals with the local grocer and a wholehearted believer in democracy. 'I have been so occupied with the presidential election,' Vivian once wrote to his mamma. 'The boys in my school knock me down and jump on me because they want me to go Democrat.'

He remained a manly little do-gooder until the end. In 1937, stout-hearted Vivian rescued four people from a capsized yacht, then died of a heart attack.

Little Lord Fauntleroy, by Frances Hodgson Burnett, was published in 1886

DENNIS THE MENACE

Henry and Dennis Ketcham
(b.1946)

There's a reason why Dennis was a menace. He had a learning disorder.

The freckle-faced scamp of the comic strip was based on the freckle-faced son of cartoonist Henry Ketcham. He was a boy who didn't believe in going to bed. On one occasion when he was told to take a nap, Dennis Ketcham decided to trash his bedroom instead. Mother Alice stormed into her husband's studio and screamed, 'Your son is a menace'. Henry started scribbling straightaway.

But that was the end of their luck. Cartoon Dennis may have got his blond hair, congenital tactlessness and parents named Henry and Alice from the real Dennis – but his happy home was a work of pure fiction. The real Alice was an alcoholic who died of a drug overdose shortly after filing for divorce. The real Dennis was sent to an overseas boarding school after Henry remarried, where he reportedly had a difficult time. He later fought in Vietnam, eventually receiving treatment for post-traumatic stress disorder.

Estranged from his father, he has since worked a series of low-paying jobs. 'I hear from Dennis about once a year, mostly when he needs money,' Henry once confessed.

Created by Henry Ketcham, the *Dennis the Menace* comic strip first appeared in 1951

KIDNAPPED'S DAVID BALFOUR

In the car-less eighteenth century, stealing a horse could get you hanged. Kidnapping, however, was just a misdemeanour. This was a bit of luck for Richard Annesley – but not so good for his nephew, James.

The son and heir of the ailing Earl of Anglesea, James Annesley was the only thing standing between his uncle and an enormous inheritance. Uncle Richard therefore had him kidnapped (nothing personal, just business), sending the twelve-year-old on a ship to America, and snaffling his title when the Earl passed away.

After a decade in the backwoods of Delaware, James returned to England to fight for his birthright. Though unlike his alter ego, *Kidnapped*'s David Balfour, he carried out the fight in court.

Nineteen years later, James was still fighting. 'It was extraordinary,' says one historian. 'Seldom, if ever, can so many people have lied so brazenly and with such apparent conviction in a court of law.'

James died 'of a broken heart' before the lawsuit could be fully resolved – a 'victim of the avarice, inhumanity and injustice of others'. Wicked Uncle Richard followed a year later, and, with the court system's customary speediness, the case was resolved just a decade after that.

The verdict? *No-one* was entitled to be Earl of Annesley. That peerage was made extinct.

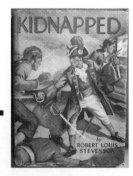

Kidnapped: Being Memoirs of the Adventures of David Balfour in the Year 1751, by Robert Louis Stevenson, was published in 1886

SALLY J FREEDMAN

Starring Sally J Freedman as Herself actually starred Judy Blume as herself. 'When I was nine and ten I was a lot like Sally – curious, imaginative, a worrier,' says the bestselling author, who, like her title character, spent a few years in Miami Beach after WWII, making up colourful stories and worrying that Hitler was still alive.

Not that that was her only worry. Like Sheila Tubman (in *Otherwise Known as Sheila the Great*), the young Blume was also scared of thunderstorms, dogs, swimming and the dark.

And like the star of *Are You There, God? It's Me, Margaret*, she also fretted about puberty. 'When I was in sixth grade, I longed to develop physically like my classmates. I tried doing exercises, resorted to stuffing my bra, and lied about getting my period. And like "Margaret", I had a very personal relationship with God that had little to do with organised religion.'

These days, Blume presumably has a very personal relationship with her daughter, Randy – whose overweight, constantly bullied former schoolmate inspired Linda in the novel *Blubber*.

Randy Blume herself inspired another novel, *Freckle Juice*. ('When she was small, she'd get into the bathtub at night and make a mess ... out of baby powder, shampoo and anything else she could mix together ... She called this concoction "freckle juice".')

Blume's son Larry, on the other hand, inspired Fudge, who appeared in several novels. The real-life model for the irrepressible toddler was 'a very interesting child', she says.

Starring Sally J Freedman as Herself, by Judy Blume, was published in 1977

LITTLE NELL

Mary Hogarth (1820–37)

As Oscar Wilde put it, 'one must have a heart of stone to read the death of Little Nell without laughing'.

That character, you see, is so angelically good, and her life just so hellishly bad. A virtuous orphan of 'not quite fourteen', Little Nell lives a lonely life in a run-down antique shop (*The Old Curiosity Shop*) until her grandfather loses both his money and his mind. Evicted by a hunchbacked moneylender, Nell trudges all the way to Shropshire, fending off various villains as she brokenly begs for food. Eventually, exhausted, she dies, having stayed strong and noble throughout her ordeal, and taken time out to spread sweetness and light.

Charles Dickens certainly *wrote* the death of Little Nell without laughing. In fact, as he noted in a letter, it 'made old wounds bleed afresh'. Dickens's heroine was based on Mary Hogarth, the 'young, beautiful and good' sister of his first wife with whom he shared his house for a time. That time ended when she fell ill after a night at the theatre, and died in the author's arms the next day. Dickens took a ring from her lifeless fingers and wore it for the rest of his life.

'That pleasant smile and these sweet words which [she would] bestow upon an evening's work in our merry bantering round the fire were more precious to me than the applause of the whole world,' Dickens wrote to Mary's mother. 'I shall never be so happy again.'

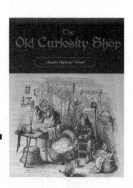

The Old Curiosity Shop, by Charles Dickens, was published in 1841

Chapter 3
Creatures

MR TOAD

Alistair Grahame (1900–20)

Parenting is magical – a wondrous, joyous, timeless miracle. So long as you get the right kid. Kenneth Grahame was one of many fathers to appreciate this caveat. Shy, semi-reclusive and a virgin until he was forty, the author's midlife marriage was quickly blessed with the arrival of Alistair – a child born with blindness in one eye, a severe squint in the other, and a deeply disturbed brain in between.

The Wind in the Willows started out as a series of bedtime stories that Kenneth created for young Alistair, based on memories of his grandmother's house by the Thames. Wild Woods is based on Quarry Woods, while Toad Hall is thought to have been inspired by Hardwick House, an eye-catching riverside manor.

As for Toad Hall's owner, he may have been Alistair himself. Dashing, debonair and just a little bit deranged, Mr Toad spends *The Wind in the Willows* working through a series of self-destructive obsessions. Various mishaps get him sent to both prison and hospital (where he probably should have been diagnosed with ADHD).

Alistair was equally impulsive – the sort of child who, when he wasn't kicking little girls, would throw himself in front of an oncoming car. His final impulse, after a 'nervous breakdown' at Eton, was to lie down on some railway tracks and not get up in time.

The Wind in the Willows, by Kenneth Grahame, was published in 1908

KING KONG

A Komodo Dragon – inspiration for King Kong

Leaving aside the minor detail that he never actually caught a thirty-foot ape that went on to terrorise New York City, Merian Cooper's *King Kong* was very nearly an autobiography. A risk-taking, pipe-smoking filmmaker like the 1933 movie's main character, Cooper had also been known to take his camera to far-off jungles, and film strange fauna at risk of death.

He never went to Skull Island, though. The most likely model for Kong's dinosaur-infested kingdom 'far west of Sumatra' was the Indonesian island of Komodo. In 1926, Cooper's friend, the naturalist William Burden, famously took a steamer there to see if rumours of a prehistoric wonderland were true.

Still more famously, he returned to New York with two komodo dragons. The enormous 'primeval monsters' attracted record crowds before dying, spirits broken, in Bronx Zoo.

Sound familiar? 'Cooper wrote at the time, "I immediately thought of doing the same thing with a giant gorilla." This is why Cooper chose the Empire State Building and modern airplanes to kill off Kong. They were fitting symbols of civilisation and the machine age that many feared were destroying nature.'

Written and directed by Merian Cooper, the first *King Kong* movie premiered in 1933

ANIMAL FARM'S NAPOLEON

Joseph Stalin (1878–1953)

If you thought *Animal Farm* was about an animal farm, it's possible you may have missed something.

George Orwell's famous satire of the Soviet Union was inspired by 'a little boy, perhaps ten years old', whom he saw driving a huge carthorse along a narrow path, whipping it whenever it tried to turn. It struck Orwell that 'if only such animals became aware of their strength, we should have no power over them, and that men exploit animals in much the same way as the rich exploit the proletariat'.

In the book, of course, we see *animals* exploiting animals. And it's Napoleon, the 'large, rather fierce-looking Berkshire boar', who's the leader of the pack. 'Not much of a talker, but with a reputation for getting his own way,' the revolutionary-turned-tyrant is clearly based on Joseph Stalin. Like the Soviet leader, Napoleon slowly and subtly builds power with the help of a secret police (puppies trained to be vicious killers), a propaganda service (his fellow pig, Squealer) and a naive workforce (the horses and sheep).

And like Stalin, he then consolidates his power by lionising a safely dead fellow revolutionary (Lenin/'Old Major'), demonising a rival one (Trotsky/'Snowball'), and going to war against a foreign power (Hitler/'Farmer Pilkington').

Animal Farm, by George Orwell, was published in 1945

LASSIE

Dogs are a man's best friend. Unless that man is a director. Fond of chasing motorcycles and barking uncontrollably, the dog who played Lassie in the TV series was notoriously hard to control.

It was a pity that they couldn't use Toots. 'The intelligence of that dog was exceptional,' said that collie's proud co-owner, Jere Knight. 'The most warm, the most loyal, the most loving, devoted dog' she had ever seen, Toots 'had an unusual range of vocabulary – an unusual number of words she could understand, and commands she could execute'.

If my relationship is any guide, Jere's husband would have executed her commands too. He created Lassie as a tribute to Toots. 'She simply would not leave where we were,' said Jere. 'If we were gone, she'd wait for us indefinitely. When Eric was in Washington, on military duty, she used to sit at the front gate of our farm, in Bucks County, Pennsylvania, and wait for him. She's buried there, on the farm.'

Lassie first appeared in *Lassie Come Home*, a 1940 novel by Eric Knight, and went on to feature in many more

STAR WARS' CHEWBACCA

An Alaskan Malamute – inspiration for Chewbacca

Dog ownership can be very rewarding. It helped earn George Lucas a few billion dollars.

The creator of the *Star Wars* franchise got the idea for Han Solo's 'gentle, hairy, non-English-speaking co-pilot', Chewbacca, from *his* co-pilot, a gentle, hairy, non-English-speaking pet dog. Lucas's enormous Alaskan malamute, Indiana, liked to ride in the front seat of his car. The dog also gave his name to another lucrative Lucas character, Indiana Jones, but did he get any royalties? Probably not.

Some cafe owner might also want his day in court. The distinctive shape of Chewbacca's spaceship was apparently inspired by a hamburger. You may think the Millennium Falcon has an outrigger cockpit, but it's really an olive on the side.

The original Princess Leia, R2-D2 and C-3PO probably preferred sushi. Versions of them first appeared in a 1958 Japanese film. Just like 1977's original *Star Wars* movie, *The Hidden Fortress* featured two hapless, faintly comical peasants trying to smuggle an endangered princess to safety so she can lead a rebellion against an evil empire.

Star Wars premiered in 1977. The movie was written and directed by George Lucas

WINNIE THE POOH

Christopher Robin Milne
(1920–96)

The real Winnie the Pooh was black.

Orphaned in 1914, when a trapper shot her mother, a small black bear cub was adopted by a Canadian soldier on his way to fight in WWI. Named after the soldier's home town of Winnipeg, she became the mascot of the 2nd Canadian Infantry brigade before being donated to London Zoo. Winnipeg ended up a much-loved tourist attraction, giving all the kiddies piggybacks and licking up condensed milk from their hands.

One of Winnie's regular visitors was Christopher Robin Milne. 'They had a glorious time together, rolling about and pulling ears and all sorts of things,' said AA Milne of the black bear and his golden-haired son. Christopher was such a fan in fact that he renamed his teddy bear 'Winnie the Pooh'. Which must have been confusing for his other stuffed animals (Eeyore, Piglet, Tigger, Kanga and Roo) when they all played games in nearby Ashdown Forest.

Not, by reports, the most attentive of fathers, AA Milne nonetheless knew a good story when he saw one. In his books, Ashdown Forest became 100 Aker Wood, Posingford Bridge became Poohsticks Bridge, and Gill's Lap became Galleon's Leap.

Christopher himself became an icon. 'It seemed to me almost that my father had got to where he was by climbing upon my infant shoulders,' the resentful adult later wrote, 'that he had filched from me my good name and had left me with the empty fame of being his son.'

Winnie the Pooh, by AA Milne, was published in 1926, and went on to spawn an entire series

MOBY DICK

Owen Chase (1798–1869)

Having a whale of a time doesn't actually sound that great. Slack-jawed, trigger-happy yokels have been harpooning these gentle mammals for years – determined to get rich on blubber, no matter the cost in blood.

The good news is that some whales hit back. One of them did some particularly fine work in the nineteenth century, surviving around 100 skirmishes with whalers, while wrecking a few dozen ships. Usually found near Mocha, an island off the coast of Chile, Mocha Dick was 'an old bull whale of prodigious size and strength'. Strikingly covered in harpoons and barnacles, he was also as 'white as wool'. When he was finally killed in 1838, after coming to the aid of a harpooned calf, Mocha Dick's huge body produced seventy barrels of oil – and a book called *Moby Dick*.

Though that wasn't the only inspiration for Herman Melville's classic novel. *Moby Dick*'s Captain Ahab (a monomaniacal sailor obsessively seeking vengeance on the white whale that took his leg) was inspired by the journal of one Owen Chase. Chase was one of the few survivors of a Nantucket whale ship that had been rammed by a large sperm whale. Like Captain Ahab, the sailor was tortured by the memory of the incident and kept obsessively reliving it in his head.

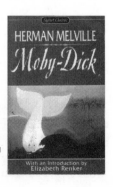

Moby Dick, by Herman Melville, was published in 1851

PEPE LE PEW

Leon 'Daffy Duck'
Schlesinger, right
(1884–1949)

If sexual harassment has a funny side, its name is Pepe le Pew.

Blissfully certain that every woman wants him (even when they are running away, shaking with fear or resorting to violence), this unflappable French skunk is the socially acceptable face of stalking. 'Zee cabbage does not run away from zee corn beef,' he will playfully reproach a terrified love interest. 'Come, my little peanut of brittle … I am zee locksmith of love!'

The inspiration for this would-be womaniser was Tedd Pierce, a Warner Bros cartoonist who felt certain that all chicks dug him. Like Pepe, Tedd could also get a little smelly. Often he would arrive at the office straight from an all-night party, then go straight to a packed bar afterwards to start the process of wooing again.

Tedd's cartoon-industry colleagues, by the way, included Ben 'Bugs' Hardaway. That artist's 'casual sketch of a proposed rabbit character' was christened 'Bugs' Bunny' by a fellow employee.

Another colleague was Warner Bros film producer Leon Schlesinger, who had a lisp just like Daffy Duck's. Equally odd-sounding was a comedian named Joe Penner, who provided the model for Elmer Fudd's voice.

PEPE' LE PEW *in*
"Two Scents Worth"
A MERRIE MELODIE CARTOON   color by
TECHNICOLOR

A WARNER BROS. CARTOON

Pepe Le Pew first appeared in *Odor-able Kitty*, a 1945 Warner Bros cartoon, and went on to feature in many more

NEMO

Neglecting your children isn't always a bad thing. Quality time together requires a lot of quality time apart.

You can also get a good movie out of it. *Finding Nemo* (the tale of a fish whose overprotective instincts drive away his defiant offspring) was inspired by writer/director Andrew Stanton's walk in the park with Ben, his young son.

'I had been working long hours and felt guilty about not spending enough time with him,' Andrew Stanton later recalled. 'As we were walking, I was experiencing all this pent-up emotion and thinking, "I miss you, I miss you," but I spent the whole walk going, "Don't touch that." "Don't do that." "You're gonna fall in there." And there was a third-party voice in my head saying, "You're completely wasting the entire moment that you've got with your son right now." I became obsessed with this premise that fear can deny a good father from being one.'

Stanton's film company had long wanted to do a feature set in the ocean and 'with that revelation, all the pieces fell into place, and we ended up with our story'.

Finding Nemo premiered in 2003. The movie was written by Andrew Stanton

GARFIELD THE CAT

Not all grandfathers are especially grandfatherly – warm, cuddly sources of interesting smells and special treats. Take J Garfield Davis, for example. The grandfather of cartoonist Jim Davis was a 'large, cantankerous man', a grump with a 'gruff exterior but a soft heart'. He contributed his name, and perhaps more, to Jim's creation, Garfield the cat – a fat, lazy, selfish orange tabby who's quite loveable, despite all that.

Jim drew on himself when creating Garfield's owner, the hapless nerdburger Jon Arbuckle. Named after a 1950s radio commercial for Yuban coffee, Jon, like Jim, is a daydreamer who was born on 28 July, and raised on a farm in Indiana.

'I hark back to my college days when I write for Jon. I didn't have a whole lot of success getting dates. I was always a bit of a geek.'

Garfield the cat first appeared in a 1978 comic strip by Jim Davis

SCROOGE MCDUCK

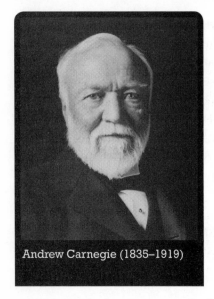

Andrew Carnegie (1835–1919)

If you're looking for a duck that symbolises the American spirit, you probably need to ask yourself why.

If you have a good reason, however, then look no further. The answer is Scrooge McDuck. Donald Duck's uncle is a classic all-American rags-to-riches tale – a shrewd businessduck who started out shining boots in Scotland, then made his fortune in the promised land. With a bit of can-do, and a touch of know-how, his story tells us, you too can have your own castle and giant money bin with 'five multiplujillion' dollars.

The real Scrooge McDuck, American steel tycoon Andrew Carnegie, had something close to that, but then he gave most of it away. Said to be the second-richest person in history (after John D Rockefeller), this son of a Scottish weaver began his career in a cotton factory, changing spools of thread for a few pence a week.

Things seem to have picked up a bit after he immigrated to America. But after cornering the steel market, this captain of industry became a king of hearts, building innumerable libraries, schools and universities (though it has to be said that he bought a castle first).

Scrooge McDuck first appeared in *Christmas on Bear Mountain*, a 1947 comic strip by Carl Barks, and went on to feature in many more

THREE BLIND MICE

Bishop Hugh Latimer
(c.1847–1555)

Next time you're captured, tortured and burnt at the stake, remember to make a pun.

Bishop Hugh Latimer certainly did. Set ablaze for being a Protestant by the Catholic monarch Mary, the churchman told his fellow martyr, Bishop Nicholas Ridley, to 'be of good cheer … For we shall this day light such a candle in England as I trust by God's grace shall never be put out'.

England's still Protestant, so I suppose he was right – but a more lasting legacy may be 'Three Blind Mice'. Some scholars argue that the nursery rhyme's ill-fated rodents are really Latimer and Ridley (plus their fellow Protestant bishop Thomas Cranmer, who was burnt at the stake the next year).

The 'farmer's wife' in this equation is of course 'Bloody Mary' herself. With her husband, Prince Philip of Spain, the sixteenth-century English queen owned endless amounts of farmland. (And, yes, she gave her name to the drink.)

She may have also given us 'Mary, Mary, Quite Contrary'. On this reading of the nursery rhyme, what sound like esoteric gardening tools are in fact instruments of torture. 'Cockleshells' are a device for squashing genitals, 'silver bells' a nickname for thumbscrews and 'maids' a kind of guillotine.

The nursery rhyme 'Three Blind Mice' first appeared in *Deuteromelia or The Seconde Part of Musicks Melodie, a* 1609 songbook by Thomas Ravenscroft, but is thought to have been written earlier

THE UGLY DUCKLING

Hans Christian Andersen
(1805–75)

It's only these days that celebrities seem 'perfect', with their carefully trimmed nostril hair, blow-dried eyelashes and shiny teeth. In Hans Christian Andersen's day they looked a bit more like Hans Christian Andersen. Pale. Bony. Gawky. Lank hair. Long nose. Big feet. The tale of a baby swan accidentally deposited among ducklings, then teased by them for looking so odd, *The Ugly Duckling* is generally seen as an autobiography of the odd-looking author.

But, unlike the ugly-duckling-turned-beautiful-swan, Andersen stayed ugly. So was the tale simply referring to the flowering of his beautiful intellect? To the talent that allowed him to escape his bullying classmates and instead mingle with arty types? That's the most likely theory.

Another is that he was really royalty. It's not actually impossible that Andersen was the illegitimate son of the Danish king – a royal 'swan' discreetly given up for adoption and thus metaphorically raised among ducks. King Christian took an unusual interest in this supposed son of an alcoholic washerwoman, covering his school fees and other expenses, and occasionally inviting him to play at the castle. When the king's son died, Andersen was the only non-family member in Denmark who was allowed to visit his coffin.

A few years later, the author also visited Charles Dickens – and remained at his house, without an invitation, for weeks. 'He was a bony bore and stayed on and on,' Dickens's daughter later recalled. *David Copperfield*'s ugly cloying, creepy clerk, Uriah Heep, might just be Dickens's revenge.

The Ugly Duckling, a short story by Hans Christian Andersen, was published in 1843

THE VERY HUNGRY CATERPILLAR

A hole puncher inspired a book

George W Bush was once asked to name his ten favourite children's books. Among other classics, he listed *The Very Hungry Caterpillar* – an illustrated tome for the very young, about, yes, a very hungry caterpillar who munches holes through different foods.

A good book. But perhaps not a good choice for Bush, given it was published when he was twenty-three.

For this instructive trivia, we can thank hole punchers, because it was with one of them that the book began. 'One day I was punching holes with a hole puncher into a stack of paper, and I thought of a bookworm and so I created a story called *A Week with Willi the Worm*,' says author Eric Carle. 'Then my editor suggested a caterpillar instead.'

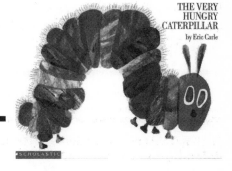

The Very Hungry Caterpillar, by Eric Carle, was published in 1969

THE LOCH NESS MONSTER

A seal may have inspired the first Loch Ness Monster sighting

There are many good things to see in Scotland – haggis, your friends eating haggis, your friends vomiting haggis – but Loch Ness isn't one of them. It's just a lake, people. Entirely empty except for some beer cans, and several gits in search of a monster.

The Loch Ness monster was first 'sighted' in the sixth century, when Saint Columba crossed paths with a 'water beast', but it didn't really come to international attention until 1934, when a prankster faked a photograph. By the time the hoax was revealed, there'd been dozens of reported sightings.

But let's just assume that at least some of these people weren't lying. So what did they *really* see? Well, the loch is connected by rivers to the North Sea, and not all that far from the Arctic Circle, so every now and then it gets a grey visitor – one with a 'long and surprisingly extendable neck'. Stray seals and their aquatic ilk (wandering walruses, disoriented otters, errant eels) are far and away the most likely explanation for 'Nessie' sightings.

People see what they want to see, even when they actually see something else.

The first recorded sighting of the Loch Ness monster may be in the *Life of Saint Columba*, a seventh-century biography by Saint Adomnán. (Right) The first 'photo' – 1934's famous hoax

THE WILD THINGS

Every child has a smelly Uncle Rupert or a weird cousin Sue. Lovely people, probably. But not great company when you're eight years old.

Maurice Sendak had a heap of them. As a child, the creator of the 'Wild Things' (hairy, scary monsters who 'roared their terrible roars and gnashed their terrible teeth') endured weekly visits from his innumerable Polish relatives, Jewish refugees from WWII.

'These people didn't speak English, only Yiddish,' Sendak later recalled. 'And they were unkempt. Their teeth were horrifying. They had hair unravelling out of their noses ... They grabbed you and twisted your face, and they thought that was an affectionate thing to do ... "Aggghh. Oh, we could eat you up", they'd say ... '

'And I knew that my mother's cooking was pretty terrible, and it also took forever, and there was every possibility that they would eat me, or my sister or my brother. We really had a wicked fantasy that they were capable of that. We couldn't taste any worse than what she was preparing.'

So that's who the Wild Things are. Tzippy, Moishe, Aoron, Emile and Bernard Sendak. 'They're foreigners, lost in America, without a language ... [As children, we] are petrified of them, and don't understand that these gestures, these twistings of flesh, are meant to be affectionate.'

Where the Wild Things Are, by Maurice Sendak, was published in 1963

MICKEY MOUSE

Charlie Chaplin (1889–1977)

When Walt Disney was a little fellow his dreams weren't all that big. He didn't set out to found a multinational entertainment conglomerate with diversified holdings in merchandising, cable television and online media. He just wanted to wear baggy pants.

Young Walt's ambition in life 'was to be another Charlie Chaplin'. 'Up and down the alley he'd swagger, with baggy trousers, derby hat, floppy shoes and a cane.' He even came second in a Chaplin impersonation contest in Kansas City.

Mickey Mouse might have been able to win the contest. 'We felt that the public, and especially the children, like animals that are cute and little,' Walt once said of his company's mascot. 'I think we are rather indebted to Charlie Chaplin for the idea. We wanted something appealing, and we thought of a tiny bit of a mouse that would have something of the wistfulness of Chaplin – a little fellow trying to do the best he could.'

Of course, with his downtrodden 'Tramp' character, Chaplin was also trying his best to criticise the capitalist system. The outspoken left-winger was given a hard time by the FBI and the McCarthyists during the Cold War, and eventually left the USA for good.

The adult Walt, sad to say, was probably happy to see him go. An extreme *right*-winger, he helped McCarthy find 'communists' in Hollywood.

Mickey Mouse first appeared in *Plane Crazy*, a 1928 Disney cartoon

UNICORNS

A rhinoceros – the likely inspiration for the unicorn

There's a reason why fantasy novels get saddled with that name. Wander over to the non-fiction section and you'll find that the olden days were filled with sad facts. Castles were always missing a toilet, damsels in distress at least a couple of teeth. And if a knight happened to be missing his shining armour, you'd find that underneath it he was about five-foot-two.

Unicorns are also disappointing. In fantasy: lithe, prancing creatures with magical horns that can cure any ill. In reality: plodding, grey herbivores whose horns could cause a nasty wound.

Many of history's unicorn 'sightings', this is to say, actually seem to star a rhinoceros. 'There are wild elephants in the country, and numerous unicorns, which are very nearly as big,' said Marco Polo of Sumatra. 'They have hair like that of a buffalo, feet like those of an elephant, and a horn in the middle of the forehead, which is black and very thick.' The Roman historian Pliny similarly described the 'unicorn' as an extremely large animal, with the 'feet of an elephant'.

But since not all that many people could read back in the day (illiteracy was another one of history's charms), such writings were generally accompanied by pictures. And since a lot of people couldn't really draw, either, the rhinos in the pictures looked a lot like horses.

Unicorns first appeared in the writings of Ctesia, a Greek physician of the fifth century BC

DRAGONS

T-Rex – the original dragon

True isolation is pretty hard to achieve these days. Go backpacking in the Himalayas, and there'll be an internet cafe waiting for you. Take a boat down the Amazon, and you'll still have reception on your mobile phone.

Of course, it wasn't always thus. The world was once a place where you rarely heard news from the next village, let alone another country or continent. Which leaves us with one big question. How was it that people all over the world – wholly isolated, disconnected tribes in Africa and Asia, the Middle East and Europe – all shared a belief in dragons?

The answer probably lies in dinosaur fossils (which were once a great deal easier to find). A Chinese book written in around 265 AD mentions the discovery of 'dragon' bones in Wucheng, an area we now know to be rich in dinosaur fossils.

Think about it. Are the dragons of myth and legend – big-jawed, lizard-like egg-hatchers – really so different from the dinos in *Jurassic Park*?

Dragons are an age-old staple of Asian, Middle Eastern, Indian and European mythologies

THE ABOMINABLE SNOWMAN

The original abominable Tibetan blue bear

Human beings have a lot of gall. We trash the planet, slaughter animals en masse and listen to music by Celine Dion, yet it's the perfectly harmless yeti that gets called 'abominable'. First 'spotted' in 1832, this reddish-grey giant ape has never actually attacked anyone – though this may just be because he doesn't exist.

A better name for the abominable snowman might be the Tibetan blue bear. While no-one has come up with an entirely satisfactory explanation for the huge, bipedal footprints that are sometimes found in the frozen uplands of Tibet, a plausible one is that they're ordinary bear prints that have melted – and thus become larger over time.

The yeti is an long-time staple of Tibetan and Nepalese mythology. It first became known in the west in 1832, when James Prinsep's *Journal of the Asiatic Society of Bengal* mentioned a tall, bipedal creature covered with long dark hair

Chapter 4
Crime fighters

DIRTY HARRY

Dave Toschi (b.1931)

In films, Dirty Harry plays by his own rules. Criminal scum get killed, innocent passers-by accidentally maimed.

In real life, he played by the book. Shortish San Francisco cop Dave Toschi isn't actually a hippie-hating, steely-eyed vigilante who shoots first then asks questions if he feels like it. He loves bow ties, bright suits and big hair, and is rather partial to a bit of 'due process'.

Now vice-president of North Star Security Services, Toschi first came to public attention in the late 1960s. He headed up the hunt for California's Zodiac Killer, a nutbag who sent police a series of taunting letters and cryptograms, along with quite a few dead bodies.

Toschi's investigation inspired 1971's *Dirty Harry*, which sees a cryptic killer named Scorpio get a few caps in his ass. Toschi went to a preview screening – and left well before the end.

'He couldn't take it. It was so simplified,' says actor Mark Ruffalo, who plays Toschi in another, rather-more-accurate film about the Zodiac killings. 'He was in the middle of one of the biggest cases in the US at the time and they were having no movement on it. He knew they had a mountain of evidence [but it was taking] them nine months to get a search warrant. He was just crawling out of his skin and [Dirty Harry] just walks up and is, like, "I don't care. If you're going to walk free, I'm going to blow your brains out." … I think it was frustrating for him. He would like to do that, probably.'

Dirty Harry premiered in 1971. The movie starred Clint Eastwood

MATLOCK

The cantankerous yet captivating Ben Matlock could make pretty much anyone confess to a crime. When that folksy attorney unleashed his Southern charm during cross-examination, even people watching from home could get a little nervous, and start planning an alibi just in case.

Bobby Lee Cook has similar skills. Dubbed 'The Lion of the Trial Bar', this Georgia legend has a freakishly successful track record, winning over 80 per cent of his murder trials. Fond of a big fee like the thrifty Matlock, Cook also shares the character's fondness for small fry – regularly opening his office for pro bono work, and receiving chickens or eggs in return. In the 1950s, he was the only lawyer in Georgia to represent the unions (who were then considered the spawn of Stalin).

Unlike the hotdog-munching Matlock, however, Cook is also a man of action. 'I walked up to the witness stand, grabbed the sheriff by the collar, pulled him down onto the floor and started whipping up on him,' he recalled of one cross-examination. 'The judge was on the bench and the jury was in the box watching me whip up on him for several minutes. They all knew the sheriff was a tyrant. After a few minutes … I pushed the sheriff back into the witness chair and finished my cross-examination.'

Matlock ran from 1986 to 1995. The TV show starred Andy Griffith

SHERLOCK HOLMES

Dr Joseph Bell (1837–1911)

When a client came to Sherlock Holmes with a problem, introductions didn't need to be made. A slight crease in the left trouser leg, combined with a distinctive 'h' sound in their 'hello', would instantly tell the legendary super-sleuth that here stood a recently widowed clerk from Surrey – one, what's more, with a dislike of badgers and a tendency to slice his approach shots. 'People see but they do not *observe*,' he liked to say.

Dr Joseph Bell agreed. A tall, lean Scotsman with piercing grey eyes, Dr Bell lectured at the University of Edinburgh and was a personal surgeon to Queen Victoria. Diagnosing a patient's disease, he would tell his students, 'depends in great measure on the accurate and rapid appreciation of small points ... In fact, the student must be taught to *observe*.' Calloused hands, for example, may mean a patient was a miner – and so more likely to have a lung problem. Sailors can be subject to tropical diseases, so look out for an anchor tattoo.

On one occasion, Bell deduced that a patient was a soldier recently returned from Barbados, where he had served in a Highland regiment. 'You see, gentlemen, the man was a respectful man but did not remove his hat. They do not in the army, but he would have learned civilian ways had he been long discharged. He has an air of authority and is obviously Scottish. As to Barbados, his complaint is elephantiasis, which is West Indian and not British.'

One of those 'gentlemen' observing him was Arthur Conan Doyle, a medical student at the University of Edinburgh who went on to create the character of Sherlock Holmes.

Sherlock Holmes first appeared in *A Study in Scarlet*, an 1887 novella by Sir Arthur Conan Doyle, and went on to appear in many more stories

INSPECTOR CLOUSEAU

Captain Matthew Webb
(1848–83)

Coordination isn't Inspector Clouseau's strong point. Lock him straitjacketed in an empty room, and this accident-prone Frenchman will still spill coffee on a priceless painting, then tumble comically down some stairs.

All quite unfair, really. The real Clouseau was actually quite the sportsman. Captain Matthew Webb first made a name for himself in 1870, when he daringly dived off his ship into the mid-Atlantic to rescue a man thrown overboard. Enjoying the press adulation that resulted, he quit the navy, smeared himself in dolphin blubber and became the first man to swim the English Channel. Similar stunts followed (along with innumerable sponsorship deals and a book called *The Art of Swimming*) until Webb decided to take a swim underneath Niagara Falls. Many people told him that the idea was suicidal. It turned out that they were right.

Webb lived on in people's hearts and pockets, however. One of his sponsors kept his picture on its matchboxes. Eighty-odd years later, the actor Peter Sellers used one to light a cigarette and saw inspiration shine forth as well. With magnificent moustache bristling above tight, black mankini, Webb's Clouseau-like pose managed to be both pompous and dignified – and not a little buffoonish as well.

Inspector Clouseau first appeared in *The Pink Panther*, a 1963 movie starring Peter Sellers

BONY

Australia's great fictional detectives can be counted on one finger. Half white, half Indigenous and not at all PC, Detective Inspector Napoleon 'Bony' Bonaparte 'combined most of the virtues of both races and extraordinarily few of the vices', according to his creator, Arthur Upfield.

A tracker in the Queensland Police Force, Bony is said to have been based on one Leon Wood, a part-Indigenous Shakespeare-quoting policeman who owned a biography of the French dictator Napoleon.

'Tracker Leon' was about thirty when Upfield met him at a cattle station on the Darling River. 'A strange and memorable character', he was 'of medium height, lean and tough of body, with brown skin and eyes that were a penetrating blue'. Like Bony, he had been educated at a convent, was 'widely read and informed' and 'spoke with a wisdom about nature and tracking that no-one could match'.

Bony first appeared in *The Barrakee Mystery,* a 1929 novel by Arthur Upfield, and became a recurring character

GK CHESTERTON'S FATHER BROWN

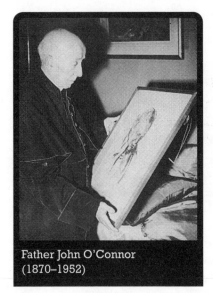

Father John O'Connor
(1870–1952)

Most fictional sleuths are like human bloodhounds – lean, coiled, watchful, and forever sniffing about for clues. But Father Brown is more like a pug. Short, fat and clumsy, with shabby clothes and a featureless face, he is one of those humble, hapless, helpless heroes that nobody takes seriously until chapter 30, when it's suddenly revealed that he knows all.

Such, GK Chesterton thought, is the life of a priest. The author, who converted to Catholicism with the help of one Father John O'Connor, was amused by the public perception of churchmen as naive, unworldly figures cloistered away from the grime of life. 'Has it never struck you that a man who does next to nothing but hear men's real sins is not likely to be wholly unaware of human evil?' asks Father Brown at one stage. Hearing confessions day in, day out has made this dumpy do-gooder far more familiar with the sordid recesses of the human psyche than any of the urbane know-it-alls who spend the first twenty-nine chapters patting him on the head.

The Secret of Father Brown was dedicated to Father O'Connor, a 'quick-witted' parish priest from Yorkshire – and Chesterton made no secret of where he got the idea. 'There is a very real sense in which Father O'Connor was the intellectual inspiration of these stories; and of much more important things as well.'

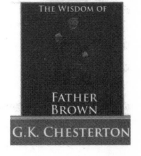

THE WISDOM OF

FATHER BROWN

G.K. CHESTERTON

Father Brown first appeared in *The Blue Cross*, a 1910 short story by GK Chesterton

AGATHA CHRISTIE'S MISS MARPLE

The Burgh Island Hotel

Brown's Hotel, Mayfair

Ever neared the end of an Agatha Christie without the faintest idea whodunnit? Then you have something in common with the Queen of Crime. According to one acquaintance, Christie would often write all but the last chapter of a book before deciding on the murderer, then go back and add a few clues.

Generally less of a mystery, however, is *where* they dunnit. *At Bertram's Hotel*, for example, is actually set at Brown's Hotel, a super-swish getaway in Mayfair, while many a bloodstained manor in the Christie canon resembles Abney Hall, her brother-in-law's estate. And if you'd rather not be a character in *Evil under the Sun* or *And Then There Were None*, avoid Devon's Burgh Island like the plague.

Near Abney Hall is one Marple Hall – which may have given its name to the Christie character. For the origins of Miss Marple's *personality*, however, we must meet the author's grandma, Margaret Miller. 'Miss Marple was not in any way a picture of my grandmother; she was far more fussy and spinsterish,' wrote Christie. 'But one thing she did have in common with her – though a cheerful person, she always expected the worst of everyone and everything, and was, with almost frightening accuracy, usually proved right ... I endowed Miss Marple with something of Grannie's powers of prophecy. There was no unkindness in [her], she just did not trust people.'

Miss Marple first appeared in *The Tuesday Night Club*, a 1927 short story by Agatha Christie

BULLDOG DRUMMOND

Captain Hugh 'Bulldog' Drummond didn't believe in post-traumatic stress disorder. The bluff, clean-living Empire builder would have seen shell-shocked soldiers as shirkers. Or pansies. Or communists. Or, indeed, Jews or Italians or Germans or anyone else not of 'the breed'.

Described as 'a sportsman and an adventurer' by his creator, and as a thuggish bigot by everyone else, Bulldog is breezily undamaged by a WWI spent murdering Germans with his meaty fists. He finds peacetime so dull, in fact, that he recruits a band of like-minded hooligans and sets out to rid England of filth.

Their adventures aren't often found on today's bookshelves, strangely enough – and the real Bulldog rests in peace too. A strapping six-footer like the muscle-bound bigot (not to mention a 'lightning and deadly shot'), the author's WWI buddy Gerard Fairlie was a heavyweight boxing champion in the Scots Guards and member of the British bobsled team in the Winter Olympics. A journalist and screenwriter, he rather concertedly ended up taking over the Bulldog franchise, writing seven more stories after the first author died.

Bulldog Drummond, **by Herman Cyril McNeile, was published in 1920**

PATRICIA CORNWELL'S KAY SCARPETTA

Corpses are people too. Such, at least, appears to be the attitude of Dr Marcella Fierro, a Virginia-based forensic pathologist who takes her scalpel work very seriously indeed.

'We are physicians and our mission is to take care of our patient – who just happens to be dead,' says the part-time FBI consultant, who helped investigate the Southside Strangler killings among other gruesome crimes. 'They have a story to tell and they tell … [it] through the physical examination … that we do – just as if they were living people.'

It was while 'hearing' such a story – presumably one involving a telltale knife wound, advanced rigor mortis and some suggestive maggots – that Fierro met Patricia Cornwell, a would-be writer working as a computer analyst at the Office of the Chief Medical Examiner. The character 'Kay Scarpetta' was the result.

'I would not be where I am today in my life were it not for Dr Fierro,' says Cornwell, who also injected a bit of autobiography into her heroine. (Like Cornwell, Kay Scarpetta is a Miami-born divorcee with a problematic dad.) What the character has in common with Fierro 'is this amazing database between her ears [and] a tremendous compassion for the victims … She has always been a tremendous advocate for those who can no longer speak for themselves'.

While conceding that they share a job and a love of Italian food, Fierro is a little less sold on the connection. 'Kay is blonde, blue-eyed and 115 pounds,' she points out. 'I've never been blonde, I have brown eyes and I haven't weighed 115 pounds since I was twelve.'

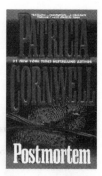

Kay Scarpetta first appeared in *Postmortem*, a 1990 novel by Patricia Cornwell

ADRIAN MONK

Mental illness is a terrible thing – but it can also be rather sweet. Ace investigator Adrian Monk, for example, suffers from a most charming obsessive-compulsive disorder. The star of *Monk* is the sort of sleuth whose first impulse upon entering a crime scene is to alphabetise the bookshelves, then rearrange a couple of lamps. Add an endearing range of phobias – including milk, beetles, mushrooms, elevators, heights, harmonicas and blankets – and must-see TV is the end result.

Monk (whose all-consuming eye for detail allows him to spot the tiny clues that others miss) was the brainchild of producer David Hoberman, who himself suffered OCD in his teens. 'Like Monk, I couldn't walk on cracks and had to touch poles. I have no idea why – but if I didn't do these things, something terrible would happen. I also had to say prayers and had to add someone new each night.'

The prayer list eventually grew unmanageably long, 'so I just went cold turkey'.

Monk screened from 2002 until 2009. The TV series starred Tony Shalhoub

CSI'S GIL GRISSOM

Once upon a time, every kid wanted to be an astronaut. Firefighters and ballerinas were quite popular too. Ask one of today's rosy-cheeked cherubs about their career plans, however, and the answer has a little less charm. Generally, it seems, their dream is to dissect the disembowelled corpse of a cheerleader then examine what remains of an old lady who's been partially devoured by her cats.

For this, we have Daniel Holstein to thank. The Las Vegas forensic entomologist was the inspiration for Dr Gil Grissom of *CSI: Crime Scene Investigation*, the show whose gruesome formula of mutilated corpses, state-of-the-art gadgets and complicated jargon has captured the imagination of so many kids.

'When my friends watch the show they'll say "Yup, that's Daniel",' says Holstein, who also works as a consultant on *CSI*, and shares his alter ego's interest in insects. (Alongside the milk and eggs, he keeps blood in his refrigerator. Plus 'maggots, in case I want to create something'.)

Another interesting item in the Holstein household is a dead fly preserved in liquid. It has grown from a pupa he removed from a corpse.

The TV show, *CSI: Crime Scene Investigation*, began screening in 2000

BONES' DR TEMPERANCE BRENNAN

If you're determined to end up in a dole queue, writing books is a good way to start. Authors don't really starve in garrets anymore, but take away their credit card and they'll probably have to go on a diet.

It's lucky, then, that the author of racy works like *Forensic Osteology* and *Cranial Suture Eccentricities* had a day job to fall back on. A ludicrously well-qualified forensic anthropologist, Dr Kathy Reichs worked as an academic when she wasn't writing about ontogenetic plasticity in nonhuman primates. She also helped Quebec police examine the occasional corpse.

'After making full professor, I was free to do what I wanted,' Reichs recalls, and it turned out that she wanted to write novels. One of the most successful crime series in history (and the inspiration for the TV series *Bones*), those novels star Dr Temperance Brennan, a quirky boffin who shares Reichs's CV. 'Everything I describe in the [first] book, I actually did.'

And that was just the start. Reichs's real-life investigation of a murder-suicide cult led to *Death du Jour*. A bikie war became *Deadly Decision*. An unidentified child skeleton inspired *Bones to Ashes*.

Meanwhile, she's on sabbatical from university. 'If you write a novel in the English Department ... you are a hero. If you write fiction in a science department, you are suspect.'

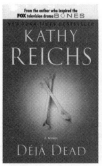
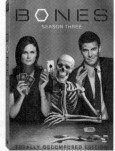

Dr Temperance Brennan first appeared in *Déja Dead*, a 1997 novel by Kathy Reichs. Emily Deschanel plays the character in *Bones*, the TV series loosely based on the books

LIE TO ME'S CAL LIGHTMAN

The human face has many muscular movements that are pretty much beyond our control. Certain emotions shape our faces in certain ways, if only for a fraction of a second. An angry London cab driver looks the same as an angry Kalahari bushman.

Or so, at least, says Dr Paul Ekman – and he wouldn't lie to you. The inspiration for *Lie to Me*'s Dr Cal Lightman proves that art sometimes needs to limit the extent to which it imitates life. Ekman's career life is less about flirting with saucy colleagues while staring murderers in the eye, and more about giving lectures, writing books and taxonomising over 3000 facial expressions on a 'facial action coding system'. The TV character is 'younger, edgier [and more] arrogant than me', the acclaimed clinical psychologist cheerfully admits.

From time to time, however, Ekman does get a little glamorous. Like Lightman, he advises the Secret Service and the Department of Defense on how to spot a liar. 'The science that [the character] does, and the applications, are exactly what I've been doing … in applying this with law enforcement and national security.'

Just don't ask him to lie himself. 'We know from our research that the ability to catch a liar and the ability to lie successfully are totally unrelated. They rely on very different skills. And although I have been asked to train liars, I don't work on that side of the street.'

Lie to Me first screened in 2009. The TV series stars Tim Roth

RUMPOLE OF THE BAILEY

Perhaps fittingly for one so fat, the cheroot-puffing Horace Rumpole was a composite of many 'Old Bailey hacks'.

First among them was James Burge, a lawyer who bravely chose to defend a 'pimp' during the Profumo scandal, and saw his career suffer as a result. 'We were defending a gang of football hooligans who had murdered a man at Charing Cross station,' Rumpole's creator, John Mortimer, once recalled. 'James leaned over to me and said "I'm an anarchist at heart, but I dare say even [a Russian revolutionary] wouldn't defend this lot." And there I had Rumpole!' Mortimer straightaway penned a play about a portly barrister who would defend anyone, however awful, and whatever the professional cost.

Burge also gave the character his habit of calling judges 'old darling' behind their back. But for Rumpole's courage in standing up to them face to face, Mortimer looked to another well-known defence silk, Lord Jeremy Hutchinson.

Rumpole's other verbal tic – incessant poetry-quoting – was apparently borrowed from the author's father. 'A barrister of the old school', he was also responsible for the character's dress sense, having 'always appeared in court dressed in old-style, starched stand-up collar, bow tie, black jacket, waistcoat and pinstriped trousers'.

Rumpole's name came from Rumpoe's, a small cafe opposite the Old Bailey (and not all that far from El Vino, the model for Pommeroy's Wine Bar). And what about the model for his wife, the irrepressible Hilda? 'Simple,' Mortimer once smirked. 'It was Mrs Thatcher – middle name Hilda.'

Horace Rumpole first appeared in *Rumpole of the Bailey*, a 1975 play by John Mortimer, and went on to appear in many more

DAVID LISS'S BENJAMIN WEAVER

Daniel Mendoza, left (1764–1836)

Once upon a time, boxing was just brutality: two hairy, sweaty primates battering one another, then lumbering groggily back to their caves. Nowadays, however, it's 'the sweet science'. Two hairy, sweaty primates battering one another with 'feints', 'swerves', 'weaves' and 'hooks'.

For this giant step in the onward march of civilisation, we have Daniel Mendoza to thank. Despite standing just five-feet-seven-inches tall, and weighing only 160 pounds, this orthodox jew became the heavyweight champion of England with the help of that little-used muscle, the brain. Before Mendoza began his career, boxers basically stood in one spot, swapping punches until someone collapsed. He was the first man to duck, weave, side-step and block – what some call 'scientific boxing' and others call 'common sense'.

Mendoza's career ended when a canny opponent grabbed his long hair with one hand and pummelled his head with the other. But he got another job 200 years later. Think of him as Benjamin Weaver, the Jewish boxer-turned-detective in David Liss's series of novels.

Benjamin Weaver first appeared in *A Conspiracy of Paper,* a 2000 novel by David Liss, 'and went on to feature in many more'

FOYLE'S WAR'S SAM

Foyle's Bookshop, London

'Jolly hockey sticks', according to the Cambridge Dictionary, 'describes a woman or girl of a high social class who is enthusiastic in a way that annoys most people'.

It also describes Sam Stewart, Inspector Foyle's driver in the TV series about police work during WWII. Cheerful, chatty and just a little bit prim, Sam is the sort of character who would be better off in a Famous Five novel, where she could have 'ripping fun' milking a cow.

She could also have this in a nursery. *Foyle's* creator Anthony Horowitz based Sam on his childhood nanny, Norah FitzGerald, a woman who 'had been in the WAAF and had lost her fiancé during the Battle of Britain. Like many displaced young women, she drifted into service after the war. When I was growing up she used to regale me with stories involving terrible scrapes, large amounts of drink and young pilots – often all three at the same time'.

Inspector Foyle himself was originally going to be called George Ransom, and do all his sleuthing in London during the Blitz. The name change occurred when Horowitz was doing some research in a bookshop: Foyle's in Charing Cross Road. 'It sort of hit me one day that it was the perfect name for the detective … It is a very 1940s shop.'

Foyle's War first screened in 2002. Created by Anthony Horowitz, the TV series stars Michael Kitchen and Honeysuckle Weeks

LORD PETER WIMSEY

Eric Whelpton (1894–1981)

Unrequited love isn't all bad. Yes, it means a spot of heartache but you can also get a good book out of it.

Dorothy Sayers got several. Her scholarly-yet-foppish detective – the food, wine and crime expert Lord Peter Wimsey – is said to have been based on an impeccably tailored fellow Oxford student on whom she had once had a crush.

Like Wimsey, Eric Whelpton had been injured in WWI and knew his way around a wine list. He too had a claim to an ancient title, and bought his white slacks in Saville Row.

Dapper unto death, Whelpton ended up one of those urbane, Panama-hatted travel writers who dash off tomes like *The Intimate Charm of Kensington* and *The Gastronomic Guide to Unknown France*.

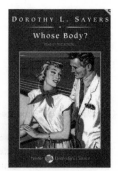

Lord Peter Wimsey first appeared in *Whose Body?*, a 1923 novel by Dorothy Sayers

BLUE HEELERS' MAGGIE DOYLE

If you're after a quiet country getaway, Mount Thomas just isn't the place. Yes, it's full of earthy characters, homespun wisdom and flannel shirts. There are more trees than you can poke a stick at, and plenty of sheep to share. The problem is that there are also murderers. And rapists. And drug runners. And kidnappers. And bank robbers.

Fortunately, Australia's crime capital is also home to the Blue Heelers: earthy, homespun police officers who combine a burning desire for justice with the need to call everyone 'mate'. Constable Maggie Doyle didn't have this need to begin with – city-bred, she only arrived in Mount Thomas in episode one – but it wasn't long before she got fair dinkum and bought a few flannel shirts of her own.

Constable Michael Winter was much the same. A city cop transferred to the small town of Yass, 'he really loved it up there because the routine was so simple and straightforward', says *Blue Heelers* creator Hal McEvoy. 'Most often you knew the victim and sometimes you knew the culprit, and someone in charge would give them a clip behind the ear and say "Wash the police car" or "Sweep the yard and don't ever do it again", rather than sending a juvenile to jail.'

McEvoy met Winter while a researching a gritty, inner-city police drama to be called *Boys in Blue* – and immediately rethought the show. 'I said to this copper "What are you called in the country? What is your nickname?" And he said they call highway patrol "tyre biters" and coppers "blue heelers". And I thought "That's the title!" So I rang [the scriptwriter] and said "Let's do a show about young cops in the country. It's called *Blue Heelers*."'

Blue Heelers screened from 1994 until 2006. Created by Hal McEvoy, the TV series starred Lisa McCune

Chapter 5
Difficult women

MRS DALLOWAY

Kitty Maxse (1867–1922)

One night in 1922, London high society was suddenly down one socialite. Kitty Maxse – 'a sharp-edged, elegant woman … who played the piano well, and was full of social graces' – fell to her death down a flight of stairs.

'How sad,' thought most people. 'How suggestive,' thought Virginia Woolf. Suspecting this apparent accident was in fact suicide, the author began *Mrs Dalloway* six days later – a novel whose well-connected title character closely matched her view of Maxse. ('A snob.' A 'foolish, thimble-pated woman living in a swarm of smart people she doesn't care about, but quite happy'.)

Originally, Woolf had wanted to show that deep down Mrs Dalloway was in fact *un*happy – that behind the glitter of a Mayfair drawing room there lurked some sad, dark and lonely souls. But in the final version of the novel, a traumatised war veteran leaps to his death instead. Mrs Dalloway herself spends the day planning a party and the evening enjoying it very much.

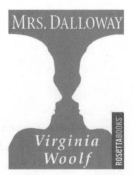

Mrs Dalloway, by Virginia Woolf, was published in 1925

DESPERATE HOUSEWIVES

On TV, Wisteria Lane is delightful – a sun-dappled oasis of white picket fences and fragrant flowers in endless bloom. In real life, it's a fairly major road in Houston – quite handy if you need some groceries, and also a good source of smog.

The original desperate housewife was Andrea Yates of Beachcomber Lane. The TV show about four outwardly contented suburban homemakers who deep down are consumed by angst was inspired by an incident in the life of that overworked, psychotically depressed Texan mother. She drowned her five children in the bath.

After seeing a TV report about the incident, the writer Marc Cherry expressed shock. But he was even more shocked that his mother wasn't. 'I've been there,' she simply said.

'I always thought of my mom as the perfect wife and mother, a woman who I felt had aspired to nothing more than to be a wife and mother,' Cherry later recalled. But it turned out that raising a heap of kids all alone in the suburbs isn't actually an unmixed delight.

Struck by the thought that 'if my mom has these moments, every woman has had a moment where she's close to losing it', Cherry started hunting about for a pen.

Created by Marc Cherry, the TV series *Desperate Housewives* first screened in 2004

THE WICKED WITCH OF THE WEST

Chicago World Fair, 'The White City'

History shows us that geniuses were sometimes unappreciated in their own lifetimes. Feminists, on the other hand, were *always* unappreciated in their own lifetimes.

Matilda Gage was a case in point. To us, the outspoken founder of the National Women's Suffrage Association was a courageous pioneer of women's rights. To her contemporaries, however, she was some kind of man-hating testicle-eater – and certainly not someone you'd want as a mother-in-law.

L Frank Baum got her, nonetheless. Many speculate that the author's love–hate relationship with his visionary (but somewhat pushy) mother-in-law inspired the good and wicked witches of Oz. Backing up this theory is the fact that Gage wrote a great deal about spiritualism and the persecution of 'witches' in medieval times.

A few years before *The Wonderful Wizard of Oz* was published, journalists wrote a great deal about the Chicago World Fair. The 'White City' (as the fair's temporary palace of tall, white tents was known) is thought to have inspired the Emerald City of Oz.

To find the yellow brick road, however, we must go to New York State. Long before he began his writing career, L Frank Baum attended military school in the small town of Peekskill. Its roads were once paved with yellow bricks.

The Wonderful Wizard of Oz, by L Frank Baum, was published in 1900, and the movie premiered in 1939

MIDDLEMARCH'S DOROTHEA BROOKE

Jeanie Senior (1828–77) – painted by George Frederick Watts

Hell, we are told, hath no fury like a woman scorned. In *Middlemarch*, George Eliot's saga of life in a provincial town, Dorothea Brooke hath plenty of fury. An idealistic, intelligent young woman, she has several schemes to help the local poor, but not a single soul to take her seriously.

Jeanie Senior knew just how she felt. Hailed by Florence Nightingale as 'a noble army of one', this real-life do-gooder was the first female civil servant in Britain. Forever butting heads with the male establishment, she was a pioneer in social work and housing reform and a co-founder of the British Red Cross.

She also wrote a few letters. Analysis of her writing reveals 'astonishing correspondences with the speech of the equally frustrated, idealistic Dorothea Brooke', says one biographer.

Note too that 'George Eliot had first known Jeanie Senior before she managed to enter public life and the novelist used the same key words, "ardent" and "diffusive", to describe both her friend and her later heroine'.

Middlemarch: A Study of Provincial Life, by George Eliot, first appeared in serial form in 1871–72, and was published whole in 1874

CATWOMAN

Jean Harlow (1911–37)

Pornography was hard to get in the 1930s, so some boys had to draw their own.

Under the mattress of the future comic writer Bob Kane, were there pictures of Jean Harlow? We *do* at least know that he drew her in adulthood. A pouty, voluptuous movie star who found underwear 'uncomfortable' ('my parts have to breathe'), Harlow 'personified feminine pulchritude at its most sensuous', says Kane. 'When we created Catwoman, I had her in mind.'

When Kane created Penguin, he probably had a cigarette in his mouth. *That* (rather less sensuous) supervillain was modelled on 'Willie the Penguin', the brand mascot for Kool Cigarettes.

Batman's other archenemy could have fit several cigarettes in his mouth. The Joker's manic, mile-wide grin was inspired by Gwynplaine, a character in the Victor Hugo novel *The Man Who Laughs*, which was made into a 1928 movie. It's about a man who joins a freak show after his face is carved into a permanent smile.

And what about Batman himself? Kane cited many inspirations for his most famous character – Zorro, Dracula, a 1928 movie called *The Bat Whispers* – but the most important was a genius from Italy. 'When I was thirteen, I discovered a book of Leonardo da Vinci's inventions … What inspired me most was his flying machine.' The teenage Kane kept his drawings of da Vinci's 'ornithopter' (basically a pair of enormous wings that could be attached to the back of a man) and reproduced them a few years later.

Bob Kane began the Batman universe in 1940, with *Batman comic #1*

ABSOLUTELY FABULOUS'S EDDIE MONSOON

Nothing is more important than a mother's love. Except, perhaps, a mother's sanity.

Lynne Franks is far from insane. The inspiration for *Ab Fab*'s Eddie built a sixty-person PR company from her kitchen table, earning millions from the likes of Tommy Hilfiger and Coke. But she's been known to be a little unconventional.

Take the Franks-style Buddhism, for example. 'It's very easy to become a Buddhist,' says Lynne's son Josh. 'You just learn the chant … Mum would chant for her clients or to win work. I'd chant for a bike … There was five minutes at the end of the hour when we'd chant for world peace and that was meant to make up for the materialism.' Come adolescence, Josh was sent to a psychic consultant. Then at eighteen came his 'rebirth': a few hours naked in a bath with his also-naked mum.

Things were no more conventional away from Lynne's mansion (with its fire-eaters, Rastafarian drummers and macrobiotic cook). 'One minute, Lynne would have been chairing a meeting with senior politicians, and the next you would hear her telling her secretary to call some hippy-dippy therapist to find out what colour we had to channel that day,' recalls one employee. She once even flew in a feng shui consultant when a canal near the office started generating negative energy.

Josh would also generate negative energy. Just like *Ab Fab*'s Saffy, 'I was very cynical, always dissing the hippies hanging around and just being a grumpy teenager'. His grandma, equally, was 'just like the one on the show': 'very prim and proper and slightly oblivious to what was going on'.

Jennifer Saunders was less oblivious. The creator of *Ab Fab* 'is in denial now, saying [the show] wasn't based on me, but of course it was,' says Lynne. 'We're not such good friends any more. It did hurt me.'

Absolutely Fabulous ran from 1992 until 2004. The TV series starred, and was created by, Jennifer Saunders

THE IMPORTANCE OF BEING EARNEST'S LADY BRACKNELL

Sibyl Montgomery, the Lady Queensberry (1848–1935)

Lady Bracknell doesn't approve of the modern sympathy with invalids. 'Illness of any kind is hardly a thing to be encouraged in others.' The imperious matriarch also takes a dim view of non-smokers, low-pedigree suitors, long engagements and hosts who fail to provide cucumber sandwiches.

The real Lady Bracknell was less judgemental. She mainly just disapproved of Oscar Wilde. A fragile, ethereal beauty who always looked 'as though she had been struck and was still quivering from the blow', Lady Queensberry was the mother of 'Bosie', Oscar's boyfriend (though as far as she knew they were just good chums).

The austere old aristocrat always tried to 'set an example of moral behaviour' to her wayward son, and apparently felt that Oscar wasn't much of a help. So in 1892, when Bosie was about to get kicked out of Oxford, she invited the playwright to her country mansion for a little chat about his 'peculiar views of morality'.

Over tea and cakes, Lady Queensberry 'spoke frankly and warningly of Bosie's vanity and extravagant habits'. The visit, for Oscar, 'had all the embarrassment associated with meeting one's beloved's mother'.

The name of the village near her mansion? Bracknell.

The Importance of Being Earnest, by Oscar Wilde, was first performed in 1895

TO DIE FOR'S SUZANNE STONE

According to some people, love means never having to say you're sorry.

According to Pamela Smart, it means shooting your husband in the face.

In 1990, this New Hampshire media teacher, who provided the model for Nicole Kidman's equally demanding newsreader in *To Die for*, seduced a fifteen-year-old student. (The two apparently bonded over a love of heavy metal.) 'How inappropriate,' you may think, but don't worry. After a while, Pamela said she'd have no more sex with him. No, not until he killed her husband.

The student did so with the help of three friends, and is now residing in Maine State Prison. Described by state prosecutors as 'an evil woman bent on murder', Pamela was secretly taped admitting her part in the affair, and ended up in prison for life.

To Die for premiered in 1995. The movie starred
Nicole Kidman

THE EXORCIST'S REGAN MCNEILL

Every mother wants to be proud of her offspring, but sometimes they make it tough. In *The Exorcist*, for example, twelve-year-old Regan may be able to levitate, projectile vomit and blaspheme in a demonic male voice – and she also likes to murder babysitters. Eventually, however, we learn that little Regan isn't to blame so much as Satan. The cloven-hoofed Prince of Darkness has gone and possessed her soul. Quite a relief.

Such a thing could never happen in the real world, of course, but it did happen in the United States. The novel that inspired the movie was based on the only documented example of demonic possession in America – a real-life exorcism conducted at St Louis University in 1949.

The real Regan was reportedly a thirteen-year-old German-American boy from Maryland who had been dabbling with a ouija board. 'Terribly draining' for all concerned, his exorcism took four priests six weeks and featured many scenes from the movie: flying furniture, projectile vomiting and strange messages that appeared on the boy's skin. 'The demon knew everyone's weakness and tailored his attacks to demoralise the team.'

The Exorcist, by William Blatty, was published in 1971. The movie version premiered in 1973

THE 101 DALMATIANS' CRUELLA DE VIL

Talullah Bankhead (1902–68)

Dogs may be man's best friend but they can also be a woman's best coat. Being cruel and evil, *101 Dalmatians'* pampered heiress doesn't care how many puppies it takes to keep her warm in winter. She just wants them skinned quick smart.

The real Cruella de Vil didn't actually wear dogs – just coats made from murdered foxes, otters, seals, rabbits and minks, which society for some reason deems okay. But that was about the only socially acceptable thing Talullah Bankhead ever did. She was better known for wandering into parties naked, or doing cartwheels sans underpants.

The quintessential Southern belle, Bankhead was born into the Alabama establishment. (Her uncle and grandpa were senators, her father a Speaker of the House). She chose a different career path, however, and became one of Hollywood's most notorious stars. Described by Marlene Dietrich as 'the most immoral person alive', and by herself as 'as pure as the driven slush', Bankhead had around 500 lovers (of both genders), enjoyed a snort of coke, and was accused of seducing several small boys.

But it was her other extravagances that caught the eye of Dodie Smith (an author who, not incidentally, owned nine Dalmatians). Like Cruella de Vil, Bankhead liked to combine skin-tight satin with long ropes of jewels and body-length furs. It's also because of her that Cruella drives an extravagant car with a noisy horn, and calls more or less everyone 'Dah-ling'.

We don't know what Bankhead called the doctor at her deathbed – but we do know her final words. 'Codeine …' she croaked. 'Bourbon … '

The 101 Dalmatians, by Dodie Smith, was published in 1956. The movie premiered in 1996

DAME EDNA EVERAGE

It's not always good to know where you stand. In his autobiography, Barry Humphries recalls asking his mother, a reproachful and unimaginative housewife who never spoke to foreigners, just how much she really loved him. '"Well," she thoughtfully replied, "naturally I love your father most of all, and then my mother and father, and after that, you and your sister, just the same."'

Ouch. The wound, it seems, was still smarting a few years later when, as a student with a bit of a drinking problem, Humphries debuted 'Edna Everage' at a Melbourne University revue. 'I invented Edna because I hated her,' he has said of his creation. (She didn't start out as a titled megastar, by the way, but as an a(E)verage suburbanite of the 1950s. She spent her dull days dusting furniture and cooking dinner for her equally conventional husband, 'Norm'.)

In her original incarnation, Edna was 'a silly, ignorant, self-satisfied housewife', says Humphries. 'I suppose one grows up with a desire to murder one's parents, but you can't go and really do that. So I suppose I tried to murder them symbolically on stage. I poured out my hatred of the standards of the little people of their generation.'

BARRY HUMPHRIES

Handling
EDNA
THE UNAUTHORISED BIOGRAPHY

Created and performed by Barry Humphries, Dame Edna Everage first appeared in 1955 at a Melbourne University comedy revue

THE READER'S HANNA SCHMITZ

Ilse Koch (1906–67)

You know you're a terrible person when even the SS draws the line.

Known as 'the bitch of Buchenwald', Ilse Koch was married to the commandant of Buchenwald concentration camp and took an unhealthy interest in her husband's work. Placed in charge of the female guards, she loved watching, as well as ordering, punishment. Sometimes she would ride through groups of prisoners on her horse, lashing them with her whip as she went. She was also said to pick out prisoners with tattoos she liked … in order to make lampshades with their skin.

At her trial, witnesses said the Nazis had disciplined Ilse for another habit: forcing prisoners to rape one another, or having a go herself. You'll be glad to know she ended up in jail, where she hanged herself after sixteen years.

She may also have ended up in *The Reader*. Hanna Schmitz, the troubled, sexually inventive tram conductor who turns out to have been a troubled, sexually inventive SS guard, is probably based on 'the bitch'. 'We are told that Ilse's son wrote poems to her in prison and that [Hanna and the teenage character she seduces] are united by reading. What also struck me was that Ilse was accused of using a riding crop to strike prisoners and Hanna, in the book, strikes [the teenage character] with a belt,' says one historian.

Moreover, 'both Hanna and Ilse selected prisoners for execution' and seemed to bring a 'sexual element' to their choice.

The Reader, by Bernhard Schlink, was published in 1995. The movie starring Kate Winslet premiered in 2008

ROME'S ATIA

Clodia Metelli (c.95 BC)

The moral standards of ancient Rome weren't all that high, but even so some managed to stand out. In a world where people spent their time raping slaves and cheering gladiators – a world where crowds could object to a criminal being crucified, but only because they wanted to see him buried alive – eyebrows could still be raised by that ancient sin: a woman who didn't know her place.

In the TV series *Rome*, Atia is one such woman. The niece of Julius Caesar and mother of the future emperor Augustus, she is 'snobbish, wilful, cunning, sexually voracious and totally amoral'. Instructive Atia quotes include 'Die screaming, you pig spawn trollop' and 'A large penis is always welcome!'

Now, Atia Balba Caesonia was of course an actual person. The real-life mother of Augustus was, however, a quiet, pious woman who spent very little time meddling in politics, and probably none at all sending her son to brothels, kidnapping and torturing rivals, and shagging everyone in sight.

The TV version of Atia, then, owes more to another real-life Roman: Clodia, the alluring, scheming, gambling, boozing sister of the politician Publius Clodius. For a few years, she was said to be his lover too. (There was space in her bed after she murdered her husband. Though she also liked to fill it with slaves.)

The TV series *Rome* ran from 2005 until 2007

MISS DAISY

Knowledge is the best weapon against bigotry. To overcome the prejudices of Miss Daisy Werthan (a seventy-two-year-old Southerner whose son hires her a black chauffeur) in *Driving Miss Daisy*, all the chauffeur Hoke Colburn has to do is show her the good man that he is. With patience, integrity, and a certain quiet dignity, he puts up with Miss Daisy's nagging, contempt and pig-ignorant comments every day for just twenty-three years, then, hey presto, they're the best of friends. Wonderful stuff. What was that Martin Luther King complaining about?

Anyway, this tale of racial harmony blooming on the highways of Atlanta was all more or less based on fact. Playwright Alfred Uhry drew *Driving Miss Daisy* from memories of his grandmother, Lena Guthman Fox, an ex-teacher forced to hire a black chauffeur who eventually steered his way into her heart.

Alfred Uhry's play, *Driving Miss Daisy*, was first performed in 1987. The Academy Award–winning movie, starring Jessica Tandy and Morgan Freeman, premiered in 1989

VANITY FAIR'S BECKY SHARP

Grandparenting is a thankless task. Change nappies, wipe away tears, mop up snot, and what do you get? In the case of granny Harriet Becher, a comprehensive character assassination.

William Thackeray based *Vanity Fair*'s scheming vixen, Becky Sharpe, on his dear granny Harriet, with whom he had lived as a child. The author wasn't the only male to live with her, though. Whether or not she seduced any man with a bank balance, like the shameless anti-hero of *Vanity Fair*, Harriet did leave quite a few in her wake. She ditched Thackeray's grandfather to elope with a well-born army officer, for example – then ran off on *him* with somebody else.

The book's title, by the way, comes from *The Pilgrim's Progress*, a religious allegory by a writer who liked his metaphors crystal clear. In it our bible-toting hero ('Christian') tries to make his way to heaven, despite the many earthly temptations that can lead us to hell. Along the way he encounters complex, subtly drawn characters like Mrs Know-Nothing, Mrs Light-Mind and Mrs Inconsiderate, and is enticed by 'Vanity', a frivolous, *do*-nothing city that is home to a year-long fair.

Vanity Fair: A Novel without a Hero, by William Thackeray, was published in 1847

MADAME BOVARY

Flaubert is generally described as the Father of Realism (realism basically being anything with poor people being miserable in it). It's fitting, then, that his most famous character was based on a real person.

Madame Delphine Delamare was born to a provincial farmer in Rouen, France (Flaubert's home town) and educated at the local convent. Whether or not she got aroused by church services like the libidinous character Madame Bovary, she was certainly just as eager to get shacked up. Delphine married the local doctor (who had been a student of Flaubert's father) at the age of just seventeen.

Nine years, several affairs and some massive debts later, Delphine was dead. Having hugely overspent on decorations and dresses, she sensibly chose to drink prussic acid, rather than show her husband the bills. When he finally saw them, and learned about her affairs, he sensibly killed himself too.

Gritty stuff. Very realistic.

Madame Bovary, by Gustave Flaubert, was published in 1856

ULYSSES'S MOLLY BLOOM

Nora Barnacle (1884–1951)

Any idea what 'ouns' means? What about 'chrysostomos' or 'christine' with a lower-case C? If you struggle with such terms, you may not enjoy page one of *Ulysses* – and things don't get much easier from there.

But while it's never entirely clear what's going on in James Joyce's incomprehensible masterwork, one fact does emerge if you read very slowly (then do some research on Wikipedia). The novel's narrator likes Molly Bloom.

Molly (who at one point soliloquises for 761 words without a single full stop or comma) is a lusty opera singer who's cheating on her husband with some man and a series of boys. (She probably does some other stuff too, but I got a bit lost.) Anyway, she's based on Joyce's eventual wife, Nora Barnacle, a self-aware, highly sexual woman about whom he was pathologically possessive. Though this twenty-year-old chambermaid had only been out with three men before she met the author (giving him 'a lasting sense of awe at the banked fires of female desire'), Joyce 'never conquered his fear of Nora's old loves' and was forever accusing her of sleeping around.

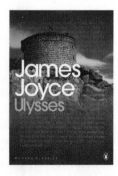

Ulysses, by James Joyce, was first published in serial format from 1918 to 1920, then as a whole in 1922

LADY MACBETH

Shakespeare was a bit of a suck. Perhaps understandably, in an age of beheadings, his plays were first and foremost about pleasing the monarch, and if others liked it too, then great.

Macbeth, for example, was written in the reign of James I, the dour and much-disliked Scottish monarch Guy Fawkes quite understandably tried to blow up. The script ambitiously attempted to remind theatregoers of an even more charmless Scottish monarch – Mac Bethad mac Findlaich, who had ruled the Highlands 500 years before.

But the real villain of the play, of course, is Lady Macbeth – a manipulative, cold-hearted schemer with a fiendish glint in her eye and blood all over her hands. As a loyal soldier, Macbeth would have happily confined his murdering to Scotland's enemies if she hadn't told him to screw his courage to the sticking point, then come up with a foolproof plan.

The thing is, though, she did nothing of the sort. The real wife of Mac Bethad mac Findlaich, Queen Gruoch, 'was universally acclaimed as a saintly and popular figure', says the playwright, David Willcock.

'We know, for instance, that she donated money and land to a group of monks, the Culdees, who lived on a tiny island in Loch Leven. And we know, from the very fact that she was the first Scottish queen to be named in history, that she was popular.'

And the real Macbeth, by the way, became king of Scotland after killing Duncan *on the field of battle*. In 1040 that was like winning an election.

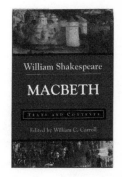

The Tragedy of Macbeth, by William Shakespeare, was first performed somewhere between 1603 and 1611

LADY CHATTERLEY

Lady Ottoline Morrell
(1873–1938)

Lady Ottoline Morrell loved love. The first cousin of the Queen Mother, and great-great-niece of the Duke of Wellington, she also loved the philosopher Bertrand Russell, the author Axel Munthe and the painters Roger Fry, Augustus John and Dora Carrington. Such was life as a society hostess on the fringes of the Bloomsbury Group (a bunch of highly sexed, party-going, endlessly self-referential artists who occasionally also found time to make art).

Not all of Lady Morrell's flings happened in Bloomsbury, however. One took place at her country house in Garsington and was more about a love of big muscles than the life of the mind. The flamboyant redhead's affair with 'Tiger', a young and sexy stonemason who was carving plinths for her garden statues, may just have inspired DH Lawrence's most famous character. (In *Lady Chatterley's Lover*, an aristocrat's quest for a purely physical sensation leads to goings-on with the gamekeeper.)

Virginia Woolf saw a resemblance, anyway. 'I was so angry I could hardly finish his letters,' she wrote to Lady Morrell in a letter. 'There you were, sending him Shelley, beef tea, lending him cottages, taking his photograph on the steps at Garsington – oft stuffing gold into his pocket – off he goes, has out his fountain pen and – well, as I say I haven't read it.'

Lady Chatterley's Lover, by DH Lawrence, was published in 1928

MERMAIDS

A sea cow or manatee

Long sea voyages were pretty unpleasant back in the day – several cramped, smelly years spent developing scurvy and hearing people say 'lubberly' and 'abaft'. But you did at least get to see naked animals.

Most scholars agree that 'mermaids' – perky-breasted sirens of the deep who like to sing haunting melodies and lure good men to their doom – aren't actually that attractive, close up. The legend likely began with manatees, dugongs and sea cows: seafaring cousins of the elephant who weigh about 3000 pounds. They have wrinkled skin, thick, coarse whiskers and a prehensile upper lip.

But, that said, they've also got boobs. With large mammary glands near their armpits, and flippers that could be mistaken for arms, they are not entirely inhuman, from a distance. 'Dugong' is a Malay term for 'lady of the sea', while 'manatee' can be translated as 'breast' in Carib Indian. 'There have been times when they come up out of the water and the light has been such that they did look like the head of a person,' says one marine biologist.

They aren't entirely un-mermaid-like, either. Fish-like from the waist down, and with no fin, these members of the order 'sirena' make a lot of noise when wooing. (They also rub their genitals on coral.)

Okay, there's not much dugong porn on the web these days, but remember that standards could be lower after a few months at sea. 'Deprivation of intimacy inflamed all these voyages … Anything in the water became a projection of the sailor's need for contact.'

The first known mermaid stories appeared in modern-day Iraq, in around 1000 BC

Chapter 6
Eccentrics

SANTA CLAUS

Nicholas of Myra (270–343)

You better watch out. You better not cry. Better not pout. I'm telling you why. You may be rendered destitute and forced to work in a brothel.

The name 'Santa Claus' came from 'Sinterklaas', the Dutch version of 'Saint Nicholas'. The man himself came from Turkey. Nicholas of Myra was a pious orphan of wealthy parents who was raised by his uncle, a bishop. He eventually became a bishop himself, whereby he produced some kind of wheat-related miracle, petitioned the emperor for tax relief, and generally proved himself a good pal of the people.

Bishop Nicholas is best remembered, however, for having given many gifts to the poor. He was famous for secretly placing coins in people's shoes, and once helped a financially strapped father who was about to force his three daughters to work in a brothel. After his death, Nicholas became the patron saint of children, sailors and merchants (and, strangely enough, archers and thieves).

He also looks after the Dutch. They, in turn, have long celebrated Nicholas's birthday on 5 December: children place their shoes in front of the chimney, and wake up to find them filled with toys. Dutch immigrants continued this tradition in America – and, wanting a way to help pass the time at Christmas everyone else thought, 'What a good idea!'

The folk feast of 'Sinterklass' was first celebrated in the twelfth century, after the saint's remains were transported from Myra to Italy

SCRUBS' JD

Want to know what being a doctor is *really* like? Then there's probably no need to watch *Scrubs*. Medical intern JD *does* see patients from time to time, but mostly he just daydreams, performs complicated song-and-dance routines, and wonders whether his on-again, off-again relationship with Elliot should be on again or switched off.

To truly learn something about medicine, a more constructive idea might be to visit the Los Angeles Medical Centre, where you can see the real-life JD in action. A well-regarded cardiologist, Dr Jonathan Doris was a college pal of *Scrubs* creator, Bill Lawrence. 'Bill … would always listen to these crazy stories I would tell him through medical school and residency. Towards the end of my internal medicine residency [at Brown University in Rhode Island], he contacted me and told me that he'd been keeping all these stories and wanted to make a show about it.'

'I distinctly remember our conversation. He said: "JD, if you would entrust me with all of your mistakes, misadventures and gaffes during your residency, I promise no-one will know it was you." So I did. Bill promptly named the main character after me. Then he sent the NBC press corps and *USA Today* over to interview me about what a bumbling intern I was. So much for anonymity.'

Scrubs first screened in 2001. Created by Bill Lawrence, the TV series stars Zach Braff

PG WODEHOUSE'S PSMITH

Rupert D'Oyly Carte (1876–1948)

The P in 'Psmith' is silent. Psmith, however, is not. The snappily dressed Old Etonian is a master of the monologue, specialising in languid, florid, gently subversive speeches that touch on communism and quote from the classics – all in answer to a question about cricket.

The real Psmith talked about props. The son of the Savoy Theatre's owner (a man best known for staging the Gilbert and Sullivan operas), Rupert D'Oyly Carte went to school with a cousin of PG Wodehouse, and clearly made quite an impression.

'[I was told that] he was long, slender, always beautifully dressed and very dignified,' Wodehouse recalled many years later. 'His speech was what is known as orotund and he wore a monocle. He habitually addressed his [fellow students] as "Comrade", and if one of the masters chanced to inquire as to his health, would reply, "Sir, I grow thinnah and thinnah" … This was all the information I required in order to start building him in a star part.'

D'Oyly Carte went on to inherit the Savoy, and smarten things up on stage. Disliking the 'dreary' and 'dowdy', he 'formed the view that new productions should be prepared with scenery and dresses to the design of first-class artists … who would produce a décor attractive to the new generation'.

Psmith first appeared in *Mike and Psmith*, a 1909 novel by PG Wodehouse, before featuring in many more

GREAT EXPECTATIONS' MISS HAVISHAM

There are many ways to mend a broken heart – but none of them occur to Miss Havisham.

After her true love leaves her at the altar, the spiteful spinster of *Great Expectations* doesn't give Time the Great Healer much chance to do his good work. Instead, she orders her servants to stop the clocks and close all the curtains and blinds. Never once removing her wedding dress, Miss Havisham broods for years in her decaying house while watching rats chew away at the cake. Eventually, you'll be cheered to learn, she adopts a daughter. Though, less cheerily, this is only so the girl can be taught to break some random man's heart. The heartwarming tale of Havisham finally ends when her wedding dress catches fire.

The tale of Donnithorne, however, was only half of it. Charles Dickens's probable model for Miss Havisham spent a further twenty-five years after *Great Expectations* was published mouldering in a darkened room – though she always kept a door ajar, in case her fiancé returned. The daughter of a judge, Eliza Donnithorne was a darling of the Sydney social scene in 1856, so the city's great and good duly gathered for her wedding. Practically the only person who didn't turn up was the groom.

Eliza duly did a Havisham, ordering that the feast be untouched, the curtains be drawn and the door be locked. She too died in her wedding dress. Though in her case death came from old age.

Great Expectations, by Charles Dickens, was published in serial form between 1860 and 1861, and in book form in 1861

PG WODEHOUSE'S EARL OF EMSWORTH

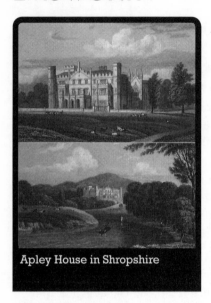

Apley House in Shropshire

There are many ways for an aristocrat to win immortality. They can become a poet like Lord Byron, enter politics like Lord Melbourne, or go charging into battle like their glorious ancestors, bellowing the king's name until they get stabbed in the throat.

There's also the pig option. William Heneage, the sixth Earl of Dartmouth, doesn't seem to have done anything very much with his career. (Yes, he was Vice-Chamberlain of the Household, but this basically means organising the occasional garden party at Buckingham Palace.) He did, however, know pigs.

This real life earl's obsessive passion may have inspired PG Wodehouse to create the Earl of Emsworth – an amiable, absent-minded old homebody whose grossly overweight Berkshire boar has won three consecutive Fat Pig silver medals at the Shropshire Agricultural Show.

Exactly where we might find his home is a question that has vexed many. The most plausible theory is that the earl's Blandings Castle was modelled on Apley House in Shropshire, a stately manor Wodehouse visited as a child.

The Earl of Emsworth first appeared in *Something Fresh*, a 1915 novel by PG Wodehouse, before going on to feature in many more

AROUND THE WORLD IN 80 DAYS' PHILEAS FOGG

George Francis Train
(1829–1904)

There are two ways to approach an election campaign. The first is to actually campaign. The second is to travel around the world for no apparent reason, completely disappearing from view. This was George Francis Train's method. Unaccountably, it lost him the 1872 US presidential election in a landslide, despite his having a great slogan ('Get on board!') and actually making the trip in the then-record time of eighty days.

Jules Verne never acknowledged the connection but can it be a coincidence that that author produced *Around the World in 80 Days* the very next year? Train certainly thought not. 'Verne stole my thunder,' he reportedly bellowed, 'I'm Phileas Fogg!' And it's noteworthy that, like Train, the novel's main character hires a private train at one point in his travels – and at another, manages to get himself imprisoned.

At the end of the book, Fogg finds love. Train found himself in jail for obscenity. Released in 1873, he was threatened with an insane asylum the next year – and seemingly spent the rest of his life doing his best to get in. After unsuccessfully campaigning for the position of 'Dictator of the United States', the multimillionaire spent his final years on a bench in Madison Square Park, handing out dimes to passers-by but speaking only to animals and children.

Around the World in 80 Days, by Jules Verne, was published in 1873

VIRGINIA WOOLF'S ORLANDO

Vita Sackville-West (1892–1962)

Some elderly folk stay young at heart. Orlando stays young in body. At one point, he also becomes female in body. Confused?

Virginia Woolf's weirdest novel sees the title character work his way into Queen Elizabeth I's pants, then ravish a Russian princess. He spends the next century or two in a slightly less macho fashion – writing poetry and decorating Knole, his stately home – then goes the whole hog and turns into a woman. Various adventures follow featuring sailors, gypsies and Turks. Then he/she publishes a poem and wins a prize. The end.

Still confused? Me too, sorry. If it's any help, Orlando is said to be 'literature's longest love letter': our hero(ine) is based on Woolf's one-time lover and long-time friend, Vita Sackville-West, who liked to be called 'Julian' when she dressed up as a man.

An androgynous-looking aristocrat, Sackville-West was born at Knole, spent years lovingly furnishing it, and won a major prize for her poetry. Like Orlando, she was prone to melancholy, loved animals, spent time in Turkey, and knew a few gypsies (her grandfather had five children by one). Most importantly, perhaps, she was bisexual – a fact the frumpy public so frowned upon, Woolf had to make her character transsexual instead.

Orlando: A Biography, by Virginia Woolf, was published in 1928. Tilda Swinton starred in the 1993 film

UNCLE SAM

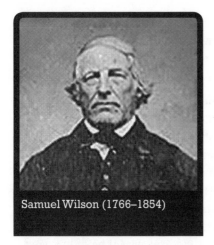

Samuel Wilson (1766–1854)

If the real 'Uncle Sam' ever did say 'I want you', he was most likely addressing a cow. The star-spangled American icon is generally thought to have been inspired by one Samuel Wilson, a meat packer from Massachusetts. During the War of 1812, this bearded businessman won a government contract to supply beef and pork to American troops – men who would otherwise have had to make do on lice. All over the country, therefore, hungry soldiers would rejoice in the arrival of Sam's barrels full of meat – all which were labelled 'U.S.' (for 'United States').

'U.S.' wasn't an especially common term at the time, so the joke went that the initials stood for the oh-so-generous 'Uncle Sam'. After a while, the term became synonymous with the US government – and, eventually, with the country itself.

As to Uncle Sam's appearance, his goatee and general gangliness probably owe a bit to Abraham Lincoln. The classic Uncle Sam image was created shortly after the Civil War by the cartoonist Thomas Nast (who also came up with the Republican elephant and the Democrat donkey).

The first written reference to Uncle Sam appeared in an allegorical book by Frederick Augustus Fidfaddy in 1816

BASIL FAWLTY

Donald Sinclair (1909–81)

Basil Fawlty was perfectly capable of running a hotel. He only had problems when it got filled up with hotel guests.

People skills also didn't come easily to Donald Sinclair. A few years after the wife of this real-life naval commander opened a hotel in Torquay, on the 'English Riviera', he 'reluctantly' agreed to join her – and did his best to run a tight ship. Snobby, 'bonkers' and 'just so bad-tempered, … [Sinclair] was a square peg in a round hole,' recalled a former waitress. 'Like Basil Fawlty he was not polite to the guests and he shouted at staff … It was as if he didn't want the guests to be there.'

He certainly didn't want Monty Python. The comedy team was considered a 'colossal inconvenience' when they came to stay in 1970, recalled group member Michael Palin, who left after one night only to be presented with a bill for two weeks. Too 'lazy' to leave, his fellow Python John Cleese stuck around and watched a sitcom pretty much write itself.

In a few short weeks, the comedian saw Sinclair yell at his cheap foreign labour (think 'Manuel'), criticise Terry Gilliam's 'clearly American' table manners (he was holding his fork in the 'wrong' hand), throw Eric Idle's suitcase behind a wall (the 'bomb' inside it was a ticking clock) and abuse builders for slacking off (they were on a tea break). Watch the *Fawlty Towers* episodes 'The Builders', 'Waldorf Salad' and 'Basil the Rat' and you can see all the fun for yourself.

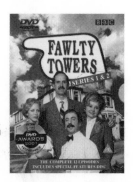

Fawlty Towers screened from 1975 until 1979. The TV series was written by, and starred, John Cleese

PUNCH–DRUNK LOVE'S BARRY EGAN

The proof isn't the only thing in the pudding these days. Along with milk and sugar (and additives and thickening agents), you can find frequent flyer miles as well.

Barry Egan did, anyway. Adam Sandler's character in *Punch–Drunk Love* was inspired by a real-life Californian civil engineer named David Phillips, who once won 1.25 million frequent flyer miles thanks to an ill-considered promotion from the Healthy Choice food company. The promotion (a few miles for every ten barcodes) wasn't all that enticing when it came to 99 per cent of Healthy Choice products – moderately expensive items like cereal and pasta sauce. Phillips did a bit of driving, however, and found one cut-price exception. Certain discount grocery stores sold tiny individually barcoded Healthy Choice pudding cups for just twenty-five cents apiece. So he bought 25,000 of them.

'It worked out great,' says the avid blackjack player – who, unlike his *Punch–Drunk Love* alter ego, is not a lonely patron of phone sex hotlines and prone to sudden fits of rage. 'I got the miles and the Salvation Army got the pudding.'

Phillips has since taken family and friends to almost thirty countries – though, unfortunately, he still needs to pay for hotels. 'There are a lot of other expenses … I'm going broke with all the free travel.'

Punch–Drunk Love premiered in 2002. The film starred Adam Sandler

ON THE ROAD'S DEAN MORIARTY

Rather astonishingly, Jack Kerouac wrote *On the Road* in just three weeks. Rather less astonishingly, it then took him nine years to find a publisher. A tale of some guy and his mate driving, drinking, doing drugs, then driving some more, it's not hard to see why so many editors initially mistook the definitive work of the Beat Generation for a definitive piece of crap.

What made the book different from some teenager droning on tediously about his big weekend (albeit only marginally) was the character of Dean Moriarty. An oft-jailed 'son of a wino' who yearns for the freedom of the open road, Moriarty was based on Kerouac's real-life driving chum Neil Cassady, a 'mad genius' and 'Nietzschean hero' who worked as a car park attendant in New York.

In and out of prison for stealing cars, Cassady's biggest mistake was going for a walk. After taking god-knows-what at a party in New Mexico, he stumbled off for a stroll in the great open spaces and collapsed with heart failure after a couple of miles.

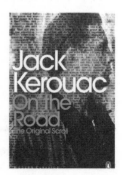

On the Road, by Jack Kerouac, was published in 1957

JEFF 'THE DUDE' LEBOWSKI

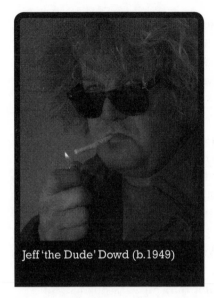

Jeff 'the Dude' Dowd (b.1949)

For such a well-known slacker, the Dude actually works pretty hard. A Vietnam War activist in the 60s (who was jailed when a protest turned violent), Jeff 'the Dude' Dowd now toils away in Hollywood, promoting independent movies.

In the 70s, however, he was less productive. 'We kind of hung out and hung pretty heavy ... drinking White Russians and Tequila Sunrises and any other drink of the moment. And smoking a little of whatever it was.'

A large man with large hair, Dowd met the Coen brothers while promoting their 1984 film, *Blood Simple*. Immediately taken by his nickname ('they used to like to get on the phone and go "Dude, Duder, Duderino"'), the filmmakers knew about his past and were thinking about the future. *The Big Lebowski* was born.

'I'm a pretty quick and easy study to mimic,' says Dowd of his iconic alter ego, Jeff 'the Dude' Lebowski – a character who passes his days bowling, smoking dope, drinking White Russians and listening to Creedence Clearwater Revival. 'But you know, I think one of the things that people like about the Dude character ... is that he's able to see through the bullshit ... So many people have to go to work every day and put on their costumes, their masks in the corporate world, and I think that they have an appreciation for somebody who understands that a lot of that's not the way it should be ... I'm an opinionated guy, and in many ways the Dude is too.'

The Big Lebowski premiered in 1998. Directed by the Coen brothers, the movie starred Jeff Bridges

119

WILL AND GRACE

Dense philosophical tracts aren't usually a source of sitcoms. There aren't many laughs in phenomenology or the metaphysics of Emmanuel Kant. Martin Buber's *I and Thou* is different, however. By revealing how to have an 'I–Thou relationship in the presence of the eternal' (you need the 'will' to go after it and the 'grace' to receive it), it gave us the sitcom title *Will and Grace*.

Another slightly less baffling source of inspiration was a casting director named Janet Eisenberg. She gave us Grace Adler – a kooky redhead never happier than when she's fretting about her foot size or dating someone inappropriate. Now based in New York, Janet went to school with the show's co-creator Max Mutchnick, and went out with him for a while as well. 'Max and Janet seemed to have a lovely rapport but the romantic element confused me and it confused them as well,' recalled classmate David Kohan.

Things became less confusing after Max came out. 'She was stunned,' says Kohan. 'It was a shocking revelation for her, so I kind of functioned as a liaison between the two of them, because they both still really loved each other.' Love triumphed after a few years of frostiness, you'll be glad to hear, and a beautiful friendship was reborn. 'We are made for each other in every way except the bedroom,' says Max.

Should any of this seem vaguely familiar, watch the first episode of *Will and Grace* and you'll find out why.

Will & Grace screened from 1998 until 2006. The TV series was created by Max Mutchnick and David Kohan

LEGALLY BLONDE'S ELLE WOODS

Elle Woods is no quitter. When *Legally Blonde*'s beautiful, bouncy sorority president is dumped by her Harvard law student boyfriend, does she let it get her down? Well … yes. But then she gets into Harvard herself, charms those dowdy intellectual types, singlehandedly wins a court case and graduates in a blaze of glory.

The real Elle, however, *is* a quitter. Like the character (whom she named after *Elle* magazine), author Amanda Brown went to a glitzy high school where she bought stuff, went to parties, glanced at a book, then bought some more stuff. Like super-rich Elle, super-rich Amanda managed to get into an Ivy League law school, nonetheless arriving with a designer wardrobe, pink legal pad and fluffy pens.

And like Elle, she got a hard time. 'This one particularly horrible Trekkie was coming in as I was going out the door, and he knocked everything out of my hands … and, of course, he didn't help me pick anything up. So I'm down on the ground … and for the first time in two years, he said something to me. He said, "Why don't you just leave and get married like you're supposed to?"'

So she did. Amanda quit law school, got married, wrote a semi-autobiographical novel – and watched the millions roll in. If there's a moral to this story, try not to tell it to kids.

Legally Blonde, by Amanda Brown, was published in 2001.
The movie, starring Reese Witherspoon, premiered in 2001

THE BIG FRIENDLY GIANT

In a world full of Childchewers, Bonecrunchers and Gizzardgulpers, it's good to have a Big Friendly Giant. A kindly vegetarian (unlike the aforementioned child-eaters), Roald Dahl's BFG spends his days doling out pleasant dreams.

In real life, he kept busy with a hammer. Roald Dahl based his loveable title character on an actual big friendly giant: a huge, sweet-natured Norfolk builder with a 'long, pale, wrinkly face'. 'When the book was written, I didn't know I was the BFG,' Wally Saunder once commented. 'It was only later that people started coming up to me and asking, "Is it you, Wally?"'

Wally was a 'wonderful man', recalled Dahl's wife. 'He had huge hands like a bunch of bananas, enormous ears and a big nose. He spoke with a very strange accent and got his words all wrong.'

His heart was in the right place, though. A WWII veteran (who was able to flap his ears), Wally built Dahl's famous writing hut and was like a second father to his kids. One of his kids' kids – Dahl's granddaughter, the model Sophie Dahl – also appears in the book as Sophie, the little girl the BFG befriends.

The BFG, by Roald Dahl, was published in 1982

MONKEY'S TRIPITAKA

Xuanzang (c.602–664)

Adolescence is a confusing period, and watching *Monkey* doesn't really help. A teenage boy grappling with the many mysteries of his sexuality really doesn't need to see a strangely alluring boy priest – all delicate cheekbones and ruby red lips – on TV day after day, without being aware that the actor is actually a girl.

Xuanzang wouldn't have had this problem. Just like *Monkey*'s sexy boy priest, Tripitaka, this real-life monk managed to transcend his sexuality, along with assorted other earthly desires. A fully ordained Buddhist by the age of twenty, Xuanzang was unimpressed with the religious texts available in seventh-century China, so set out on a *Monkey*-like journey to India, Buddhism's birthplace, to see if they had any better scriptures there. Returning after seventeen years, he built a monastery, founded a school of Buddhism and, of course, wrote a lengthy travelogue.

Eight hundred years later, that book inspired another. *Journey to the West* is a classic Chinese novel about a boy priest sent by Buddha to obtain some holy scriptures. The TV show *Monkey* is just one of many adaptations – though it's the sauciest by far.

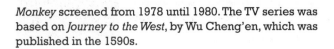

Monkey screened from 1978 until 1980. The TV series was based on *Journey to the West*, by Wu Cheng'en, which was published in the 1590s.

ALL CREATURES GREAT AND SMALL'S SIEGFRIED FARNON

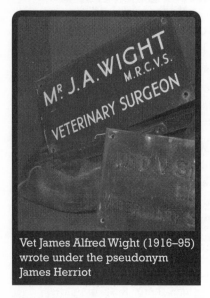

Vet James Alfred Wight (1916–95) wrote under the pseudonym James Herriot

Sometimes being a war hero means sticking your hand up a sick cow's bum.

When WWII was declared, a Yorkshire vet named Donald Sinclair immediately joined the RAF, hiring a young assistant to take care of his practice. Given the severe food shortage, however, the authorities decided that England would be better served by healthy farm animals, so sent the vet back to work.

Bad news for Donald. Good news for us. For that young assistant was none other than would-be author James Herriot. In Herriot's *All Creatures Great and Small*, the eccentric, demanding, endlessly disorganised Donald became the eccentric, demanding, endlessly disorganised Siegfried Farnon. His brother Brian Sinclair became Tristan Farnon, and the town of Thirsk in North Yorkshire, where the practice was based, became the *All Creatures* town of Darrowby.

The publicity-shy Donald is said to have resented the novels, telling Herriot that it was 'a real test' of their friendship. We can't ask him if that's true because, a few months after his wife – and then Herriot – passed away, Donald swallowed some poison and died.

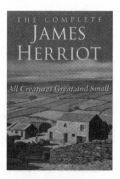

All Creatures Great and Small, the compilation of James Herriot's vet stories, was published in 1972

HOWARDS END'S MARGARET WILCOX

Rooksnest, in happier times

In EM Forster's novel of the same name, Howards End represents a retreat from the vulgar world – a cosy, thatched pocket of ye olde England tucked away amid trees and shrubs.

In real life, Howards End *is* the vulgar world. Once owned by the Howard family, Forster's childhood home, Rooksnest, is these days surrounded by Stevenage. In place of England's green and pleasant land, Rooksnest snuggles up to several grey and unpleasant business parks – home to GlaxoSmithKline, Tubetec Tube Fitting and Guy Mace Industrial Chemical Consultants, among others, and conveniently close to the A1.

Forster himself hated the development, describing it as 'like a meteorite upon … ancient and delicate scenery'. The married couple who lived at Rooksnest after him, the Postons, probably disliked it too. Just like their *Howards End* alter egos, Mr and Mrs Wilcox, the Postons were a successful but slightly unlikely match: a widowed, rather conservative father and a lively, 'charming and cultivated' second wife.

Perhaps, thought Forster, this pairing of opposites worked simply because Rooksnest was so nice? 'It was almost as if it was the house that was the stability and the harmony, not a particular wife,' as one biographer puts it – 'as if the strength and spirit of the house transcended individuality'.

Howards End, by EM Forster, was published in 1910

SHAKESPEARE'S FALSTAFF

The burning of Sir John Oldcastle (1370–1417)

Shakespeare could be a little smutty. His plays contain around 400 gags about genitals and at least 700 puns on sex. He didn't just do blue material, though. Falstaff, *Henry V*'s 'fat, vainglorious and cowardly knight', is apparently subtle political satire – or, at least, some say that he was going to be, until the playwright lost his nerve.

Originally called Oldcastle, the character seems to have been conceived as a parody of Sir John Oldcastle, a real-life counsellor to Prince Hal. The similarities end there, however: Oldcastle was a capable advisor, successful military leader and Puritan reformer. He ended up being burnt for heresy after taking on the corrupt authorities of the church.

Falstaff's original incarnation as Oldcastle, then, was an exercise in political satire. Making Henry's counsellor ever-so-pious in theory and a bawdy, boozy braggart in practice would have been a neat anti-Puritan joke.

Or so, at least, the theory goes.

Falstaff first appeared in *Henry IV*, William Shakespeare's 1597 play

THE VICAR OF DIBLEY

In 1994 the Church of England ditched 400 years of tradition and allowed the ordination of female priests. (Its other tradition, closet atheism, continues to this day.) For a punk-rocking former barmaid and schoolteacher this was a stroke of luck. Joy Carroll became a curate in Southwark, south London – and the model for the Vicar of Dibley.

TV writer Richard Curtis came up with the idea of a sitcom about a female vicar after seeing one marry some friends ('I thought to myself, "This is so much more apt than getting married by some weird man"') – but it was meeting Carroll that gave the character shape.

'I had been having seriously cold feet. I couldn't imagine a female priest young enough or spunky enough or credible enough to base the character on,' says Dawn French, who played the hard-partying, chocoholic churchwoman. But 'there were sufficient empties lined up in [Caroll's] kitchen to reassure me that this girl knew how to party'. Not to mention a mug with the inscription 'Lead me not into temptation, I can find it myself'.

'I knew it was so right that women should be ordained. Women are good at this job, it comes naturally to us, providing spiritual guidance and succour. I could finally see how [the character] might work.'

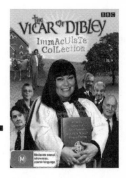

The Vicar of Dibley screened from 1994 until 2007. Created by Richard Curtis, the TV series starred Dawn French

Chapter 7
Geniuses

CHITTY CHITTY BANG BANG'S CARACTACUS POTTS

Count Louis Zborowski
(1895–1924)

On average, someone once calculated, we each spend about two weeks waiting at traffic lights.

Caractacus Potts never waited at all. The inventor of Chitty Chitty Bang Bang, the magical flying car, was himself invented by Ian Fleming, a man better known for giving us James Bond. Fleming's one and only children's novel was based on a memory of his own childhood.

With his parents, the author once visited the Kentish home of Count Louis Zborowski, a racing car driver, squillionaire and loon.

In 1920, the count was anxious to put those squillions to further use (he had already married a showgirl), so he hit upon a fine idea. Why not take the body of a lightweight Mercedes and throw in the engine of a military jet? He christened the resulting sports car/bomber 'Chitty Chitty Bang Bang' and used to drive it across the Sahara and win a race or two.

The Italian Grand Prix went less well, however. Racing in a more conventional car, the count crashed into a tree and died.

Chitty Chitty Bang Bang: The Magical Car was published in 1964. In 1968, the Ian Fleming novel was made into a movie starring Dick Van Dyke

JEEVES

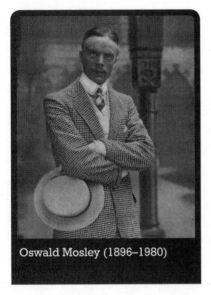

Oswald Mosley (1896–1980)

Genius is a burden bestowed on very few. Newspaper columnists often feel that they are carrying it, but it's generally self-importance instead. Jeeves, on the other hand, *does* have genius, and is always happy to put it to use. As his creator PG Wodehouse puts it, the all-knowing manservant 'takes a size 14 hat, eats tons of fish and moves in mysterious ways his wonders to perform'.

He probably also knows a bit about spiders. Jeeves is said to have been based on Wodehouse's butler, Eugene Robinson, whom he once described as a 'walking encyclopaedia'.

Jeeves's foppish master may have been drawn from life too. Bertie Wooster has a prototype in George Grossmith Jr, an Edwardian music hall star best known for playing dimwitted 'fop' characters. Grossmith was well known to Wodehouse, who occasionally wrote for the stage.

Bertie's fictional aunts, Dahlia (the good one) and Agatha (the one who 'chews broken bottles and kills rats with her teeth'), are said to resemble the author's aunts, Louisa and Mary Deane, while his mortal enemy, the would-be dictator Roderick Spode, is a clear parody of a real-life would-be dictator, the famously deranged Oswald Mosley.

Jeeves first appeared in *Extricating Young Gussie,* a 1915 short story by PG Wodehouse, before going on to appear in many more

IAN FLEMING'S Q

Charles Fraser-Smith (1904–92)

How can you possibly save the world without a dagger shoe, a ski pole gun or plastic explosives disguised as ordinary toothpaste?

The answer, of course, is that you can't. Which is why the world must be forever grateful to Q, James Bond's gadget man, and Charles Fraser-Smith, the boffin who inspired him. A former Christian missionary in Morocco, who later ran a dairy farm in Devon, Fraser-Smith officially spent WWII at the Clothing and Textile Department of the UK Ministry of Supply.

Unofficially, he was working for MI6, devising snazzy gadgets for secret agents. A little more low-tech than Q, Fraser-Smith mostly put things inside other things. Mini-cameras went into cigarette lighters, mini-compasses into golf balls. Maps were squeezed into hairbrushes, and secret agents' shoes contained little saws.

For one week a year until his death, Fraser-Smith would himself squeeze into a little booth at Exmoor steam railway station and share his war work with passers-by. 'He was always delighted to explain to visitors the workings of the gadgets.'

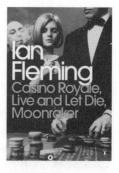

Q first appeared in *Casino Royale*, a 1953 novel by
Ian Fleming

MALCOLM IN THE MIDDLE

Every parent thinks their child is a genius. The ability to dress oneself and poo in a toilet may not seem that remarkable to outsiders, but when you spend your first six months lying on your back gurgling, pretty much anything represents amazing progress.

Malcolm's parents, however, *knew* he was a genius. It said so on all the tests. Placed in a class for 'gifted' students, and duly ostracised by the rest of the school, *Malcolm in the Middle*'s teenage whiz-kid also has trouble relating to his less-than-intellectual brothers, his dimwitted teachers and his disciplinarian mum.

Linwood Boomer knew just how he felt. The Canadian TV producer created Malcolm as a 'very self-serving, highly exaggerated version' of himself. 'I was a troubled kid with very few social skills and did not connect to the people around me,' says Boomer, who was put into 'gifted' classes just like the character, and was also known to war with his three brothers. 'I was not a sociopath, but I wasn't social. I was always telling the principal he was stupid and arguing with my teachers … So basically I took a belligerent jackass and turned him into a charming eccentric.'

Though that wasn't the only difference. 'My mom would never tell me what my IQ was, so when I wrote *Malcolm*, I said his IQ was 165. My mom then told me that mine was never that high.'

Malcolm in the Middle screened from 2000 until 2006. The TV series was created by Linwood Boomer

HANNIBAL LECTER

Eating human flesh can be good for you. Sure, there's a chance of brain malformation (or dementia or paralysis or death) but it also offers up plenty of fibre, plus protein to power through the day.

William Coyner would have been a healthy man. A peckish killer from Cleveland, he had a pretty open mind when it came to snacks. After escaping from jail in 1934, the cannibal went on a major killing/snacking spree. He apparently needed 200 armed guards after he was finally re-caught.

The Silence of the Lambs author Thomas Harris was born in Cleveland six years after Coyner was executed and we can be pretty sure he would have heard a few tales. So was Dr Hannibal 'I-ate-his-liver-with-some-fava-beans-and-a-nice-chianti' Lecter inspired by the real-life loony? According to one biographer, Harris once privately confessed that the answer was 'yes'.

Hannibal Lecter first appeared in *Red Dragon*, a 1981 novel by Thomas Harris, and became a recurring character

RAIN MAN

Kim Peek (1951–2009)

Not all body parts get the credit they deserve. We hear a lot about legs and teeth and bowels and nostril hair but what about the good old corpus callosum, that splodge of gooey membrane that connects our right and left brains? Where do you think you'd be without it?

Quite possibly, you'd be in *Rain Man*. Kim Peek, the inspiration for Dustin Hoffman's Oscar-winning turn as autistic savant Raymond Babbitt, was born without said splodge – and *with* a remarkable memory. Possibly because, lacking their usual lines of communication, his neurons went and made other connections, this prodigy managed to memorise the contents of over 12,000 books. Since reading each tome took less than an hour (he would simultaneously scan the left page with his left eye, and the right page with his right), 'Kimputer' also liked to mentally add up the numbers in a phone book, for the sake of a mental challenge.

On the other hand, Kim was cursed with a range of developmental difficulties and had trouble doing things like buttoning up his shirt and walking. Like Rain Man, he never completed high school. He also had the character's rapid monotone, swaying motions and general childishness.

Rain Man premiered in 1988. The Academy Award–winning film starred Dustin Hoffman and Tom Cruise

THE WEST WING'S JOSH LYMAN

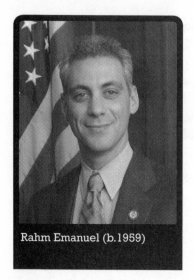

Rahm Emanuel (b.1959)

In *The West Wing*, Josh Lyman is said to be 'the finest political mind in the party'. His real genius, though, lay in being able to talk so fast while pacing around the corridors of power. A little like Rahm Emanuel, Barack Obama's real-life former chief of staff: hot-headed to the point of rudeness and a bit of a loose cannon to boot.

Actually, he is *exactly* like Rahm Emanuel. A tough, fast-talking apparatchik. Prone to profanity and career-damaging outbursts. *Loathes* Republicans. Rumoured to have once mailed a colleague, Mafia-style, a rotting fish.

Rahm's brother, it turns out, is the Hollywood agent of *The West Wing*'s creator, and also of Brad Whitford, the actor who plays Josh. Rahm's 'uh, blunt,' says Whitford. 'I think that if you played Rahm Emanuel like Rahm Emanuel actually is, I don't think people would believe it.'

'People think Rahm is a bad guy but he really has a soft side,' President Obama once joked. 'He volunteers to teach profanity to underprivileged kids.'

Or should that be 'President *Santos* once joked'? Matt Santos, *The West Wing*'s young, charismatic congressman who rises above racism to win the White House, was based on Obama himself. 'I drew inspiration from him in drawing this character,' said a *West Wing* writer. 'Obama was just appearing on the national scene. He had done a great speech at the convention and … was mobbed wherever he went … Santos's insistence on not being defined by his race, his pride in it even as he rises above it' came from Obama, along with his 'celebrity aura'.

The West Wing screened from 1999 until 2006. Created by Aaron Sorkin, the TV series starred Brad Whitford

SAUL BELLOW'S HUMBOLDT

Delmore Schwartz (1913–66)

Before embarking on this opening sentence, I ate a banana, took my dog for a walk, and made sure all was well with my sock drawer. After I complete *this* one, I'll probably give the floor a quick sweep and see if the roses need pruning.

Such is life under the 'Delmore effect' – a psychological condition whereby one devotes a lot of time to low-priority goals at the expense of what needs to be done.

It was named after Delmore Schwartz. A poet and short-story writer of genius, Delmore was also very good at writing nothing. After beginning his career in a blaze of glory – he was labelled 'the American Auden' at just twenty-five, and showered in fellowships and prizes – the heavenly poet slowly slipped into a blaze of hell. Beset by alcoholism, drug abuse, mental illness and procrastination, Schwartz spent his last dozen years in semi-isolation in a New York hotel, and died forgotten at just fifty-three. Hotel staff discovered his body a few days later.

Luckily, one of Delmore's friends was a bit more productive. Saul Bellow (a resident of Humboldt Park, Chicago) later turned Delmore into Von Humboldt Fleisher, a depressed poet who dies in a run-down hotel, having wasted pretty much all of his gifts.

Humboldt's Gift, by Saul Bellow, was published in 1975

DOOGIE HOWSER

If you're convinced your child's a genius, it's probably best that you don't watch *Doogie Howser, MD*. (Though that rule also applies even if you *don't* think your child's a genius. The show wasn't very good.)

Blessed with an eidetic memory, Dr Doogie Howser completed high school in nine weeks, graduated from Princeton at ten and became America's youngest licenced doctor at the age of fourteen. He was performing colonoscopies, sigmoidoscopies and positron emission tomographies while your pride and joy was still watching reality TV shows and working out how to download porn.

So what's the *real* Doogie doing now? Many things, as it turns out. The cousin of a TV programmer, Dr Howard Zucker has one of those CVs that make you wonder what you've been doing with your time. Once one of America's youngest doctors, he's also been a lawyer, a White House fellow, a member of the Council on Foreign Relations, an Assistant Director-General of the World Health Organization and a professor at Yale, Columbia and Cornell. On top of that, Zucker once worked at the Massachusetts Institute of Technology, designing space shuttle microgravity experiments for NASA.

Must stop now. Feel sick.

Doogie Howser, MD screened from 1989 until 1993. The TV series starred Neil Patrick Harris

IRONMAN'S TONY STARK

Howard Hughes (1905–76)

Hypochondria isn't a quality often found in superheroes. They're generally too busy leaping over tall buildings to fret about a case of the sniffles.

Every rule has an exception, however, and this one's called Tony Stark. *Ironman*'s brilliant playboy/industrialist (who, when he isn't inventing weapons for the US military, becomes a superhero so as to kill people himself) was based on the hypochondriac Howard Hughes.

Hughes 'was one of the most colourful men of our time,' says the comic writer Stan Lee, who created Tony Stark in homage. 'He was an inventor, an adventurer, a multi-billionaire, a ladies' man and finally a nutcase.' And like Stark, Hughes was also a 'one-man Halliburton empire'. By inventing weapons for the US government during and after WWII, he also helped invent the military-industrial complex.

He was equally creative when it came to his health. The germ-phobic gazillionaire rarely washed, shaved or brushed his teeth during his final years (though he did wear tissue boxes on his feet). Much of his last decade was spent in a darkened hotel room, specially designed to be a germ-free zone.

Iron Man first appeared in *Tales of Suspense #39*, a 1963 comic by Stan Lee. The film *Iron Man*, starring Robert Downey Jr, premiered in 2008, and its sequel was released in 2010

ARTEMIS FOWL II

Not all children are evil geniuses. Some of them are just evil.

Donal Colfer *did* have the brainpower to carry out his wicked schemes, however. The Irish architect was 'a bit of an artful dodger as a kid,' recalls one of his brothers, the author Eoin Colfer. 'With my brothers you have to be on top form or you'll be destroyed.' Donal, in particular, was 'a mischievous mastermind who could get out of any trouble he got into'.

Seeing an old photo of Donal in his first communion suit led the author to another literary comparison. 'He looked like a little James Bond villain.' Thinking about 'how funny ... a twelve-year-old James Bond villain' would be, he duly created Artemis Fowl, a dastardly, prepubescent villain in the habit of kidnapping leprechauns.

Donal, we're told, was 'delighted' to have inspired Artemis but another brother is 'not so happy'. *Eamonn* Colfer appears as Mulch Diggums, the book's portly, flatulent dwarf. 'He should've been nicer to me as a kid,' says the author.

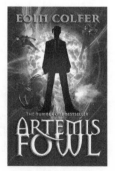

The first *Artemis Fowl* book, by Eoin Colfer, was published in 2001

DR FRANKENSTEIN

Castle Frankenstein, Darmstadt

Frankenstein was actually a bit of a wuss. Honestly, a twelve-year-old girl could have beaten him up, provided she had some kind of weapon and was reasonably big for her age. Frankenstein, you see, wasn't actually the huge, remorseless killing machine of popular imagination, but the weedy scientist who invented him. Referred to as 'the monster', 'the fiend' and 'the daemon' throughout the book, 'Frankenstein's monster' started being shortened to 'Frankenstein' somewhere along the way, proving that hardly anyone has actually read the book.

The horror story was famously created by the poet Percy Bysshe Shelley's wife Mary, while the couple was on holiday in Switzerland. Some say that, en route, they may have visited Castle Frankenstein ('stone of the Franks'), a picturesque ruin in southwest Germany. If this is true, then they certainly would have been told about its former owner, the kooky alchemist Johann Konrad Dippel.

Dippel didn't just wish to create gold, says one academic; 'he always wanted to perpetuate life'. Not unlike Dr Frankenstein, the mad scientist 'claimed he had an oil that could make you live to over a hundred and he dug up graves and collected cadavers to use for this purpose.'

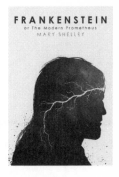

Frankenstein; or, The Modern Prometheus, by Mary Shelley, was published in 1818

CASINO ROYALE'S LE CHIFFRE

Aleister Crowley (1875–1947)

Throughout human history, great minds have managed many great feats, in everything from chemistry to physics to the arts. It took the genius of Le Chiffre, however, to think of tying James Bond to a chair and beating his testicles with knotted rope.

Also a mathematical whiz, and more than handy with a deck of cards, *Casino Royale*'s sinister supervillain may have had more than just torture in mind. In the book, at least, this bad man is manifestly bisexual, disconcerting Bond with his odour of 'unmentionable vice'.

That trait came courtesy of Aleister Crowley, a notorious English 'black magician' once considered 'the wickedest man in the world'. Crowley also gave Le Chiffre his small stature, strange eyes (all white around the iris) and habit of calling people 'dear boy'.

Fond of heroin, benzedrine and sadomasochism, Crowley founded 'the Magickal philosophy known as Thelema' and knew his way around a ouija board. It's said that when Hitler's deputy, Rudolph Hess, was captured by the British during WWII, he spoke in strange ramblings that some interpreted as occult. Bond author Ian Fleming worked in intelligence at the time and apparently sought to involve the black magician in the interrogations. He was vetoed, to his great chagrin.

Le Chiffre first appeared in *Casino Royale*, a 1953 novel by Ian Fleming

DR JEKYLL (AND MR HYDE)

If you're going to have dual personalities, surely at least one of them should be likeable? William Brodie, sad to say, failed in this basic courtesy. By night, this married, eminently respectable cabinet-maker and city councillor would sneak out into the mean streets of Edinburgh to rob banks, gamble heavily and quietly accumulate mistresses and kids. By day, he was, well, a city councillor.

Despite his best efforts to survive the noose (legend says he smuggled in a steel collar), Brodie's double life ended eighteen years after his first robbery, when a fellow crim ratted him out.

A century later, he was granted two more lives, however – as Dr Jekyll and Mr Hyde. Robert Louis Stevenson grew up in Edinburgh, in a house containing one of Brodie's cabinets. The author wrote a play called *Deacon Brodie, or The Double Life* early in his career, then ditched it and used the theme for a novel.

In that novel Dr Jekyll is a friendly, seemingly normal fellow – until he creates a potion that lets out the beast within. That beast's name, of course, is Mr Hyde. Exactly what this 'cruel', 'lustful', 'remorseless' subhuman does on his nocturnal excursions is never made entirely clear. We can only hope that he didn't become a city councillor.

The Strange Case of Dr Jekyll and Mr Hyde, by Robert Louis Stevenson, was published in 1886

DR STRANGELOVE

Wernher von Braun (1912–77)

Evildoers will always be punished, unless they can make themselves useful.

Dr Wernher von Braun was a useful Nazi. This brilliant rocket scientist may have designed Hitler's V-2 ballistic missiles. And, yes, he may have built them with slave labour. The point was, he could do the same kind of thing in the US.

After WWII, von Braun worked for the US military, and then for NASA, where he designed the rocket that took the first man to the moon. And wrote about how it could be used to launch missiles …

In 1975, he received America's highest medal for science. Yes, it's a heartening tale.

Less heartening is the story of *Dr Strangelove*. This is mostly because it sees the world get destroyed by a nuclear apocalypse. To find one of the models for the movie's crazy scientist (a warped, irrationally rational ex-Nazi prone to saying 'Sieg Heil!') we need look no further than von Braun himself.

Dr Strangelove, or: How I Learned to Stop Worrying and Love the Bomb premiered in 1964. Directed by Stanley Kubrick, the movie starred Peter Sellers

FAUST

Johann Sabellicus
(c.1480–1540)

Even if you *really* want something, it's best not to sell your soul.

Faust did, of course – handing it over to Satan in return for some knowledge and power. Good times followed for a decade or two but now that he's roasting for eternity in the fiery pits of hell, he may just feel a certain regret.

'Regret' isn't a word usually associated with Johann Sabellicus, on whom the character of Faust was based. He more often gets 'con man' and 'swindler'.

An alchemist, astrologer and magician, Sabellicus received a degree in divinity in 1509, then renamed himself 'Johann Faustus' ('the fortunate'). The rest of his career seems to have been spent wandering around Germany, displaying various dark arts in exchange for cash.

When a churchman denounced Sabellicus as the Devil's agent, that savvy marketer was more than happy to agree. 'I have pledged myself to the Devil with my own blood, to be his in eternity, body and soul.'

The Devil took his body, at least. Legend says Sabellicus's corpse was found on a dungheap. Horribly mutilated limbs still twitching. Eyes glued to a nearby wall.

The Tragical History of Doctor Faustus, by Christopher Marlowe, was first performed in the 1590s

SVENGALI

The biggest-selling book of the nineteenth century wasn't *War and Peace* or *Pride and Prejudice* or anything else you might have actually heard of. It was *Trilby* by George du Maurier, an elderly cartoonist who took up writing for fun.

You've heard of the book's main character, however. Now a byword for shadowy puppetmasters, the hook-nosed hypnotist Svengali is a musical virtuoso – a man who knows pretty much everything about timbre, pitch and tone. Unfortunately, he also knows that he can't sing. A solution comes to hand in the form of Trilby O'Farrell, an artist's model who's tone deaf but blessed with some excellent pipes. Unwittingly put under hypnosis, she becomes an opera diva and the darling of Paris.

A good news story, I would have thought, but *Trilby* treats Svengali as some kind of bad guy. We read about his 'sinister' and 'sallow' face, his 'black beady eyes' and his 'big yellow teeth'. His voice is 'thin and mean and harsh'. When he smiles, it's 'a mongrel canine snarl', when he laughs, it's a sound 'full of malice'.

All of which was doubtless quite offensive to the real Svengali, who was actually one of the author's good pals. A hypnotist and dab hand at the piano, Felix Moscheles roomed with du Maurier during their university days in Antwerp. 'Hypnotism formed [a] frequent … topic of conversation and speculation between du Maurier and myself,' he later recalled. 'It was on one or the other of these excursions, I feel confident, that du Maurier was inoculated with the germs that were eventually to develop into Trilbyism and Svengalism.'

Trilby, by George du Maurier, was published in 1894

THE USUAL SUSPECTS' KEYSER SÖZE

Parenting, as they say, is the hardest job in the world – and the how-to books aren't much help. Do *this*, says one. Do *that*, says another. Don't even contemplate doing either, a third one solemnly intones.

There is one point, however, on which all authorities agree. It is not good to murder your three children, and their mother, then disappear for eighteen years.

John List was one such deadbeat dad. In 1971, this churchgoing New Jersey accountant had serious financial problems, having taken on a big mortgage then lost his job. He also had a wife with increasing dementia. If things continued like this, List decided, his family would sink into poverty and perhaps even begin to question their Christian beliefs. So he sent them to heaven to save their souls.

He then focused on saving himself. Like the *Usual Suspects'* criminal mastermind Keyser Söze (a similarly bad husband and father), List managed to just disappear. Masquerading as 'Robert Clark', a churchgoing accountant in Virginia, he was only found after a 1989 episode of *America's Most Wanted* aired. The program featured a mock-up of how the wanted man might have aged, complete with grey hair and drooping jowls. It was so accurate one of Robert Clark's neighbours promptly called the police.

The Usual Suspects premiered in 1995. The movie starred Kevin Spacey

Chapter 8
Killers

BIG BROTHER

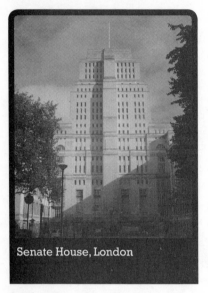

Senate House, London

George Orwell got it wrong. The problem with society today isn't that Big Brother is watching us, it's that we're watching crap like *Big Brother*.

Studying at Bennetts' Correspondence College would be a much better use of our time. The now-closed distance-education school was established by a Mr Bennett in 1930s London. His gentle, kindly face would appear in advertising posters around that city, alongside the slogan 'Let me be your father'.

When Mr Bennett died, however, his rather less comely son took over. Beside *his* faintly unfriendly face on the new posters, therefore, went a new slogan: 'Let me be your big brother'. This gave Orwell a name for the all-powerful dictator of *1984* (whose personality was of course modelled on Stalin).

If you didn't want to study at Bennetts', another option was University College, London. Senate House at the college is a towering grey pyramidal building, like the *1984* 'Ministry of Truth', with vast basements and innumerable rooms.

Room 101, however, can be found at the BBC. The Ministry's torture chamber was named after the room where the broadcaster's Indian radio division held its meetings during WWII. Sitting in those torturously long meetings was Orwell, who had joined the BBC to support the British war effort, but was uncomfortable with the propaganda he sometimes had to produce. Keeping Indian listeners loyal occasionally involved keeping them ignorant.

1984, by George Orwell, was published in 1949

COUNT DRACULA

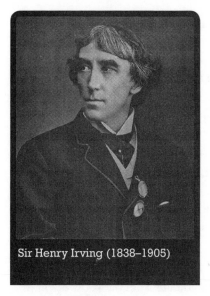

Sir Henry Irving (1838–1905)

The real villain in Bram Stoker's life wasn't 'Dracula', the bloodsucking creature of his imagination. It was the bloodsucking boss he had to face every day.

The first actor to ever be knighted, Sir Henry Irving was the Victorian era's most famous A-lister. He also managed London's Lyceum Theatre, ruling it with a rod of iron and a rather haughty tone.

As his personal assistant, Bram Stoker was governed rather more than most. Like Irving, his Count Dracula is tall and thin. Moody and menacing. Pale and patrician. The undead one's dramatic presence, polished manners and sweeping hand gestures were all taken from Irving – along with his tendency to abuse his underlings.

Dracula's *name*, however, came from Romania. The link between the character and Vlad the Impaler, a fifteenth-century prince from the region, is often overstated. It's true Vlad wasn't very nice to people (he impaled thousands of them, frequently through the anus), but he never actually drank their blood.

What he *did* do was adopt the nickname 'Dracul-a' ('son of Dragon': Vlad's dad was part of a group of knights called 'The Order of the Dragon'). Bram Stoker came across the name while researching his novel about a vampire character called 'Count Wampyr', and decided to call him 'Dracula' instead.

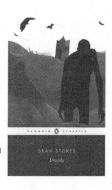

Dracula, by Bram Stoker, was published in 1897

TAXI DRIVER'S TRAVIS BICKLE

Arthur Bremer (b. 1950), in handcuffs

Next time you have a bad cab ride, reflect that it could have been worse. Yes, *Taxi Driver*'s taxi driver keeps the bad music to a minimum and generally knows how to read a map. But on the other hand he's psychotically unstable: a crazy loner with some enormous guns.

In the movie, Travis Bickle wants to use these guns to kill a presidential candidate. Unable to get past the Secret Service, he makes do by shooting a few pimps instead.

The real Travis Bickle *did* get past the Secret Service. A janitor who largely lived in his car, Arthur Bremer shot George Wallace four times at point-blank range in 1972, paralysing that presidential candidate from the waist down. Bremer's motive – as his diary, published from jail the next year, revealed – was not so much a hatred of Wallace as a hatred of life. I want 'to do SOMETHING BOLD AND DRAMATIC, FORCEFUL AND DYNAMIC, A STATEMENT of my manhood for the world to see,' Bremer, later diagnosed with schizophrenia, wrote. 'Nobody ever ... took interest in me as an individual with the need to receive or give love.'

Screenwriter Paul Schrader used Bremer's tale of urban dislocation as a starting point for *Taxi Driver* – and went to write a bit about himself. Unemployed and recently divorced, Schrader was 'very suicidal' at the time he wrote the movie. 'I was enamoured with guns, I was drinking heavily, I was obsessed with pornography in the way a lonely person is ... One day I went to the emergency room in serious pain. While I was in hospital talking to the nurse I ... noticed that I hadn't talked to anyone in two or three weeks. It really hit me; I was like a taxi driver floating around in this metal coffin in the city, seemingly in the middle of people but absolutely, totally alone.'

Taxi Driver premiered in 1976. Written by Paul Schrader, the movie starred Robert De Niro

THE COUNT OF MONTE CRISTO

Some say that living well is the best revenge. Other people prefer homicide.

Pierre Picaud was in the second camp. When this Parisian shoemaker was falsely denounced as a spy by three friends, he simply refused to see the funny side. Okay, the joke meant he got sent to prison for several years, but all turned out well in the end. Picaud was bequeathed a 'hidden treasure' by a dying inmate, tracked it down upon his release, and returned to France with a false name and fine clothes.

Placed in a similar situation, Alexandre Dumas's Count of Monte Cristo is a little testy to begin with, but ends up able to forgive. Picaud was less broadminded. He instead elected to stab two of the jokesters and then poison the third (burning down the latter's restaurant for good measure, which forced the man's daughter into prostitution and his son into a life of crime).

Eventually put in prison, Picaud also found a place in *Police Dévoilée*, a history of Parisian police work shamelessly plagiarised by Alexandre Dumas.

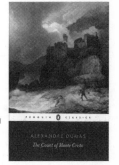

The Count of Monte Cristo, by Alexandre Dumas, was published in 1844

DEAD MAN WALKING'S MATTHEW PONCELET

Elmo Sonnier (1951–84)

In the US legal system, two wrongs make a right. Grieving for a brutally murdered relative? Then come see the killer get killed himself. Placed beside every electric chair is a front-row seat for families.

Nuns can check it out too. When Elmo Sonnier was strapped into 'Gruesome Gertie', Louisiana's 2000-volt killing machine, Sister Helen Prejean was watching on. After meeting him as part of her convent's community outreach program, she had agreed to serve as the convicted murderer and rapist's spiritual adviser – persuading him to apologise for his crimes, and doing her best to avert his death.

Sonnier's last words were said to her. 'I love you.' The last words he heard came from her. 'I love you too.'

The nun also loved Robert Willie, another Louisiana murderer who was murdered, in turn, by the state. Together, Willie and Sonnier became Matthew Poncelet, the unpleasant but utterly pitiable death-row inmate of *Dead Man Walking*.

Dead Man Walking premiered in 1995. Based on a memoir by Sister Helen Prejean, the film starred Susan Sarandon and Sean Penn

NATURAL BORN KILLERS

We all want our kids to do well in school and be the very best they can be. Mr and Mrs Hawking would have been delighted by Steven's science reports, and we can be sure that David Beckham excelled in phys ed.

Charles Starkweather was a good knife fighter. 'Even as a little kid, things would build up in him 'til he'd go berserk,' his father once fondly recalled. 'I don't think he would have stopped at shooting me.'

Short-sighted, bowlegged and with a mild speech impediment, Starkweather felt that he'd suffered at the hands of the world, and so did his best to return the favour. Thrown out of school for fighting, he became a garbo (where 'he would lean out of the … truck to perfect strangers and start yelling, "Go to hell"') and then a storeman ('He was the dumbest man we had').

These were the well-adjusted years, however. At age twenty the 'schizophrenic paranoid with an obsessive death wish' went to a petrol station to buy a stuffed dog for Caril Fugate, his equally deranged girlfriend. The attendant refused to sell him one (not unreasonably, given he had no money), so Starkweather got a shotgun and blew off his head.

Like Mickey Knox in *Natural Born Killers*, Starkweather then shot his girlfriend's parents and got her to join him on a lengthy killing spree. *Unlike* the film duo, both of them were eventually caught. She was released after seventeen years, and now works as a janitor in Michigan. *He* got electrocuted, leaving behind this eloquent note: 'i'm not sorry for what i did cause for the 1st time me and caril had more fun … all we wanted to do is get out of town.'

Natural Born Killers premiered in 1994. Directed by Oliver Stone, the movie starred Woody Harrelson and Juliette Lewis

PSYCHO'S NORMAN BATES

Ed Gein (1906–84)

You know a film is scary when even the actors get spooked. Janet Leigh never took another shower after filming *Psycho*'s famous stabbing scene. 'I suddenly said to myself, "My God, we're so vulnerable and defenceless in the shower. You can't hear because the water's running. You can't see. You're there and you're easy picking".'

Bernice Wordden was also easy picking. She was the owner of a hardware shop in Wisconsin who, in 1957, suddenly disappeared. As part of their routine inquiries, police visited the home of her last known customer, a local odd-job man named Ed Gein … and found her decapitated, mutilated corpse.

But that was just for starters. Among many, many other things, the police also found a pair of lips on a string and a vest made out of breasts. And nine masks made out of human faces. And some salted genitals in a box. It turned out that, in mourning for his recently deceased (and weirdly puritanical) mother, Gein had been raiding the local graveyard. By making and wearing a 'woman suit' (out of, yes, women), he was able to pretend that she was still alive.

Bad news for humanity – but good news for Robert Bloch. The novelist, who lived thirty-five miles away, was struck by 'the notion that the man next door may be a monster unsuspected even in the gossip-ridden microcosm of small-town life', and began scribbling straightaway. Interestingly, many details of Gein's 'insane transvestite ritual' were kept out of the press at the time. Bloch only discovered years later how closely Norman Bates, his dead-mother-recreating psycho, 'resembled the real Ed Gein in both overt act and apparent motivation'.

Psycho, by Robert Bloch, was published in 1959. The movie based on it, directed by Alfred Hitchcock, premiered the following year

BLUEBEARD

Gilles de Rais (1404–40)

Skeletons in the closet are best left undisturbed. Generally omitted from fairytale compilations these days, the story of Bluebeard features a deranged, closet-owning aristocrat who keeps mysteriously misplacing his wives. No-one is ever told what became of them, and (what with him being deranged and all) they don't quite like to ask. You can probably guess what they found in his dressing room.

Gilles de Rais, on the other hand, *didn't* keep skeletons in his closet. That's because there wouldn't have been enough room. Born in 1404, this wealthy knight won wealth, acclaim and the title 'Marshal of France' fighting alongside Joan of Arc in the Hundred Years War. The acclaim faded somewhat in 1440, however, when it was discovered that the would-be Satanist had also kept busy by raping, torturing and sacrificing around about 200 kids.

Gilles de Rais's confessions were so gruesome (think phrases like 'wallowed in the elastic warmth of their intestines' and 'wounds enlarged and opening like ripe fruit'), a judge at his trial drew a curtain over a nearby picture of Jesus.

Let's draw a veil over his confessions ourselves.

Bluebeard first appeared in *Stories or Fairy Tales from Bygone Eras,* a 1697 collection by Charles Perrault

LORD OF THE RINGS'S SAURON

The Two Towers ...
of Birmingham

Did you read the previous entry about the French Satanist, Gilles de Rais? And have you also read JRR Tolkien's fantasy saga, *The Lord of the Rings*?

If so, read this. Tolkien's Sauron the Necromancer might be based on de Rais too. A fictionalised version of the notorious Satanist appears in *The Black Douglas*, an adventure novel Tolkien loved as a child. Just like Sauron, the Lord of the Rings he later created, this fictionalised version of de Rais was an evil necromancer who commanded an army of wolves and tortured his enemies in a tower.

Some of Sauron's best work, of course, was done in and around the Two Towers. Or in and around Birmingham, if you take a more literal view. Tolkien grew up in a rural hamlet on the outskirts of that city. On his way to school, he would pass two enormous towers: the Edgbaston Waterworks (which has a sort of Italianate chimney) and Perrott's Folly (a strangely shaped hunting lodge). He also lived near Moseley Bog, later immortalised as the 'Old Forest', and Sarehole Mill, which became 'the Old Mill'.

Tolkien didn't spend all his life in Birmingham, though. In 1911, he went to Switzerland, where he picked up a postcard of Josef Madlener's painting, *The Mountain Spirit*: an old man in a forest with a white beard, wide-brimmed hat and long cloak. Tolkien kept the postcard in an envelope his whole life. On the envelope he wrote 'Origin of Gandalf'.

The 'Lord of the Rings', Sauron, first appeared in *The Hobbit*, a 1937 novel by JRR Tolkien

GANGS OF NEW YORK'S BILL THE BUTCHER

The death of Bill Poole (1821–55)

If you think the Jets and the Sharks are the only gangs of New York, you need to stop watching musicals. As Martin Scorsese showed us, the nineteenth century contained plenty more frisky hooligans – and song and dance weren't their weapons of choice.

In that director's *Gangs of New York*, one gang is led by 'Bill the Butcher'. A moustachioed psychopath who enjoys hacking people to death with meat cleavers, Bill also likes to drape himself in the American flag.

In real life, this noble patriot was William Poole, a butcher and bare-knuckle boxer who led an excitable group called the No-Nothings. 'The most ferocious rough-and-tumble fighters that ever cracked a skull or gouged out an eyeball', the No-Nothings (like the film's 'Natives') were workers who hated cheap immigrant labourers – but loved a good excuse for a riot.

Poole himself weighed well over 200 pounds and could throw a knife through a plank from 20 feet away. (From two feet away, he could kick you in the balls and smash a bottle in your face.) Just like Bill the Butcher, he died after a brawl with an Irish Catholic gang, parting with the words, 'Goodbye boys; I die a true American.'

Poole had rather more time to think of the words, though. Despite having bullets lodged in his heart and abdomen, it took him a full fourteen days to die.

Gangs of New York premiered in 2002. Directed by Martin Scorsese, the Academy Award–winning movie starred Leonardo diCaprio and Daniel Day Lewis

THE TEXAS CHAINSAW MASSACRE'S LEATHERFACE

Elmer Wayne Henley (b.1956)

Good people can still do bad things – to err is human and so forth. But can a good person impale someone on a meat hook?

Such is the philosophical question posed by *The Texas Chainsaw Massacre*. Despite killing multiple innocents, eating their bodies and wearing their faces, the intellectually disabled 'Leatherface' has his warm and cuddly side. He's a 'big baby', says the film's co-writer and director Tobe Hooper: a lumbering, disfigured dimwit who's so frightened of his cannibalistic family that he will kill anyone on their orders.

Elmer Wayne Henley would have empathised. In the early 1970s, this Texan teenager was paid to find boys for an electrician named Dean Corll – who would then torture, rape and kill them for kicks. Henley ended up killing Corll himself, after the older man threatened to rape *him*. He was duly arrested not long after.

'I saw some news report where Elmer Wayne ... said, "I did these crimes, and I'm gonna stand up and take it like a man",' recalled *The Texas Chainsaw Massacre*'s co-writer Kim Henkel. 'Well, that struck me as interesting, that he had this conventional morality at that point. He wanted it known that, now that he was caught, he would do the right thing. So this kind of moral schizophrenia is something I tried to build into the character.'

Leatherface first appeared in *The Texas Chainsaw Massacre*, a 1974 film by Tobe Hooper and Kim Henkel

LONG JOHN SILVER

William Henley (1879–1903)

Treasure Island was no Fantasy Island. To snaffle his share of the loot, our youthful hero has to flee home, steal money, witness a murder and spend months in a boat with several violent, overdressed alcoholics saying things like 'thar', 'avast' and 'me hearty'.

First among them was Long John Silver. With his peg leg, parrot and rum fetish, Robert Louis Stevenson's villainous quartermaster is the template on which all fictional pirates are based.

Or, rather, a poet named William Henley is. A 'great, glowing, massive-shouldered fellow with a big red beard' who had had a leg amputated thanks to tuberculosis, Henley was 'jovial, astoundingly clever, and with a laugh that rolled like music … He had an unimaginable fire and vitality; he swept one off one's feet'. 'It was the sight of your maimed strength and masterfulness that begot Long John Silver,' wrote Stevenson in a letter to his friend. 'The idea of a maimed man, ruling and dreaded by the sound [of his voice alone] was entirely taken from you.'

Treasure Island itself may have been taken from Stevenson's uncle. A designer of lighthouses all over the world, some say he bored young Bob with tales of his travels to Norman Island – 600 acres of Caribbean scrubland mostly inhabited by wild goats. Back in 1750, however, it also housed silver coins. The crew of a Spanish treasure galleon mutinied off the coast of North Carolina and used the island to stash the cash.

Treasure Island, by Robert Louis Stevenson, was published in 1883

THE DEPARTED'S FRANK COSTELLO

With a cop posing as a criminal, a criminal posing as a cop, a bunch of unintelligible Irishmen and doublecrosses galore, *The Departed* is one of those deeply confusing movies from which it's tempting to depart.

In the 1980s, it was also a good idea to depart South Boston. With the US's highest concentration of white poverty, that neighbourhood's blood-drenched, drug-soaked, litter-strewn streets were simply swimming with organised crime.

Overly focused on the Italian mafia, the FBI largely let James 'Whitey' Bulger's Irish mafia have its way in the area, in exchange for the occasional tip-off. But this cosy relationship got a little too cosy after a while. Agents and mobsters even started exchanging Christmas presents, along with good times, gossip and jokes. It also didn't hurt that Whitey Bulger's brother was president of the State Senate and his childhood chum, John Connelly, was a fellow criminal employed as a cop.

Eventually, the house of cards tumbled down. Connelly (who inspired *The Departed*'s Leonardo diCaprio character, Billy Costigan) is currently in prison for racketeering and obstruction of justice. Whitey (the Jack Nicholson character, Frank Costello) managed to escape before charges could be laid. Last seen in Sicily, he could now be your next-door neighbour.

The Departed premiered in 2006. The Academy Award–winning movie starred Jack Nicholson, Leonardo diCaprio and Matt Damon

SCARFACE'S TONY MONTANA

Al Calpone (1899–1947)

Al Capone was not a blood-crazed cocaine dealer who got too high on his own supply. He was Italian, rather than Cuban, portly, rather than slim. And he never killed dozens of people with a grenade launcher before being sensationally shot by 'The Skull'.

Nonetheless, he was the basis for the character Tony Montana. *Scarface* was loosely based on a 1938 movie of the same name – about Chicago mobster, Al Capone.

The prototypical gangster (it's because of him that movie mobsters always wear fedoras and pinstriped suits), 'Scarface Al' got his nickname in a bar fight, when he was a junior member of the Brooklyn Rippers. Bigger, better gangs followed (along with investigations for murder and rape), until the pudgy tough guy decided to branch out on his own. Capone more or less ruled Chicago during the 1920s – making up to $100 million a year from speak-easies and casinos (and quite a bit from prostitutes he liked to 'interview' himself).

But just like Tony Montana, Capone's lavish lifestyle eventually proved his undoing. Since he kept managing to get away with murder, the authorities jailed him for tax evasion instead.

The gangster's other extravagance caught up with him too. In jail, his syphilis became neurosyphilis, taking away his mind. Then his empire. Then his life.

Scarface premiered in 1983. The movie starred Al Pacino

GOODFELLAS' TOMMY DEVITO

Playing cards can be fun, but you must pick your opponents with care. Start beating Tommy DeSimone, for example, and he'd start throwing darts at you. Start objecting to this, and he'd get out a gun.

'It didn't take anything for these guys to kill you,' says Henry Hill of the real-life 'goodfella' and his crew. DeSimone and his associates 'liked it. They would sit around drinking booze and talk about their favourite hits'.

Born into a well-known LA crime family, and thought to have been responsible for at least ten deaths, this 'pure psychopath' was a foot taller and 30 kilos heavier than his *Goodfellas* alter ego, Tommy DeVito (played by Joe Pesci) – but he had the same homely charm. DeSimone 'would murder someone just because he wanted to try out a new firearm', says Hill. His first victim was a random pedestrian. 'Hey cocksucker!' the then–eighteen-year-old yelled at a passer-by, before pulling a trigger and strolling away.

DeSimone's last victims were close friends of the New York godfather, John Gotti. He then became a victim himself.

GoodFellas premiered in 1990. The movie starred Robert De Niro and Joe Pesci

NEW JACK CITY'S NINO BROWN

In the drug trade, discretion is all. You do not flaunt a dozen sports cars. You do not buy fifty leather coats, a hundred pairs of shoes and 300 expensive suits. You do not convert an entire apartment building into a crack factory. And most of all, you do not pose for a smug cover photo in the *New York Times* magazine under a heading like 'Mr Untouchable'.

Leroy Barnes learned this lesson a little too late. After the magazine came out in 1977 an enraged President Carter ordered his attorney general to pursue the drug kingpin. Barnes ended up jailed for life.

'Life', as so often happens, ended up being about twenty years, after Barnes turned informant on over a hundred other dealers (including, amusingly enough, his wife). He's now hidden away somewhere in the witness protection program – but can still be seen on DVD. *New Jack City*'s Nino Brown has a crack factory much like Barnes's, and a gang very similar to his Chamber Brothers. And Nino also walks free when he 'turns state evidence'. But, with a gunman hiding outside the courthouse, the character doesn't get to walk very far.

New Jack City premiered in 1991. The movie starred
Wesley Snipes

MACK THE KNIFE

Jack Sheppard (1702–24)

Australians might like to deny this, but not all eighteenth-century convicts simply stole a loaf of bread. Some were murderers. Some were rapists. Some probably bungled a fraud scheme or committed some kind of malfeasance or tort.

Jack Sheppard was a thief. Though not a very good thief, it's true, as he kept getting caught. This hapless highwayman's real skill lay in escaping: he managed to slip out of jail a remarkable four times in 1724, until he was caught a fifth time, put in shackles and hanged.

Naturally, this whole saga made Sheppard wildly popular with the masses – everybody loves a high achiever, and the authorities of the time were famously corrupt. So when John Gay wrote *The Beggar's Opera* in 1728, Sheppard was a natural model for the play's affable gangster, Macheath. Over the centuries, the character evolved into Mack the Knife – a killer, rapist and arsonist – but in Gay's original he's all Cockney charmer: dashing, debonair and beloved.

Rather less beloved was England's leader at the time, Prime Minister Robert Walpole. Some say that Macheath was also intended to be a caricature of this ever-so-refined English politician – the gag being that a robber can act like a gentleman, and a gentleman can act like a robber.

Macheath first appeared in *The Beggar's Opera*, a 1728 play by John Gay. The character morphed into Mack the Knife in Bertolt Brecht's 1928 musical, *The Threepenny Opera*

SCREAM'S GHOSTFACE

Okay, undergraduates can be annoying, but is that any reason to kill them? Yes, said Danny Rolling. Raised in Louisiana, then razed in an electric chair, this maladjusted son of a violent policeman was no friend of campus life. Over one busy weekend in 1990 (and just a week after it was declared to be the thirteenth-safest place to live in America), Rolling terrorised the Florida college town of Gainsville, killing eight people in all.

Just like Ghostface, the serial killer he inspired in *Scream*, Rolling targetted college students – and didn't stop when they were dead. He was fond of 'posing' his victims: stripping, mutilating and positioning the corpses for maximum shock value, then adding some mirrors to shock a bit more.

All in all, a very bad man. But not a bad character, if you're writing a film.

Scream premiered in 1996. Directed by Wes Craven, the movie starred David Arquette, Neve Campbell and Courteney Cox

Chapter 9
Ladies' men

WUTHERING HEIGHTS' HEATHCLIFF

Brooding, tortured outsiders need a place to be tortured and brood. In *Wuthering Heights* the Byronic Heathcliff does most of his enigmatic sighing in Thornfield Manor – a grim, Gothic mansion just perfect for being dark-eyed and passionate (or, if more appropriate, mysterious and moody).

It's also a good place to breed sheep. The inspiration for Heathcliff's home is generally held to be Top Withens, a ruined farmhouse five kilometres from author Emily Brontë's village, which is perched romantically atop a moor-laden hill.

The inspiration for Heathcliff never lived there, though. In 1796, a low-born orphan named Richard Sutton was adopted by a wealthy Yorkshire couple, only to be bullied by their three snobby boys. His one consolation was the couple's daughter, with whom it's thought that he fell in love. Being of 'so base a nature', however, Sutton 'lost the good opinion of the lady by his misconduct and [was] not permitted to come into her presence for two years'. On the plus side, he inherited the house when she and her siblings died.

All very Heathcliff. (Though it's also worth noting that a Brontë biographer sees Brontë's father as another source for the character. A 'strange', bad-tempered and 'half-mad' man, he was the sort of dad who these days would be closely monitored by Social Services.)

Wuthering Heights, by Emily Brontë, was published in 1847

PRIDE AND PREJUDICE'S MR DARCY

Tom Lefroy (1776–1869)

If our legal system punished bad movies, the makers of *Becoming Jane* would be rotting in jail. A soulless, sappy slog through the life of Jane Austen, it purports to show how a short-lived romance with one Thomas Lefroy may have led her to create Mr Darcy, the snooty stud-muffin of *Pride and Prejudice*.

Could they plead truth as a defence? No-one really knows. What we *do* know is that Lefroy was the closest thing Austen ever had to a romance. In letters she admitted to having enjoyed a 'shocking and profligate ... flirt' with this 'very gentlemanlike, good-looking [and] pleasant young man' (who went on to become Lord Chief Justice of Ireland and a right-wing scourge of Catholics).

And we also know that, after Austen died, Lefroy admitted to having had a 'boyish love' for the author, and travelled all the way to England to pay his respects. But when all's said and done, their relationship basically amounted to three winter balls while he was visiting relatives in her village – and it doesn't sound like he behaved very snootily.

Pride and Prejudice, by Jane Austen, was published in 1813

DORIAN GRAY

John Henry Gray (1866–1934)

The Dorian tribes of ancient Greece (Sparta, Crete, etc.) didn't practise 'Don't ask, don't tell'. Far from discouraging homosexuality, their armies actively encouraged it, pairing young soldiers with old ones in the belief that rougher sex maketh the man.

Which perhaps helps explain why Dorian Gray was given that name. Condemned by critics as 'effeminate' and 'unclean', Oscar Wilde's most famous novel sees a beautiful young man remain beautiful and young while his portrait grows ugly with age. Roughly half the book waxes lyrical about male bodies. The other half talks interior design.

So who was this 'young Adonis'? On a physical level, at least, the character was based on a poet named John Gray – a man so good looking it's said that opera-goers would lean out of their boxes to peer at him through binoculars. Like Dorian, Gray was blond of hair, pouty of lip, babyish of face and shell-like of ear. He too had skin like 'ivory and rose leaves' and a liking for crisp white suits.

It's said that Gray was initially flattered by *The Picture of Dorian Gray*, and would sign himself 'Dorian' in his letters to Wilde. Fear kicked in shortly afterwards, however, and he was soon threatening to sue newspapers for noting the resemblance, and studying hard to become a Catholic priest. He ended his days 'a living example of priestly virtue', doing good works among 'the hopeless poor'. And quietly shagging a poet named Marc-Andre.

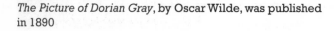

The Picture of Dorian Gray, by Oscar Wilde, was published in 1890

MAD MEN'S DON DRAPER

Draper Daniels (1913–83)

Life was easier in the 1950s, so long as you were a rich, white male. When *Mad Men*'s Don Draper wants a woman, he doesn't need to ask her about her feelings or sensitively discuss his own. He just lights up a cigarette, slams down some scotch, and reaches out with a masterful paw.

The real Don Draper kept his paws to himself. Or so, at least, says his wife. Draper Daniels 'became a one-woman man after we married,' recalled Myra Daniels, a colleague-turned-conquest of the legendary Chicago adman. Fond of a 'martini lunch', Daniels also 'quit drinking when I told him I didn't want to work with a lush' and 'stopped smoking cold turkey' after a minor heart attack.

Described as 'one of the great copy guys' by *Mad Men* creator Matt Weiner, the tall, distinguished-looking Daniels was 'a brilliant wordsmith and conceptualist'. Like his alter ego, he attracted women like 'flies to flypaper' in between creating ads for shoes, cheesy snacks and car radios. He also came up with the Marlboro Man campaign in 1954 (see page 13) – and died of cancer a few decades later.

Mad Men first screened in 2007. Created by Matt Weiner, the TV series star Jon Hamm

DON JUAN

No-one's ever actually called me 'a real Don Juan', sadly enough – but if they did I would say they were wrong. The real Don Juan was Miguel de Manara.

The leather-panted libertine of legend started out as a Spanish morality tale. In the Middle Ages 'sullying' virgins was considered a bad thing, so the 'Seducer of Seville' ends up paying for it, spending eternity in the pits of hell. Over time, however, Don Juan became more like a loveable rogue. In Molière's play, Mozart's opera and Byron's poem, the character is more of a charming ne'er-do-well than virgin-soiling servant of Satan.

Why the change? It may be because the wholesome life story of a real-life Spaniard eventually became entwined with the legend. Born in Seville in 1625, the fabulously wealthy Don Miguel de Manara had a strict religious upbringing – and so naturally spent his youth wasting money, fighting duels and shagging a nun.

A strange vision changed all that, however. De Manara imagined his own funeral procession. Contemplating the pits of hell that awaited him, the thirty-year-old very noisily changed his ways. Now a 'Venerable' of the Catholic Church (a few miracles short of a saint), de Manara founded a hospital for the poor, took over the Brotherhood of Holy Charity, and told the nun to get out of his bed.

It's said she died of grief.

Don Juan first appeared in print in *The Trickster of Seville and the Stone Guest*, a 1630 play by Tirso de Molina, but had been around as a legend for many years beforehand – painting, right, by Max Slevogt

FOUR WEDDINGS AND A FUNERAL'S CHARLES

Life can be very unfair. So convincingly did Hugh Grant play Charles, the bumbling, floppy-haired commitment-phobe in *Four Weddings and a Funeral*, people assumed he wasn't acting at all. Anyone with a grudge against gits hurled any number of insults his way.

They really should have been attacking the film's writer, Richard Curtis. 'When I read the script, I thought "I've never met anyone like this",' recalled Grant. 'Then I went to the first rehearsal and saw Richard and thought: "I see, it's you." Really I just aped him.'

'Where I got so lucky,' says Curtis, 'is that I'm a fairly dull fellow and so we found Hugh, who's so attractive and funny'.

Sweet and softly spoken like his alter ego, the Harrow-educated Curtis was inspired to write *Four Weddings and a Funeral* after attending seventy-two weddings in just a few years. Like Charles, Curtis was habitually late to these events, and used them to pursue a romance of his own.

Four Weddings and a Funeral premiered in 1994. Created by Richard Curtis, the film starred Hugh Grant and Andie MacDowell

SHAMPOO'S GEORGE ROUNDY

Jay Sebring (1933–69)

According to one biographer, Warren Beatty has shagged 12,775 women.

He's pretended to bed a few too. As *Shampoo*'s highly sexed hairdresser George Roundy, Beatty spends the movie flirting and shagging, then shagging and flirting, and every now and then cutting hair. *Shampoo* ends when his girlfriend finds him wiggling away with another woman, and stalks off in a bit of a huff.

Things ended badly for the real Roundy too. In the 1960s, Jay Sebring was the 'hairdresser to the stars'. He owned shiny salons in West Hollywood, Palm Springs, San Francisco and Las Vegas, and had sports cars parked outside each one. This debonair, dressy playboy cut the hair of Beatty, Steve McQueen, Paul Newman, Kirk Douglas and Jim Morrison, appeared on the *Batman* TV show, and used a contact to launch Bruce Lee's career.

Another contact was the actress Sharon Tate. Sebring and two friends had dinner with her at a Mexican restaurant on 8 August 1969. Returning to her house, they came face-to-face with some brand new contacts – three armed followers of the cult leader Charles Manson – and were ordered to lie down on the floor. Sebring protested that Tate was eight months pregnant. For speaking up, he was promptly gunned down.

Shampoo premiered in 1975. The film starred Warren Beatty

HIGH SCHOOL MUSICAL'S TROY BOLTON

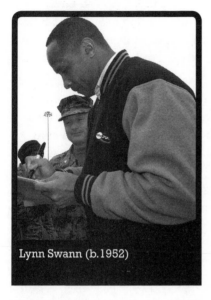

Lynn Swann (b.1952)

High School Musical has a positive message. By choosing to ponce it up in his school musical, instead of playing basketball with his fellow jocks, hunky Troy Bolton shows us that you should be who you choose to be, not simply the person who people expect.

The real Troy Bolton chose to be a Republican. Screenwriter Peter Barsocchini based the character on the Pittsburgh Steelers football player Lynn Swann, with whom he played sport at school. 'One day we were riding on a bus to a game and he said "You know, I'd really like to try ballet",' Barsocchini once recalled. 'There's the character. There's so much pressure on kids to be cool that it's tough to do something different.'

With people like Swann in high places, it's also tough to be an American. A former Republican nominee for the governor of Pennsylvania, Swann opposes abortion, supports gun rights and wants private firms to help fund education.

High School Musical premiered in 2006. Written by Peter Barsocchini, the movie (and its two sequels) starred Zac Efron and Vanessa Hudgens

ALFIE

Doug Hayward (1934–2008), left, and Michael Caine

For around 200 years the English toff was a creature of habit, who rarely strayed from his club in St James. If he needed a hat, he shopped at Locks. For boots, he went to Lobbs. And for natty tailoring, he visited Savile Row.

All that changed a few decades ago, however, thanks to the slick, spivvy son of a boiler-stoker and his twinkly-eyed Cockney charm. With grey flannel suiting for wallpaper, and champagne forever on tap, Doug Hayward's gentlemen's outfitters in Mount Street was a magnet for dressy aristocrats in the 1960s – not to mention celebrities like Roger Moore, Peter Sellers, Clint Eastwood and Bobby Moore.

'It's not Savile Row pompous,' said the cheeky chappie, who James Coburn called 'the Rodin of tweed'. 'There are no stags' heads coming through the walls, no pictures of the Queen Mum. I can get away with more bad suits because people like the atmosphere. It's relaxed, nice and easy – and, besides, I get a lot of birds in.'

That he did. So when Michael Caine was asked to play Alfie, the larrikin Cockney lady-killer with a heart of gold, it was on the tailor that his performance was based. 'It's impossible to look at that film and not recall the young Doug Hayward,' he says.

Others may feel the same way about John le Carré's *The Tailor of Panama*. Hayward is also said to have inspired *its* title character, the devious Harry Pendel.

The play *Alfie*, by Bill Naughton, was first performed in 1963. The play has been made into two movies, one starring Michael Caine, the other Jude Law

30 ROCK'S JACK DONAGHY

Lorne Michaels (b.1944)

Condoleezza Rice is pretty hard to get – unless your name's Jack Donaghy. *30 Rock*'s smooth-talking executive has taken his tuxedo off in quite a few celebrity bedrooms – Beyoncé's, Martha Stewart's and Dusty Springfield's, to name a few more.

The real Jack Donaghy tends to keep his pants on. What the happily married *Saturday Night Live* executive producer Lorne Michaels *does* have in common with the character, however, is an active interest in the lives of his staff. 'There's this world view that Jack has of "You should have a great life", "You should have a great house", "You should rise above what you think you should be" and that is the part that comes from Lorne,' says *30 Rock*'s creator, Tina Fey. 'It's kind of sweet the way he wants everyone to get rich.'

Fey says, 'I may be the only *Saturday Night Live* alumnus who has created a character based on Lorne who's not lying about it'. (Dr Evil of the Austin Powers series is said to have some of Lorne's mannerisms, as is Don Roritor in *Brain Candy* and the Bill Murray character in *Scrooged*.)

Fey also based a character on herself, of course. *30 Rock*'s comedy writer Liz Lemon is Fey 'five or six years ago, when I first started at my job [as *Saturday Night Live* head writer] and had to figure out how to … get through the day being sort-of-scared of everyone'. Both Liz and Fey came to New York via Chicago, love food, rules and *Star Wars* and wear glasses that they don't really need.

Written by Tina Fey, *30 Rock* first screened in 2006. The Emmy Award–winning TV series stars the writer and Alec Baldwin

JERRY MAGUIRE

It's not always about the plot. *Jerry Maguire*, for example, is supposed to be about a sports agent who is disillusioned with his profession and tries to persuade his colleagues to put morals above money. But it's really just ninety minutes of Renée Zellweger looking doe-eyed and Southern and Tom Cruise being cocky yet vulnerable. They exchange zingers like 'You complete me' and 'You had me at "hello",' and someone else says 'Show me the money'. And that's about all you need to know.

Unless, that is, you're Leigh Steinberg. One of the US's leading sports agents, the California-based author of *Winning with Integrity* has negotiated $2 billion dollars worth of deals for his athletes over the years, and given them a lot of love as well. 'It's fashionable now, after the movie, for a lot of agents to talk about heart,' says *Jerry Maguire*'s writer Cameron Crowe. 'But Leigh was the only one talking like that in 1993, when I began research.'

'Cameron followed me around for a good couple of years to do research for the film,' says Leigh. 'He went to the NFL draft with me, to player workouts, the NFL meetings, and even the 94 Superbowl.'

The movie's most famous line came from Tim McDonald, a footballer the agent was hawking to various teams. 'Cameron was in Tim's room one night, asking him what he was looking for in the process. CNN's *Money Line* was on the TV in the background, and Tim answered "the money". Now, Tim meant a lot more than cash – he meant "respect" and a home and a whole lot of values beyond a salary – but he gestured to the screen and Cameron laughed and wrote the line, "Show me the money".'

Jerry Maguire premiered in 2006. Created by Cameron Crowe, the movie starred Tom Cruise and Renée Zellweger

ZORRO

Joaquin Murrieta (c.1829–53)

Women like their swash and buckle. In 1920, Douglas Fairbanks was a shortish, slightly baby-faced comic actor best known for shagging Mary Pickford. Given black tights, fancy hat, flowing cape and flashing blade, however, he became Hollywood's first great sex symbol. *The Mask of Zorro* made wives all over the world wistful, and one or two husbands gay.

The real Zorro didn't have a cape, however. In fact, after 25 July 1853, he didn't even have a body. For it was on this date that Joaquin Murrieta stopped being 'the Mexican Robin Hood' and became 'the head in the jar'.

A hot-blooded bandit out to punish the authorities who had hanged his brother for stealing a horse, Murrieta had a colourful career until he was shot dead by bounty hunters. Then he was chopped up, doused in alcohol and put on a shelf for all to see. For decades, his head was on show in San Francisco at a competitively priced dollar per view.

Zorro first appeared in *The Curse of Capistrano*, a 1919 story by Johnston McCulley, before going on to appear in many movies

ROBIN HOOD

Robin Hood didn't just rob the rich. He stole storylines from other outlaws too.

The origins of the Lincoln-green legend are pretty much lost in time. The word 'Rabunhod' (or 'Robehood' or 'Hobbehod') appears in several legal documents from 1228 onwards, which suggests it might even have just been a term for a thief. But it's likely that the actions of a few real-life felons did a bit to develop the character.

One such felon was Fulk FitzWarin. A medieval nobleman from Shropshire, Fulk was a childhood friend of Prince John – until he fell out with the future king over a game of chess, rather rashly kicking him in the stomach. When he got the crown, John also got his revenge, handing Fulk's title and castle to another nobleman.

Still being rather rash, Fulk then murdered that nobleman and fled to the woods, where he lived as an outlaw for the next three years. His not-so-merry men never gave to the poor, as far as we know, but on one famous occasion they did capture King John, chivalrously giving him dinner then releasing him with purse intact.

This story quickly became part of the Sherwood mythology. Before Fulk came along, the Robin Hood of legend and song was a yeoman (sort of like a member of the middle class, only smellier) of no fixed date in time. Post-Fulk, he's generally presented as an outlawed nobleman, who's waging war against the wicked King John.

The subject of innumerable TV shows, novels and films, Robin Hood first appeared in print in 1228, and was famously played by Errol Flynn in the 1938 movie

HARRY (WHO MET SALLY)

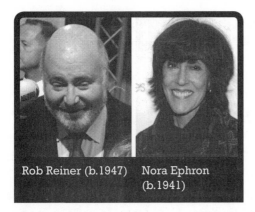

Rob Reiner (b.1947) Nora Ephron (b.1941)

Men and women can never be friends. In part, this is because men refuse to watch *When Harry Met Sally*. If they did, they would learn about when Rob Reiner met Nora Ephron. Hollywood's definitive romantic comedy was born when the director met the writer to pitch an idea for a film project – which she rejected before the first course even arrived.

Faced with an hour of awkward silence, the meeting soon morphed into a conversation about single life. This topic became the movie instead.

Harry Burns is the then–recently divorced Reiner: depressed, cynical, confused. 'I was in the middle of my single life … I'd been out a number of times, all these disastrous, confusing relationships one after another.' Whether or not he had Harry's ability to make a woman 'miaow', Reiner was also battle-scarred when it came to relationships but simultaneously inclined to see single life as a series of chores.

Sally Albright is Ephron: bubbly, optimistic, controlling. Like that character, she 'takes an hour and a half to order a sandwich' and insists that her salad dressing be 'on the side'. Sally's 'I just like it the way I like it' is a direct quote of hers.

Reiner and Ephron both married again, you'll be glad to hear (though not to one another). And they are still married to this day.

When Harry Met Sally premiered in 1989. Created by Rob Reiner and Nora Ephron, the movie starred Billy Crystal and Meg Ryan

BAYWATCH'S MITCH

Greg Bonann may have saved a few people from drowning, but he has never defeated a shark in hand-to-hand combat and is not a former navy SEAL. He does not solve murders, bust drug rings, defuse hostage situations or catch diamond smugglers. He has never found Spanish treasure or run in slow motion along the beach.

Nonetheless, Greg is probably Mitch Buchannon, the lifeguard/private investigator played with saggy-chested relish by David Hasselhoff. A below-average athlete who was picked on by school bullies, Greg trained hard to turn himself into a champion swimmer and then became a LA County lifeguard.

He then became a below-average TV producer. Greg spent ten years trying to get a reasonably serious show made about lifeguards (one about waves and currents, rather than boobs and bums) and failed at every turn. So we got *Baywatch* instead.

'If I had a daughter and she wanted breast enhancements,' says the slightly sheepish producer, 'I would spend the $5000 on professional counselling'.

Baywatch screened from 1989 until 1999 (and from 1999 to 2001 as *Baywatch Hawaii*). The TV series starred David Hasselhoff and Pamela Anderson

WIMBLEDON'S PETER COLT

The main attraction of being a sportsman, is, of course, the chicks. An athlete may have a thick neck, a broken nose and be awaiting trial for assault – but he'll still find someone blonde and perky to take home on awards night.

Peter Colt, the journeyman tennis player contemplating retirement in *Wimbledon*, also likes a perky blonde. Particularly after she inspires him to win the tournament. The so-unpredictable-it's-deeply-predictable romantic comedy was supposedly inspired by Goran Ivanisevic's Wimbledon win. In 2001, he became the only player to ever do so on a wildcard.

Injuries forced the poorly ranked thirty-year-old to retire not long afterwards. 'I said to God "If I win this one, I don't care if I never play again". I guess he was listening.'

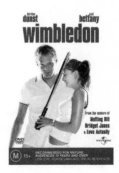

Wimbledon premiered in 2004. The movie starred Paul Bettany and Kirsten Dunst

ROXANNE'S CD BALES

Cyrano de Bergerac (1619–55)

According to biologists, what does a man's having a big nose indicate?

Generally, that he has a bad love life. A glowing exception to this rule is, of course, CD Bales, the Steve Martin character in *Roxanne*. Quick of wit and big of soul, this lonely small-town firefighter has everything going for him as a wooer, except for a nose that's four inches long. Some fisticuffs, several heartfelt poems and one or two comic misunderstandings later, however, Roxanne sees her way past the proboscis and finds some love in her heart.

It's probably better that this didn't happen in real life. CD Bales is based on Cyrano de Bergerac – a big-nosed French poet and swordsman who was full of panache, joie de vivre and élan. Immortalised in a nineteenth-century play (upon which the movie was based), de Bergerac was an 'audacious freethinker' with a 'daring temper'. He fought over a hundred duels, openly mocked the all-powerful church and was considered a madman by the likes of Voltaire.

In fact, he probably *was* a madman. Scholars these days say he had syphilis. And, being gay, de Bergerac wouldn't have wanted Roxanne. He instead had a decade-long affair with Charles d'Assoucy, a musician who travelled with an 'entourage of winsome choirboys'.

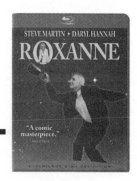

Roxanne premiered in 1987. The movie starred Steve Martin and Daryl Hannah

SATURDAY NIGHT FEVER'S TONY MANERO

Next time you tell a white lie, be aware that someone might make it into a movie.

Saturday Night Fever was inspired by 'Tribal Rites of the New Saturday Night', a 1970s magazine article about Brooklyn's disco subculture. The only problem was that its writer came from England.

'My story was a fraud,' Nik Cohn later admitted. 'I'd only recently arrived in New York. Far from being steeped in Brooklyn street life, I hardly knew the place. As for Vincent, my story's hero [upon whom John Travolta's Tony Manero was based], he was largely inspired by a Shepherd's Bush mod whom I'd known in the 60s, a one-time king of Goldhawk Road.'

Who was this king? One possibility is Pete Meaden – a former manager of The Who and roommate of Mick Jagger. Whether or not he wore white flares, this prominent mod would often strut his way through the Goldhawk Club to hushed whispers and respectful stares, then pull out some smokin' moves.

The king didn't live long, however. Back living with his parents after years of drug abuse and a nervous breakdown, Meaden died of an overdose at just thirty-six.

Saturday Night Fever premiered in 1977. The movie starred John Travolta

Chapter 10
Military men

THE HUNT FOR RED OCTOBER'S CAPTAIN RAMIUS

The Soviet frigate Storozhevoy

We *don't* all live in a yellow submarine. In *The Hunt for Red October*, for example, Captain Ramius lives in a communist-red submarine – though he's very keen to paint it red, white and blue and defect to America with it. Played by Sean Connery with an impeccable Scottish accent, the movie's Russian commander defects from the Soviet Union in this nuclear-armed sub and hands it over to the US.

Unlikely, you say, but you say wrong. In 1975, a middle-ranking Soviet officer named Valery Sablin led a mutiny aboard the Soviet missile frigate *Storozhevoy*, in protest against the corruption of the Brezhnev regime. No-one is entirely sure what he was planning to do next. What he *did* do, after the ship was recaptured, was get shot by a firing squad.

'Trust the fact that history will judge events honestly and you will never have to be embarrassed for what your father did,' Sablin wrote in a final letter to his son. 'On no account ever be one of those people who criticise but do not follow through with actions. Such people are hypocrites – weak [and] worthless.'

The Hunt for Red October, by Tom Clancy, was first published in 1984. The movie, starring Sean Connery and Alec Baldwin, premiered in 1990

GI JOE

Gary Lockwood (b.1937)

Given the choice between (a) a rich, happy life filled with close, loving relationships and (b) being the model for an action figure, many men would need time to think.

B-grade actor Gary Lockwood got both, the lucky devil. One of this former college football star's many gigs was *The Lieutenant*, the first TV show from the creator of *Star Trek*. Cancelled after just one season, it followed the entertaining adventures of Lieutenant William Tiberius Rice of the Marine Corps, until it turned out that they weren't entertaining.

Rather more successful than the show was the merchandise that accompanied it. Someone had the bright idea to market the lieutenant with a plastic figurine for boys. US patent number 3,277,602, 'Toy figure having movable joints', was eventually renamed after a popular 1945 movie, *The Story of GI Joe*.

'Government Issue' Joes, incidentally, came just two years after an equally iconic plastic doll for girls. Barbie certainly wasn't modelled after any real woman (indeed, it's been calculated that someone with her measurements would lack the body fat needed to menstruate). But she was named after one Barbara Handler, daughter of the doll's creator, Ruth. Barbie's boyfriend Ken, rather creepily, got *his* name from Ruth's son.

GI Joe was first produced as an action figure by Hasbro Toys in 1964, and became an enduring figure in pop culture

BIGGLES

Captain WE Johns, the creator of Biggles, wasn't actually a captain at all. This low-ranking-pilot turned low-quality-author cannily gave himself a promotion after WWI, reasoning that no-one would read a novel by Flying Officer Bill Johns.

Biggles, on the other hand, *was* a captain. Despite his tendency to exclaim 'Great Scott!', 'Holy mackerel!' and 'By jingo!', the high-flying star of *The White Fokker* and *Biggles Gets His Men* was a man whose word we could trust.

But who was this 'dashing champion' of the skies? This clean-living chum of Ginger and Bertie who preferred cigarettes to women and malted milk to beer? Biggles is thought to have been inspired by one Air Commodore Cecil Wigglesworth, a Derbyshire-born first-class cricketer who shared some man-time with Johns in the mess.

Biggles first appeared in *The White Fokker*, a 1932 short story by Captain WE Johns, and became a recurring character

PRIVATE RYAN

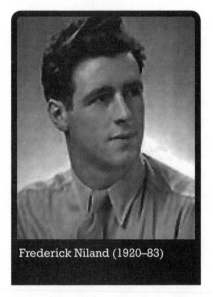

Frederick Niland (1920–83)

The real Private Ryan had to save himself.

Steven Spielberg's WWII epic (which sees some soldiers get sent to save a paratrooper whose three brothers have recently died) was loosely based on the story of Sergeant Frederick Niland. Like Ryan, Niland was a paratrooper with multiple brothers who was dropped into Normandy on D-Day. Unlike Ryan, he made his own way back.

It was only on Niland's return that the army discovered that the soldier, who had already lost a brother in the jungles of Burma, had now lost another two to the fighting in Normandy. They therefore sent him back to New York, where he rather glamorously became a dentist.

After all that, incidentally, the army discovered something else. The brother who'd been killed in Burma was actually alive and well.

Saving Private Ryan premiered in 1998. Directed by Steven Spielberg, the movie starred Tom Hanks and Matt Damon

THE LAST SAMURAI

Jules Brunet (1838–1911)

Say what you will about Tom Cruise, but at least the man isn't French.

One of his characters was, though. The inspiration for the last samurai, Captain Nathan Algren, was probably a French officer named Jules Brunet. While he left Japan a decade before the Satsuma Rebellion (the ill-fated uprising with which the movie deals), Brunet was also a Western soldier sent to modernise Japan's army, who then ended up fighting against that country's emperor in an ill-fated civil war.

'A fine soldier and a talented artist', he had the good sense to abandon a lost cause, however. Brunet slipped away a few days before his forces surrendered, and hightailed it back to Europe.

The Tom Cruise character has less good sense. He ends the movie by getting dressed up in fancy armour and galloping straight at a machine gun.

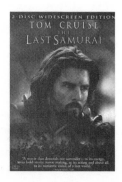

The Last Samurai premiered in 2003. The movie starred Tom Cruise

MADAME BUTTERFLY'S LIEUTENANT PINKERTON

Thomas Glover (1838–1911)

Lieutenant Pinkerton just isn't a great name for a soldier. If you were charging into battle – guns blazing, blood splattering – wouldn't you rather be alongside a 'Butch'? Or a 'Duke' or a 'Pete' or a 'Hank'?

'Tom' isn't too bad either. Which is fortunate, because it was Lieutenant Pinkerton's real name. Puccini's poignant opera (which sees an American officer marry and impregnate a Japanese teenager, who commits suicide after he callously discards her) may have been based on a real-life romance. In the late nineteenth century, Kaga Maki was a performer at a Nagasaki teahouse under the stage name 'Miss Butterfly'. Much-loved by her customers, she was loved and left by one Thomas Glover.

Glover went on to become a key figure in the industrialisation of Japan, modernising its navy, helping to create its coal and beer industries, and eventually receiving the Order of the Rising Sun. Some say that the moustache of the creature on Kirin beer labels is in fact a tribute to his very prominent fuzz.

Madame Butterfly first appeared in a story by John L Long, published in 1898. The Puccini opera, which made the character internationally famous, premiered in 1904

THE PATRIOT'S BENJAMIN MARTIN

Francis Marion (1732–95)

Patriotism may be the last refuge of the scoundrel, but it's the first place Hollywood turns. If your movie's looking like a stinker, wave a flag (*Pearl Harbor*), play an anthem (*The Sum of All Fears*) or put the president in a jetfighter (*Independence Day*). Then watch those tickets sell.

The problem, however, is that some patriots are still scoundrels. According to a source at Sony Pictures, Mel Gibson's movie about a noble guerilla soldier in the US War of Independence was intended to be a straightforward biography of one Francis Marion. Known as the 'Swamp Fox', this real-life soldier led a small band of desperados in several guerilla actions during the war, his cunning and courage helping to forge a home for the brave and land for the free.

Unfortunately, he was also a 'thoroughly unpleasant dude who was, basically, a terrorist'. The Swamp Fox 'tortured prisoners, hanged fence-sitters, abused parole and flags of truce, and shot [his] own men when they failed to live up to the harsh standards [he] set'. Outside work hours, he enjoyed hunting Native Americans for sport and raping his many female slaves.

Wholesome stuff. Sony Pictures supposedly got wind of Marion's seedy side after production had started, so 'the patriot' became 'Benjamin Martin'. He too was a guerilla fighter in the swamps of Carolina. But a nice one, with excellent hair.

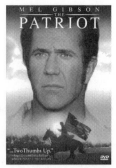

The Patriot premiered in 2000. The movie starred Mel Gibson and Heath Ledger

A FEW GOOD MEN'S DANIEL KAFFEE

In *A Few Good Men*, Daniel Kaffee is a charismatic hot shot – a wisecracking navy lawyer who says things like 'I'm gonna slam dunk this guy!', then flashes a winning smile.

In real life, he's a right-wing evangelical Christian and former member of the Bush administration. Sigh. 'Trim', 'straight-backed' and boasting 'movie-star good looks of his own', David Iglesias was one of three naval lawyers sent to Guantanamo Bay to deal with the case of a group of Marines who nearly killed one of their colleagues in a 'hazing' ordered by a superior officer. 'It was one of those things when I look back, I can see the hand of the Lord in it,' he says. (Sigh.)

God's hand must have been elsewhere a few years later, however, when Iglesias became one of eight US attorneys controversially sacked by the White House. An official inquiry eventually found that he had been wrongfully dismissed. The 'ethical straight shooter' had refused to prosecute some New Mexico Democrats in time to assist the Republican Party at an upcoming election, so suffered vengeance at the party's hands.

Iglesias later said that he felt disappointed and betrayed by the sacking. 'To use a *Star Wars* kind of imagery, I thought I was working with the Jedi Knights and [it turned out] I was working for the Sith Lords.'

The play *A Few Good Men* was first performed in 1989. In 1992, the Aaron Sorkin play was made into a movie starring Tom Cruise, Jack Nicholson and Demi Moore

APOCALYPSE NOW'S COLONEL KURTZ

Leon Rom (1861–1924)

'War! Huh! Yeah! What is it good for?' sang some one-hit wonder. The answer, of course, is movies. If you've never enjoyed seeing masses of people murder one another with guns or tanks, then you've probably never been a thirteen-year-old boy. *Apocalypse Now*, however, is better suited to adults. This is largely because of the crazy Colonel Kurtz – a sadistic US soldier who goes AWOL during the Vietnam War. Having found a bunch of troops to follow him, the character creates a kind of tin-pot dictatorship in the jungle, and grows more brutal and insane each day.

If he had been a soldier in the Belgian Congo, Kurtz wouldn't have needed to go AWOL. Brutal, insane tin-pot dictatorships had the Belgian army's full support. *Apocalypse Now* was based on *Heart of Darkness*, Joseph Conrad's novella about 'the vilest scramble for loot that ever disfigured the history of human conscience': Belgium's slave camps in nineteenth-century Africa.

Like the movie, *Heart of Darkness* features a deranged Western tyrant, Kurtz, living in the middle of the jungle, where he has managed to persuade the locals he's some kind of god. He too collects human heads. And he too comes to a gruesome end, plaintively murmuring 'The horror! The horror!'

It's thought that Joseph Conrad based the character on one Leon Rom, a poorly educated Belgian officer whose 'brutality knew no bounds'. He 'kept a gallows permanently erected in front of the station' and had 'the reputation of having killed masses of people for petty reasons'. And like Kurtz, Rom was also famous for having a flowerbed that he liked to decorate with human heads.

Kurtz first appeared in *Heart of Darkness*, Joseph Conrad's 1902 novella. The movie *Apocalypse Now,* starring Marlon Brando as Colonel Walter E Kurtz, premiered in 1979

KING ARTHUR

Glastonbury Tor, Somerset

If you're disillusioned with democracy, relax: it's just a phase. One day, it's said, when the world needs him most, King Arthur will rise from his resting place at Avalon, smite down the people's enemies, and replace parliament with a nice round table.

Wonderful news, though there's one slight problem. We don't know who Arthur was. The best guess is that he was Lucius Artorius Castus, the commander of a group of foreign mercenaries who guarded Roman Britain from the 'barbarian' Scots. Seven of Artorius's battles resemble battles in Geoffrey of Monmouth's *The History of the Kings of Britain* – the source of the Arthur legend. And, like Geoffrey's Arthur, Artorius once suppressed a mutiny and also led an expedition to France. Along with his name (a variation of 'Arthur'), other similarities include his pennant (a large red dragon, much like Arthur's 'pendragon') and his rank (Arthur was 'a commander of war', not necessarily a king).

So where was Arthur himself buried? For those keen to find 'Avalon', Glastonbury Tor is a good place to start. A conical mountain set amid the apple orchards of Somerset, the Tor was once surrounded by flood lands but today by hippies. It has been a candidate for the magical 'Isle of Apples' since 1190, when monks found a grave reading 'Here lies renowned King Arthur in the island of Avalon'.

The 'find', it should perhaps be noted, represented a major propaganda coup for Glastonbury Abbey, which promptly applied for more funds.

King Arthur first appeared in *The History of the Kings of Britain*, an 1136 book by Geoffrey of Monmouth – pictured here in a painting by NC Wyeth

THE BRIDGE ON THE RIVER KWAI'S COLONEL NICHOLSON

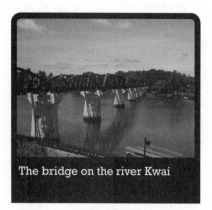

The bridge on the river Kwai

Building bridges isn't always a good way to build bridges. During WWII, for example, constructing a railway bridge over the River Kwai didn't bring British POWs and their Japanese captors closer together. If anything, relations grew positively frosty.

Around 12,000 slave-labouring Allied soldiers are thought to have died building the Burma–Siam railway, along with up to 100,000 civilians.

Still more might have carked it, however, had it not been for the efforts of one Lieutenant Colonel Philip Toosey, who negotiated for more food and medicine on behalf of 2000 Allied prisoners, despite enduring regular beatings as a result. The colonel (who lost over 30 kilograms during the ordeal, along with many of his teeth) also did everything possible to delay the construction of the bridge, ordering his fellow prisoners to mix weak concrete and smuggle in white ants to eat away at the wood.

Unfortunately – and unjustly – the years have also eaten away at his reputation. Many officers were horrified by *The Bridge on the River Kwai*, which depicts a Toosey-like colonel willingly collaborating with the Japanese. 'He wasn't that bothered until he realised that people were beginning to believe that it was a depiction of historical reality,' says Toosey's granddaughter. 'Then he was really upset about it because he felt the prisoners were not well served by a fiction which was so very far from what had actually happened during the war.'

The Bridge on the River Kwai, by Pierre Boulle, was published in 1952. The movie starring Alec Guinness premiered in 1957

THE COLONEL IN *ONE HUNDRED YEARS OF SOLITUDE*

One Hundred Years of Solitude took fifteen months of solitude to make. Struggling with writer's block, Gabriel García Márquez reportedly barricaded himself in his house while working on his magnum opus. 'Everyone's my friend since [the ultra-successful book was published],' the author once noted, 'but no-one knows what it cost me to get there'.

It probably would have been quicker if he'd worked in his grandfather's house. The novel's character Colonel Buendía was directly based on Colonel Nicholás Mejía, Márquez's devoted poppa and 'umbilical cord with history and reality'. He would speak of his wartime experiences as if 'they were almost pleasant – like youthful adventures with guns'.

Both the real and the fictional colonels were small-town silversmiths and big-time ladies' men, who fathered scores of illegitimate children. Both were also world-weary liberals, having fought countless civil wars against Columbia's conservatives.

One Hundred Years of Solitude, by Gabriel García Márquez, was published in 1967

TOP GUN'S MAVERICK

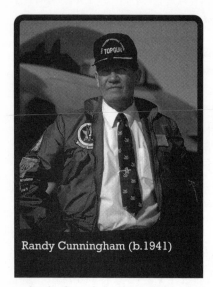

Randy Cunningham (b.1941)

What movie features gleaming abs, pert buttocks, some mantastic hairdos and about two dozen references to 'ass'? *Top Gun*, of course. The film naturally appeals to Republican Party supporters, which may be why one cocky former congressman has always insisted he helped inspire Maverick, its cocky main character. A much-decorated Vietnam War veteran, Randy 'Duke' Cunningham studied at Top Gun, the fighter pilot training school on the San Diego coast. While there, Duke says, he invented Maverick's famous 'hit the brakes and he'll fly right by' manoeuvre, and was indeed a bit of a maverick himself.

Interesting. Also probably untrue: the 'hit the brakes' manoeuvre has been in use since WWI. Duke *was* a maverick, though. An 'aggressive ... assaultive person', he has had two wives apply for restraining orders and was reportedly almost court-martialled at Top Gun. After being elected to Congress, his statesmanlike contributions included calling gay people 'homos', calling for war protesters to be 'lined up and shot', and telling President Clinton to 'get tough on drug dealers'. (Four months later, his son was arrested for smuggling marijuana. Duke cried in court as he pleaded for leniency.)

The congressman did a bit more pleading in 2005 – pleading guilty to tax evasion, mail fraud, wire fraud and conspiracy to commit bribery.

He is currently serving an eight-year prison sentence. Hopefully no-one is on his ass.

Top Gun premiered in 1986. The movie starred Tom Cruise and Kelly McGillis

MASTER AND COMMANDER'S CAPTAIN JACK

Admiral Thomas Cochrane
(1775–1860)

If you're interested in the finer details of rigging, then Patrick O'Brian is the author for you. Set during the Napoleonic Wars, his nautical novels also cover jiggermasts, lugsails, orlop decks and bilge keels in some detail. We get a few pages on forestays and sou'westers – and learn all we ever needed to know about shift tides.

Good stuff (according to my dad). Admiral Thomas Cochrane is at least one other person who would like it, but this is because it's on him that the novels' Captain Jack Aubrey is based.

Like Jack, Cochrane was born to a 'good' family fallen on bad times (his father was a penniless earl). Dubbed 'the greatest man afloat', the fiery Scot was often at odds with the authorities, who at different points court-martialled him and sent him to jail. In the course of a colourful career, he defeated numerous French and Spanish ships, commanded the navies of Greece, Chile, Brazil and Peru and still found time to be an active MP. Lord Byron once said that 'there is no man I envy so much' and Sir Walter Scott wrote a poem in his honour.

Patrick O'Brian wrote an entire series of novels. The first of them, *Master and Commander*, was directly based on Cochrane's *Autobiography of a Seaman,* which described his unlikely victory over an enormous Spanish frigate with a tiny fourteen-gun sloop. Cochrane's *HMS Speedy* became Jack's *HMS Sophie.* James Guthrie, Cochrane's surgeon friend who played an important role in the battle, became *Jack*'s surgeon friend Stephen Maturin.

Jack Aubrey first appeared in *Master and Commander* by Patrick O'Brian, published in 1969. The movie, starring Russell Crowe, premiered in 2003

M*A*S*H'S RADAR O'REILLY

The Korean War lasted three years. *M*A*S*H*, the TV show set during the war, lasted eleven years – and one of its characters may be going still.

Don Shaffer spent the Korean War as a company clerk at a mobile army surgical hospital (MASH). Now a retired history lecturer, he says he was the model for a rather better-known MASH company clerk, Radar O'Reilly – a character in a novel by one of his colleagues, which eventually spawned the show. 'My two sons were watching this new TV program and they came and … said, "Dad, this sounds like your nutty war stories."'

The colleague disagreed. Through his lawyers.

Who's right? Let's examine the facts. Like Radar (who transformed from a worldly shyster into a naive farm boy as *M*A*S*H* progressed, and somehow managed to regain his virginity), Shaffer was from Ottumwa, a tiny town in Iowa. He too was an animal lover, keeping multiple dogs around the MASH unit. And he too had exceptionally good hearing. 'I was observant … It was just that I would listen for things when no-one else was listening [like] helicopters coming.'

They are the facts. Make of them what you will.

Radar O'Reilly first appeared in *MASH: A Novel about Three Army Doctors*, Richard Hooker's 1968 novel. The Robert Altman film premiered in 1970 and the TV series screened from 1972 until 1983

THE THREE MUSKETEERS' D'ARTAGNAN

Ever had a rude dinner guest? A former French finance minister knew just how you felt. In 1661, Nicolas Fouquet hosted a banquet at his magnificent chateau. He lavished exotic delicacies upon Louis XIV and assorted other distinguished guests, generously giving each a horse. Feeling upstaged and suspecting embezzlement, Louis immediately ordered his guard to arrest his host, and sent him to jail for life.

That guard was Charles de Batz-Castelmore, the Count of Artagnan. These days he's better known as the inspiration for the fictional D'Artagnan, hot-headed leader of the three musketeers. But while the author Alexandre Dumas borrowed de Batz's title, birthplace and job description when creating the character, he also left rather a lot out. Family connections, not timeless heroics, allowed de Batz to join the musketeers, and a certain toadiness characterised his career from there. 'Charles de Batz was no flashing blade ... [but] rather a dull, literal-minded career soldier who followed the rule-book and furthered his ambition with a generous measure of sly patience.'

He also technically wasn't 'of Artagnan'. The lands belonged to a distant relative, which gave him no right to use the title.

The three musketeers themselves, by the way, were all based on real men too. Dumas drew on the careers of Arnaud de Sillegue d'Athos, Isaac de Portau and Henri d'Aramitz to create the characters of Athos, Porthos and Aramis. Each man really did serve in the musketeers, though it's unlikely that they were ever in the same room together, let alone worked as a team.

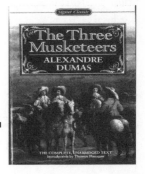

The Three Musketeers, by Alexandre Dumas, was first published in 1884

THE WHITE COMPANY

Sir John Hawkwood (1320–94)

To really appreciate the glamour of the Middle Ages, it's best to avoid non-fiction.

In Arthur Conan Doyle's novel of the same name, the White Company is a blue-blooded band of dashing do-gooders. Prancing throughout Europe in shining armour atop noble steeds, they are led by Sir Nigel Loring, a chivalrous servant of country and king.

In the history books, things read a bit differently. The real White Company was a mobile army of mercenaries who would kill for whoever paid them. They fought for Pisa against Florence. Then for the Pope against Florence. Then for Milan against Pisa. Then for Perugia against the Pope.

They sometimes also killed the people who paid them, or threatened pillage to jack up the price. According to one historian, the White Company 'dismembered their enemies, raped women and savagely murdered peasants … [Their] raids on the cities of Faenza and Cesane in 1376 were widely considered two of the cruellest and most violent acts of the entire fourteenth century'.

The real White Company's leader was Sir John Hawkwood, an illiterate tanner's son from Essex who at least had his chivalrous moments. It's said that, while plundering a monastery, Sir John once came across two of his soldiers bickering over who got to rape a nun first. He nobly came to the young girl's rescue. By plunging a dagger straight into her heart.

The White Company, by Sir Arthur Conan Doyle, was published in 1891

GLADIATOR

***Gladiator* begins with** a battle. We see General Maximus Decimus Meridius, war dog at his heels, telling his troops to send their enemy to hell.

At this point, a pedant might say three things: (a) 'Maximus' is actually a surname, so should come after 'Decimus', not before; (b) that breed of German shepherd didn't exist in antiquity; and (c) Romans didn't believe in hell. At this point you tell the pedant to shut up.

If they've done their reading, the pedant might then add that Maximus was partly based on Marcus Nonius Macrinus, a real-life Roman general whose tomb was discovered in 2008. Like Maximus, Macrinus was a hairy-chested warmonger who won major victories for the Emperor Aurelius and eventually became one of his closest friends. Unlike Maximus, he died of old age, a wealthy man and proconsul.

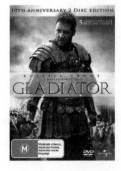

Gladiator premiered in 2000. The Academy Award–winning film starred Russell Crowe

A KNIGHT'S TALE'S WILLIAM

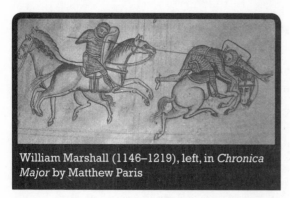

William Marshall (1146–1219), left, in *Chronica Major* by Matthew Paris

In 1152, when William Marshal was six, he was taken hostage by his father's enemies. They ruthlessly declared they would hang him unless his father immediately surrendered his castle. 'Go ahead,' Daddy Marshal replied. 'I still have the hammer and anvil with which to forge still more and better sons.'

Psychologists weren't around in the Middle Ages, so we don't know what this did to young William's mental health. Brutal, violent jousting tournaments *were* around, however, and we know that he took to them with relish.

Never defeated in over 500 fights, William has been called 'the greatest knight that ever lived'. Opponents 'put every effort they could into doing him harm and capturing him, but they dared not stand there and take his blows', read one medieval biography.

Such, you may have noticed, was not precisely the story of 'William' in *A Knight's Tale*. But the scriptwriters did borrow a few biographical elements. Like Marshall, the character is knighted by a prince for his glorious jousting, and – less gloriously – gets to visit a blacksmith after his battered helmet gets stuck on his head.

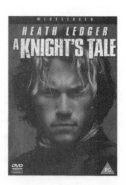

A Knight's Tale premiered in 2001. The movie starred Heath Ledger

GONE WITH THE WIND'S RHETT BUTLER

'Red' Upshaw (centre) on his wedding day

It's true: Rhett Butler *really* didn't give a damn. The debonair scoundrel of *Gone with the Wind* is thought to have been based on the author's husband, 'Red' Upshaw – a bad man who beat her, raped her and cheated on her (and – a more forgivable crime – also worked as a bootlegger).

We don't know too much else about the life of this thrice-married gambler and ex-football-player, and his death is a bit of a mystery too. In 1947, Red and another man plunged to their deaths from the fifth floor of a Texas hotel. Rumour says that they were pushed out for gambling debts. The inquest said it was suicide.

As to Scarlett O'Hara, the woman Rhett didn't give a damn about, her probable model is Ohara's grandmother, Annie Fitzgerald. Like Scarlett, Annie was the beautiful, somewhat feisty daughter of a rich Irish plantation owner. Like Scarlett, she had two sisters and an American mum called Ellen. And while Scarlett's plantation was called Tara, Annie's was on Tara Road.

Gone with the Wind, by Margaret Mitchell, was published in 1936. The Academy Award–winning movie starring Clark Gable and Vivien Leigh premiered in 1939

BARRY LYNDON

Andrew Robinson Stoney
(1747–1810)

The fictional fortune-hunter Barry Lyndon appears in both a William Thackeray novel and a Stanley Kubrick film – and in neither does he come off well. But Thackerayish terms like 'rogue' and 'rakehell' don't begin to describe the real version. Barry was based on a low-born lieutenant called Andrew Stoney, an Irishman who liked to lock his first wife in cupboards and feed her one egg a day.

But she actually got off pretty lightly compared with wife number two. Stoney wooed Countess Mary Bowes, the richest heiress in England, by planting slanderous stories about her in a newspaper, then challenging the editor to a duel to defend her good name.

A fake duel, that is. Drenched in animal blood, and with a bribed doctor in tow, the 'wounded' martyr brokenly told Mary that his one dying wish was to marry her. Expecting a funeral, she compassionately agreed.

After Stoney's miraculous recovery, he soon proved himself 'Georgian England's worst husband'. Mary (a great-great-great-great-grandmother of Queen Elizabeth II) was beaten, raped and bullied for eight years, and effectively deprived of both money and freedom. Stoney also had affairs with maids and wet nurses, and hosted prostitutes in the family home. He was finally jailed after Mary fled their house and he illegally dispatched some hoodlums to kidnap her back.

The Luck of Barry Lyndon, by William Thackeray, was published in 1844. The Stanley Kubrick movie based on it premiered in 1975

Chapter 11
Performers

BILLY ELLIOT

Sir Thomas Allen (b.1944)

In rough, tough English mining country, it doesn't do to be a lord of the dance. In *Billy Elliot*, the title character may have a private passion for ballet, but in public he's mad about boxing.

The real Billy Elliot is mad about singing – and, in fact, probably can't even dance. The opera star Sir Thomas Allen grew up amid the coal pits of Durham, but is now more often onstage in Paris and Rome. 'I did get a bit of stick for singing in the church choir from boys from the other side of the tracks, but it wasn't as bad as for Billy,' the world-renowned baritone recalls. 'The great thing about my school was that you could play rugby and sing in the choir as well.'

Allen 'was the inspiration for that sort of career', says *Billy Elliot*'s writer, Lee Hall. 'I've never met him, but I've always been interested in music and so I knew about what he'd done.'

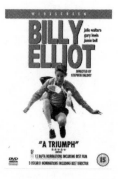

Billy Elliot premiered in 2000

KRUSTY THE CLOWN

Rusty Nails (b.1928)

In *The Simpsons,* Krusty likes dirty limericks ('There once was a man named Enus'). In life, he prefers the Bible. Jim Allen is a clean-living Baptist minister who once hosted a Christian kids' variety show in Portland. His clown character on that show, Rusty Nails, was 'a nice guy, a very nice guy and a very sweet clown,' says *Simpsons* creator Matt Groening. 'But he had that name which I found incredibly disturbing as a child because, you know, you're supposed to avoid rusty nails.' So, with the chain-smoking, pill-popping, problem-gambling Krusty, Groening decided to invent an incredibly disturbing clown character of his own.

Groening grew up in Portland – not far from Flanders Street and Quimby Street, as well as a nuclear plant and a gorge. The city was, of course, also home to his family: father Homer, mother Marge and sisters Lisa and Maggie. Their names were about the extent of their influence on *The Simpsons*, however. (The real Homer, for example, was a tertiary-educated documentary filmmaker with a full head of hair.) But Groening did once say that older brother Mark was 'the actual inspiration for Bart'. He too had a comics-filled tree house from which he'd use a slingshot on passers-by.

Mr Burns, of course, should be shot with a gun. Some say the evil billionaire resembles a Norwegian shipping magnate named Fred Olsen. The businessman appeared on US TV quite often in the 80s, and shares the character's long nose, bald head and thin body.

Mayor Quimby has more in common with the Kennedys. Also a wealthy Democrat, he speaks with a Irish Boston accent and thinks with the thing in his pants.

Not many people want to see inside Moe's pants, sadly – but the bartender's alter ego might be a different story. 'I suspected that Moe was based on me because I used to write with … one of the original writers on the show,' says the sad-faced writer and TV personality Rich Hall. 'Then Matt confirmed it.'

The Complete *Seventh* and *Eighth* Season

Created by Matt Groening, *The Simpsons* **first screened in 1989**

(ALL ABOUT) EVE

Elisabeth Bergner (1897–1986)

All about Eve was actually all about Martina. The tale of a scheming young actress (who becomes an assistant for Betty Davis's ageing Broadway star, then attempts to ruin her life) was inspired by the real-life machinations of one Martina Lawrence, a former assistant to Elisabeth Bergner.

In 1943 Bergner was on Broadway, performing in the hit melodrama *The Two Mrs Carrolls*. Night after night, she noticed, the same person stood devotedly by the stage door. Describing herself as a huge fan, Martina Lawrence eventually befriended the actress, telling a tale of misfortune that later turned out to be lies.

Taking pity on the 'waiflike young woman', Bergner offered her a job. Martina then tried to take over her career – showing casting agents how *she* would tackle Bergner's parts – and, more insidiously, also went for her husband.

A few years after getting rid of 'the terrible girl' (who, unlike Eve, never made it onstage), Bergner described the scheming wannabe to a writer friend. 'Three weeks later I was at the hairdresser and someone gave me a copy of this magazine and there was the whole story.' A few years after that, someone made a film as well.

The Wisdom of Eve, by Mary Orr, was published in 1946. The Academy Award–winning movie based on it, *All about Eve*, premiered in 1950

RONALD MCDONALD

In Japan, Ronald McDonald is known as 'Donald McDonald'. Everywhere else, he's known as deeply annoying.

For this, we must blame Willard Scott. The long-time NBC weatherman created the hamburger chain mascot in 1963 (somewhat spookily wearing a paper cup for a nose and a cardboard tray as a hat).

The idea, he says, came from Bozo the Clown, the white-faced, red-haired host of *The Bozo Show* whom Scott had played on Washington TV for a couple of years. 'At the time, Bozo was the hottest children's show on the air ... [and] there was something about the combination of hamburgers and Bozo that was irresistible to kids ... So, I sat down and created Ronald McDonald.'

Sadly, Scott was dumped after the company took the ad campaign national. 'I was too fat,' he says.

Ronald McDonald the Happy Hamburger Clown first appeared on a Washington local TV advertisement in 1963

ENTOURAGE'S VINCENT CHASE

Mark Wahlberg (b.1971)

There's no business like show business. At least, not if you're hoping to have sex. In the TV series *Entourage*, movie star Vincent Chase and his working-class buddies take full advantage of the Hollywood lifestyle. Premieres, parties, money, mansions, cars, cocktails, blondes, brunettes – it's a fun life for the fellas.

Mark Wahlberg has a good time too. This real-life Hollywood star acts as a producer on the show – and was also the man who inspired it. 'My assistant wanted to film my friends around me, because he thought it was just hilarious,' says Wahlberg. What started as a documentary eventually turned into a comedy. Mark became Vincent. His assistant Donnie 'Donkey' Carroll became Turtle. Cousin Johnny 'Drama' Alves became brother Johnny 'Drama' Chase. And real-life agent Ari Emmanuel became fictional agent Ari Gold.

Why did they abandon the documentary format? In part it was because the real entourage had a little bit too much grit. Raised in the mean streets of Boston, Wahlberg wasn't a teen idol like the blue-eyed, floppy-haired Vincent so much as a teenage delinquent. He even spent time in jail after one robbery, in which he attacked a middle-aged Vietnamese refugee with a hooked stick and ended up taking out an eye.

'We didn't think that, like, the entourage fighting amongst themselves, like hitting each other with bottles, was going to, like, work,' says the now-reformed producer (who has a third nipple – 'it's dope: bitches like to suck it' – and dedicated his autobiography to his 'dick'). 'We wanted it a little bit lighter.'

Entourage first screened in 2004. Produced by Mark Wahlberg, the TV series stars Adrian Grenier

BOOGIE NIGHTS' DIRK DIGGLER

Life can be tough with an enormous penis. I know this because I have seen *Boogie Nights*.

Sporting a thirteen-inch schlong, the movie sees high-school dropout Eddie Adams become 70s porn star 'Dirk Diggler', a cocaine-snorting party boy with a big mansion and an orange corvette. All good so far, but Dirk slowly spirals into a nightmare of drug abuse. To support his habit, he also turns to crime.

John Holmes knew just how he felt. And many women knew just what it was like to feel John Holmes. The real-life porn star featured in around 2500 movies in the 1970s and somehow also found the energy to use prostitutes. Well-known for his thirteen-inch willy, Holmes also had a secret life, running drugs for criminals to help fund an enormous coke habit.

This side venture didn't always go smoothly. On 1 July 1981, four members of the Wonderland Gang, drug dealers based in LA's Wonderland Avenue, were found killed. Holmes was charged with murder but eventually was acquitted. Seven years later, he died of AIDS.

Boogie Nights premiered in 1997. The movie starred
Mark Wahlberg and Heather Graham

GENTLEMEN PREFER BLONDES' LORELEI LEE

Lillian Lorraine, centre, (1892–1955)

Not all gentlemen actually prefer blondes. According to a study at the Kyoto Institute of Technology, hair colour preferences are culturally determined.

HL Mencken quite liked them, though. Known as the 'Sage of Baltimore', this ferociously intellectual essayist was once turned into a giggly schoolboy when a voluptuous blonde sauntered by. Watching on was Anita Loos, a writer who some say had a crush on the sage. Whether or not that's true, she was immediately prompted to create 'Lorelei Lee' – a gold-digging, hip-waggling showgirl who always manages to dazzle smart men, despite having the IQ of a lobotomised sheep.

The character was also partly based on Lillian Lorraine, a saucy, blonde star of the Ziegfeld Follies (elaborate spectacles then staged on Broadway). Described as 'the most beautiful woman in the world' by her producer Florenz Ziegfeld, with whom she had a long-running affair, Lillian apparently wasn't much of an actress, but she knew how to get a man to give her some diamonds.

Justly, perhaps, her 'heavy drinking and violent temper ruined her career, leaving her destitute in her final years'.

Gentlemen Prefer Blondes, by Anita Loos, was published in 1925. The movie starring Marilyn Monroe and Jane Russell premiered in 1953

DREAMGIRLS

Diana Ross (b.1944)

Prepare to be shocked. This is big, I say. Perhaps it would be best if you could strap yourself in, and then move to the edge of your seat.

Here goes. The Dreams (that sexy, Detroit-based Motown trio in *Dreamgirls*) were actually based on the Supremes (that sexy, Detroit-based Motown trio from real life). Yep, it's true. Blew me over too.

Only no, it's *not* true. According to the musical's writers, *Dreamgirls* has nothing to do with the Supremes. (In the movie, for example, the demoted-for-not-being-sexy-enough member of the Dreams gets a happy ending. In real life, the demoted-for-not-being-sexy-enough member of the Supremes died a poverty-stricken, depressed alcoholic, aged just thirty-two).

A Hollywood journalist says that Supremes lead singer Diana Ross 'hates *Dreamgirls* because she feels like she's been ripped off, like its creators changed just enough key elements of her story so they didn't have to pay her royalties and then refused to give her any input on how her story would be told'.

All Ross herself will say is that 'I hear they use my image and likeness. Maybe I should go see it with my lawyer'.

Dreamgirls the stage musical was first performed in 1981. The movie based on the musical, starring Beyoncé Knowles and Jennifer Hudson, premiered in 2006

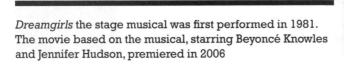

CABARET'S SALLY BOWLES

'All the world's a stage,' said Shakespeare. Geologists have since proven this to be untrue. In the 1930s, however, Berlin was largely filled with stages – a state of affairs welcomed by Christopher Isherwood when he went to Germany 'in search of boys to love'.

He also found a woman to despise. Sally Bowles – the flighty, talentless cabaret singer in Isherwood's novel *Goodbye to Berlin* and the movie it spawned, *Cabaret* – was based on the author's housemate in Berlin, an actress named Jean Ross. Only she wasn't flighty. Or talentless. She was 'gentle, highly intelligent and cultured, as well as being very elegant in behaviour and dress' – 'not a bit like the vulgar vamp displayed by Liza Minnelli'.

An active member of the Communist Party, who eventually moved to Aberdeen, Ross is even said by some to have been in Berlin as a British spy. We at least know that she was a good enough performer to have been cast in a Max Reinhardt production of *Peer Gynt*, and a good enough writer to have made a living as a journalist. Why Isherwood so despised her remains a bit of a mystery.

Goodbye to Berlin, by Christopher Isherwood, was published in 1939. *Cabaret*, the Liza Minnelli movie based on the book, premiered in 1972

WITHNAIL AND I

There are two drinks out there that will really get your head spinning. One is 'pure' whisky, which is made by getting some used filters from a distillery and sticking them in a spin dryer to concentrate the alcohol. The other is lighter fluid.

Vivian MacKerrell drank them both. Which may help explain why this unemployed alcoholic actor's housemate eventually moved out. 'We had lots of expectations that we would all become film stars, which of course never happened,' recalls filmmaker Bruce Robinson. 'People were getting married or getting jobs until there was just me and Vivian living in the house. I literally had one light bulb. I guarded it like a Russian prisoner of war. At night I'd take the light bulb up and put it in the bedroom, and in the day I'd go down and put it in the kitchen and get the oven open, sit there in an overcoat and get warm.'

Instead of becoming a star, Robinson eventually became a screenwriter – and, of course, the 'I' in *Withnail and I*. The 'wild, aristocratic and highly educated' Vivian in turn became Withnail, the silver screen's most silver-tongued drunk.

Sadly, that was about the only time he made it on-screen (apart from a small role in the schlock-horror film, *Ghost Story*). So obscure was the struggling actor that, when he died, the Internet Movie Database spelled his name wrong, accidentally listing him as an actress.

Withnail and I premiered in 1986. Created by Bruce
Robinson, the movie starred Richard E Grant

TROPIC THUNDER'S TUGG SPEEDMAN

Sylvester Stallone (b.1946)

Sometimes actors take themselves a bit too seriously. The rest of the time, they take themselves *way* too seriously.

The Vietnam War films of the late 80s were a good case in point. 'It seemed like there was a time when all these actors were going away to fake boot camp and talking about these incredible experiences that they had and how it really changed their lives,' recalled Ben Stiller. 'There was something there that seemed funny to me ... I was like, "What about people who actually go to war?"'

Twenty years later, Stiller made a Vietnam War movie of his own. Named after 'Tropic Lightning' (the infantry division portrayed in *Platoon*), *Tropic Thunder* sees a bunch of prima donna actors accidentally placed in real danger in the heart of the jungle.

Who was who? For starters, Stiller admits that the movie's highly paid action hero Tugg Speedman was a send-up of a young Sylvester Stallone. Robert Downey Jr's turn as self-important Australian method actor Kirk Lazarus was a mixture of Russell Crowe and Daniel Day-Lewis, while *Tropic Thunder*'s chubby coke-head comedian Jeff Portnoy was probably based on real-life *Saturday Night Live* star Chris Farley (who eventually died of an overdose).

Who else? Well, no-one involved in the film has ever said who Les Grossman is supposed to be. But Tom Cruise's turn as a bald-headed, hairy-armed, foul-mouthed film producer may owe something to Stiller's long-time producer, Stuart Cornfield, who's said to share one or two of those features.

Tropic Thunder premiered in 2008. The movie starred Ben Stiller, Robert Downey Jr and Jack Black

TENDER IS THE NIGHT'S ROSEMARY HOYT

Lois Moran (1909–90)

Being young and innocent can take a lot of know-how. When a sweet, wholesome-looking sixteen-year-old named Lois Moran became a silent-film star, the studio told her to stay sweet and wholesome-looking, no matter what it took. The pink-cheeked child-wonder may have been 'exceptionally intelligent' and able to quote from Einstein and Spinoza, but if she 'rolled her stockings, drank a cocktail or uttered one small faint "damn", her contract was automatically forfeited'.

Sleeping with married men was probably a no-no too. The alluring actress (whose career didn't survive the transition to 'talkies') met F Scott Fitzgerald at a Hollywood mansion 1927, and is thought to have begun an affair with him soon afterwards.

Whether or not that's true, it seems certain that she provided the template for 'Rosemary Hoyt', the wide-eyed ingenue of *Tender is the Night*. 'Her body hovered delicately on the last edge of childhood,' wrote Fitzgerald, rather creepily. 'She was almost eighteen, nearly complete, but the dew was still on her.'

Tender is the Night, by F Scott Fitzgerald, was published in 1934

MISS PIGGY

Peggy Lee (1920–2002)

Not all publicity is good publicity. A certain jazz diva, for example, would probably rather not have been immortalised as a pig, but such, I'm afraid, can be life.

The mother of *Muppets* designer Bonnie Erickson 'used to live in North Dakota where Peggy Lee sang on the local radio station before she became a famous singer'. She says, 'When I first created Miss Piggy I called her Miss Piggy Lee – as both a joke and an homage. Peggy Lee was a very independent woman, and Piggy certainly is the same. But as Piggy's fame began to grow, nobody wanted to upset Peggy Lee, especially because we admired her work, so the Muppet's name was shortened to Miss Piggy.'

A sexy, breathy, blonde glamour girl, Peggy Lee recorded more than 600 songs over six decades, during which she got somewhat less sexy and glamorous. In her late seventies, she was still singing in the tight, white satin of her heyday, despite a number of weight and glandular problems, and a history of diabetes, strokes and heart surgery.

As a diabetic, Lee wouldn't have had much use for the Swedish Chef. A real-life Swedish chef claims to have inspired *that* muppet, after he made an amusingly unsuccessful appearance on *Good Morning America*. 'I was so nervous,' recalled Lars Blackman. 'I was shaking and didn't know what to do. And all the time I was mumbling strange words.'

The real Oscar the Grouch also knew his way around food. That muppet (from *Sesame Street*) was based on a grumpy waiter who once served *Muppets* creator Jim Henson.

Miss Piggy first appeared in *The Muppet Show*, a 1976–81 TV series by Jim Henson

CHICAGO'S ROXIE AND VELMA

Annan Beulah (1899–1928)

If you ever get charged with murder, get a slick lawyer and a low-cut dress. That seems to be the moral of *Chicago*, anyway – and also of the real-life story on which the musical was based.

In 1924, a 'gorgeous young flapper' named Beulah Annan (*Chicago*'s Roxie Hart) shot her lover in the back. For the next four hours, she played a foxtrot record in their Chicago flat, drinking cocktails as she watched him die. When the police finally came, it's said that Beulah drunkenly confessed to the crime, but changed her story when she sobered up.

While in jail, 'the beauty of the cell block' met the 'most stylish [woman] of Murderess Row': Belva Gaertner (Velma Kelly in the movie), a hard-drinking cabaret singer who had recently woken up drunk … and drenched in her boyfriend's blood.

The two Chicago glamour girls were often photographed together as they awaited trial. Both seemed to revel in the media attention – not to mention the chocolates, flowers and proposals they received in the post. Both also received verdicts of 'not guilty', for reasons no-one has ever quite discerned.

Maurine Watkins's play, *Chicago*, was first performed in 1926, and became a stage musical in the 1970s. Starring Renée Zellweger and Catherine Zeta-Jones, the Academy Award–winning movie version premiered in 2002

BETTY BOOP

Helen Kane (1904–66)

Can a cartoon character be sexy? Yes, if her name's Betty Boop.

The first animated character with cleavage (not to mention big brown eyes and a little black dress), Betty was once the subject of a two-year lawsuit alleging theft of image, filed by one Helen Kane.

Like Betty, Kane was a short, slightly plumpish, Bronx-born jazz singer, with brown eyes and black hair and the signature line 'boop-boop-a-doop'. But the judges eventually decided that she was *not* the model for Betty Boop. Why, I'm not entirely sure.

The coquettish Kane is also said to have influenced Blondie and Tweetie Bird, though that too has yet to be established in a court of law.

Betty Boop first appeared in *Dizzy Dishes*, a 1930 cartoon by Max Fleischer, and became an enduring character

THE ROCKETEER'S NEVILLE SINCLAIR

Errol Flynn (1909–59)

You shouldn't kick a man while he's down. But you can say what you like when he's dead. That seems to be the attitude of one biographer, anyway. In 1980, the journalist Charles Higham argued that, when he wasn't swashing and buckling onscreen, Errol Flynn kept busy being a Nazi agent.

The claim has been dismissed by all subsequent biographers. A close buddy of Fidel Castro, Flynn was a communist, if anything. The actor also sought to fight against Hitler during WWII, but was rejected from the army because of health issues.

But that didn't stop *The Rocketeer* from featuring Neville Sinclair, a debonair, devil-may-care 1930s movie star who moonlights as a German spy.

The Rocketeer comic strip first appeared in 1982. The movie, starring Timothy Dalton, premiered in 1991

SISTER ACT'S DELORIS

Dolores Hart (b. 1938)

It's not actually *that* inappropriate when a teary-eyed Academy Award winner tremulously gives thanks to God. One of the Academy's voters is actually a nun.

Once compared to Grace Kelly, Academy member Sister Dolores Hart made her film debut opposite Elvis Presley, and went on to star alongside Robert Wagner and Montgomery Clift. The real star for her, though, was God. At age twenty-four, the actress gave away all her worldly possessions and joined a Benedictine Abbey in Connecticut.

The writer of *Sister Act* – a Whoopi Goldberg movie about Deloris van Cartier, a nightclub singer turned nun – came up with the concept before he had heard of Hart but, in the interests of research, tried to track her down. Like the film's Deloris, Hart uses art to reach out to the local community (the abbey holds musicals and runs an arts school). *Unlike* the film's Deloris, Hart also chants in Latin eight times a day.

Sister Act premiered in 1992. The movie starred Whoopi Goldberg

SINGIN' IN THE RAIN'S LINA LAMONT

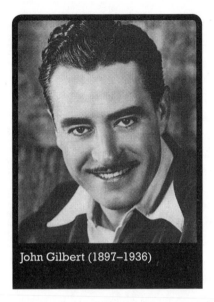

John Gilbert (1897–1936)

Video killed the radio star. Audio killed Lina Lamont. In *Singin' in the Rain*, the classic satire of 1920s Hollywood, the career of this great-to-look-at-but-horrible-to-hear movie star suffers at the hands of technology. The introduction of 'talkies' reveals that some stars should be seen but not heard.

John Gilbert didn't like talkies either. The real-life inspiration for Lina Lamont was one of the most popular film stars of the silent era – a dashing romantic lead with 'penetrating black eyes [that burnt] like basilisks' and a 'fascinating combination of mastery and savage desire'.

He also had a squeaky voice. First heard by filmgoers in *A Glorious Night*, Gilbert's high-pitched wooing 'caused a large female contingent in the theatre ... to giggle and laugh', reported the *New York Times*. 'Oh beauteous maiden,' the great lover squeaked, 'my arms are waiting to enfold you!'

Gilbert's career never quite recovered. Abandoned by film studios (and by girlfriend Greta Garbo, at the altar), he instead became a great drinker, dying of alcohol-related causes before forty.

Singin' in the Rain premiered in 1952. The movie starred Gene Kelly, Debbie Reynolds and Jean Hagen

Chapter 12
Secret agents

CHRISTOPHER ISHERWOOD'S MR NORRIS

If you can't say anything nice about someone, it's best not to say anything at all. Alternatively, you could say that they 'radiated evil'. Your call, really.

Most of Gerald Hamilton's acquaintances went with option two. The well-travelled writer and critic has also been described as 'snobbish', 'racist' and 'close to fascist'. His face, we are told, was 'grotesque, a canvas of debauch'.

Born to a 'faintly ducal' family, and educated at Rugby School, Hamilton seems to have stepped on one or two toes. Some said he was a Nazi. Others said he was a Stalinist. Everyone said he was shady. Interned by his own government in WWI and WWII, he was nonetheless popular with foreigners, receiving a few solid-gold decorations in Eastern Europe, which he unabashedly sold for cash.

The author was introduced to Hamilton in Berlin when he was trying to get foreign citizenship for his boyfriend (a German wanted by the police for draft evasion). Hamilton took £1000 to see what he could do – and then did nothing at all. *Mr Norris Changes Trains*, featuring Mr Norris, a shifty spy with an ill-fitting wig, was Isherwood's revenge.

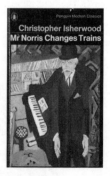

Mr Norris Changes Trains, by Christopher Isherwood, was published in 1935

JAMES BOND

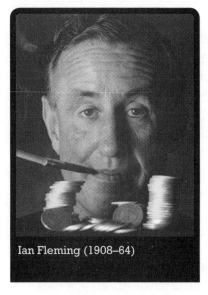

Ian Fleming (1908–64)

Just as many actors have played James Bond, many spies could claim to *be* him. Ian Fleming, 007's creator, worked in Intelligence during WWII, and just which of his lynx-eyed colleagues may have inspired Bond is a question to which some devote books.

The short answer is that Bond is no-one in particular. The slightly longer answer is that he's largely Fleming himself.

Consider the facts. Both Bond and his creator were chain-smoking, heavy-drinking naval commanders, fond of boating, short-sleeve shirts and scrambled eggs. Both were Old Etonians, heavy gamblers and members of an exclusive London club. They shared the same height, hair and eye colour, together with a 'longish nose' and 'slightly cruel mouth'. And both were, shall we say, pre-feminist. The jet-setting, Jamaica-based Fleming had innumerable, somewhat brutal affairs.

He was also a birdwatcher. The name 'James Bond' was borrowed from the author of *Field Guide to the Birds of the West Indies*, a book sitting in Fleming's Jamaica home.

The name of that Jamaica home, incidentally, was 'Goldeneye', while 'Octopussy' was the boat moored outside. And they weren't the only names Fleming reportedly plundered from real life. Another was 'Scaramanga', the triple-nippled man with the golden gun. That was George Scaramanga, an old school friend. 'Blofeld' was a fellow member of Fleming's club (and father of the cricket commentator, Henry). And 'Drax' was borrowed from an admiral who had plenty of names to spare: Sir Reginald Aylmer Ranfurly Plunkett-Ernle-Erle-Drax.

James Bond first appeared in *Casino Royale*, and went on to appear in many stories and films

IAN FLEMING'S M

The biggest secret about secret agents is that they're often rather dull. Lean, hard-bitten men of affairs aren't all that common in the offices of MI6. Look for expensive suits and telltale scars, and you'll probably look in vain. Most spies are balding bureaucrats who get most of their intelligence from Google.

The second-biggest secret is that most of them love their mums. The most attractive theory for the origins of James Bond's boss, M, is that offered by one of Ian Fleming's biographers. He points out that Bond's creator called his mum 'M' and that, like the fictional spymaster, she could be a bit of a martinet.

The most *plausible* theory, however, is that M was inspired by Admiral John Godfrey, Fleming's real-life boss at the Naval Intelligence Department. Awarded the Order of the Nile of Egypt, and made a Chevalier of the French Legion d'Honneur, Godfrey (like M) was said to inspire a mixture of fear and loyalty in his underlings, and boast some 'damnably clear' blue eyes.

Espionage requires original thinking, and Godfrey was the man for the job. One of his theories was that good-looking women were less likely to blurt out secrets, as they didn't need interesting conversation to attract men. Naval Intelligence thus employed some saucy numbers. A good guess as to which of them inspired 'Miss Moneypenny' is Dame Victoire Ridsdale, Fleming's formidable secretary of the time. Like Moneypenny, she was 'never taken in by his charm'. 'He'd go off and do something brave and come back with silk stockings and lipsticks for me [but] I always kept him at arm's length.'

M first appeared in *Casino Royale* and has most recently been played on screen by Judy Deuch

THE GOOD SHEPHERD

James Angleton (1917–87)

You'd think being a good shepherd would involve not being afraid of sheep. Not so. James Angleton, the paranoid founder of the CIA, was freaked out by his flock. Shepherding America through the Cold War for this chain-smoking insomniac meant accusing more or less everyone of being a spy. President Gerald Ford, Secretary of State Henry Kissinger and various members of Congress were all considered overly close with Russia during Angleton's twenty-nine years at the helm, as were the prime ministers of Britain, Canada and Sweden.

The painstaking patriot (whose hobbies also included writing poetry, growing orchids and dressing in black) was finally forced to resign during the Nixon era, when it emerged that he had been using the CIA to spy on students.

Being so very paranoid, Angleton probably would have thought *The Good Shepherd* was all about him. In this, at least, he would have been right. That movie's spymaster, played by Matt Damon, is also a Yale-educated insomniac, known to the Soviets as 'Mother', who's never happier than when rooting out spies.

The Good Shepherd premiered in 2006. Directed by Robert De Niro, the movie starred Matt Damon

AUSTIN POWERS

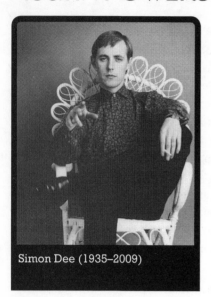

Simon Dee (1935–2009)

A lack of any discernible talent doesn't have to hold an entertainer back these days. They can always release a hit single or join a radio station's wacky breakfast crew.

Simon Dee helped start the trend. In 1967 this super-groovy DJ, actor, vacuum-cleaner salesman, cafe manager, nightclub bouncer and photographer miraculously became a super-groovy TV chat show host. This was despite his apparently being hopelessly stoned half the time, and shagging blondes in his Jaguar the rest. 'He was talentless, out of his depth, a fantasist – truly the first person famous for being famous,' says a former PA of the colourfully dressed swinger, who 'behaved as if he had divine right to every woman'.

Dee's luck finally ran out in 1969 when, somewhat carried away by his success, he walked out of the BBC over a pay dispute. His new employers were less tolerant of their out-of-control presenter's drinking and drug habits, and cancelled his contract after a couple of months. The fallen star never worked in the industry again, going from unemployment benefits to a job as a bus driver, to a short spell in prison for being unable to pay council rates.

Still, at least he made it into the movies. The co-star of the first *Austin Powers*, Elizabeth Hurley, once said that Dee's 'sixties grooviness' helped inspire the secret agent.

Austin Powers: International Man of Mystery premiered in 1997. The movie starred Mike Myers and Elizabeth Hurley

JOHN LE CARRÉ'S GEORGE SMILEY

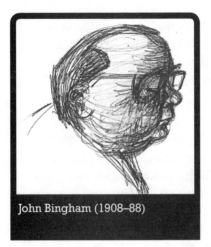

John Bingham (1908–88)

Not all spies spend their time sipping martinis in high-priced casinos and shagging shapely vixens named Pussy Galore. George Smiley, for example, is rarely seen in sports cars. John le Carré's fictional MI6 agent mostly shuffles paper from the safety of his desk. Short and overweight, with thick glasses, he battles bureaucracy, not supervillains; he dresses in cardigans, not tuxedos. 'A brilliant spy and totally inadequate man', Smiley not only *doesn't* shag around, he has a wife who *does*. (She eventually leaves him for a Cuban racing driver.)

All of this may help explain why the real-life model for this fictional spymaster was less than impressed with the books. John Bingham, the seventh Baron Clanmorris, was le Carré's 'professional mentor' when the author was 'going mad with boredom' working at MI5 but they parted 'on terms of bitter animosity'. 'As far as he was concerned, I was a shit … [who] had betrayed the Service by writing about it,' le Carré recently recalled. 'The fond apprentice had turned wrecker.'

Bingham did, perhaps, have a point. An Ulster nobleman, he also worked as a novelist during his thirty years in the Secret Service, but managed to keep his plots spy-free. Bingham's seventeen novels instead deal in simple, old-fashioned crime. I recommend *Murder off the Record*, *The Tender Poisoner* and *Ministry of Death*.

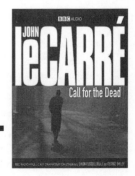

George Smiley first appeared in *Call for the Dead*, a 1961 novel by John le Carré

JASON BOURNE

Robert Ludlum (1927–2001)

A writer's life is quite forgettable. Get up. Procrastinate a bit. Write a bit. Procrastinate some more. Give up. Drink heavily. Go to bed. Repeat the next day.

One writer's life, however, was even more forgettable than most. *The Bourne Identity* came about in 1979, after thriller writer Robert Ludlum received a call at his Connecticut home. '[My accountant was] saying "Why aren't you in New York? You were supposed to be here at 11.00!"' Ludlum once recalled. 'I said "You never told me that", and he said "Well, I was up at your house yesterday. We were talking about it!"'

'What had happened to me was that I had lost about twelve hours of my life. I hadn't been drinking, it wasn't a question of alcohol or anything like that, but the stresses of just finishing a book or something had led me to just forget twelve hours. There is a medical term for it. It's called temporary amnesia.'

The author had promised his wife that he 'wouldn't sit down and start another book for at least a couple of weeks' but, inspired, he forgot that too. Jason Bourne was born. Named after Ansel Bourne, one of the first patients to be diagnosed with temporary amnesia, the character can speak five languages, handle guns, knives and bombs, and murder pretty much anyone in hand-to-hand combat. If only he could remember his past.

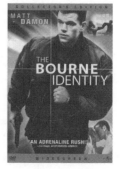

The Bourne Identity, by Robert Ludlum, was published in 1980. The movie of the same name, the first in a trilogy starring Matt Damon, premiered in 2002

A PERFECT SPY

David Cornwell (b. 1931)

Espionage isn't really a job for the well adjusted. People blessed with a happy childhood and loving relationships would generally rather potter about the garden than spy, lie, maim and kill.

Magnus Pym was *A Perfect Spy*. John le Carré's fictional spook had a twice-jailed manipulative con man for a father, a German nanny who abandoned him, and a mother who left when he was five.

So did David Cornwell, the real spy on whom the character was based. He once referred to his upbringing as a process of 'clandestine survival', saying that 'the whole world was enemy territory'. Like Magnus Pym, Cornwell studied German in Oxford and Switzerland, and was recruited by the Secret Service to report on the 'subversive' activities of more left-wing students.

In contrast to Pym, however, Cornwell did not spend his career as a Czech double agent, then end it with suicide. He became a well-known novelist called 'John le Carré'.

A Perfect Spy, by John le Carré, was published in 1986

RUDYARD KIPLING'S KIM

Rudyard Kipling may have been racist, but at least he wasn't ageist. In *Kim*, the Empire-builder's most famous book, 'the white man's burden' becomes a white boy's burden: England recruits a thirteen-year-old Pakistani street urchin, Kim, to be a secret agent in central Asia.

But don't worry; Kim can be trusted. Despite speaking Hindi better than English, and having skin 'burned black as any native', our hero is European to the core. He is actually the orphaned son of an Irish soldier and a British nursemaid, who was tragically abandoned in the mean streets of Lahore. But after being identified by the certificate he wears around his neck, and getting some polish from a public school, Kim soon proves himself worthy of 'the breed'.

We don't know whether things ended up so well for the real Kim. All we *do* know is that, a few years after the Indian Mutiny of 1857, there 'one day … appeared in the Darjeeling bazaar a strange youth with fair hair and blue eyes but who spoke no English. Around his neck, however, was hung an amulet-case containing papers which showed him to be the son of [a] missing soldier'.

This solder was Sergeant Doolan, a 'wild, harum-scarum' Irish trooper who had fled the mutiny in the company of his Tibetan lover. Neither he nor his son was ever seen again.

Kim, by Rudyard Kipling, was published in 1901

THE MEN WHO STARE AT GOATS

Not all 'intelligence' organisations necessarily deserve the name. The CIA, for example, may be very good at killing tin-pot dictators, and it certainly knows how to incarcerate Arabs without a trial, but it can struggle when it comes to common sense.

So says Jon Ronson, anyway. Immortalised as Bob Wilton, the journalist played by Ewan McGregor in *The Men Who Stare at Goats*, Ronson spent years investigating the First Earth Battalion, a secret network of 'psychic' spies employed by the CIA.

Allegedly formed to interrogate prisoners at Guantanamo Bay, the 'battalion' included one Major General Albert Stubblebine III, who believed that people could walk through walls, and Guy Savelli, who said he could kill goats just by staring at them.

The Men Who Stare at Goats premiered in 2009. Based on a book by Jon Ronson, the movie starred George Clooney

THE THIRTY-NINE STEPS' RICHARD HANNAY

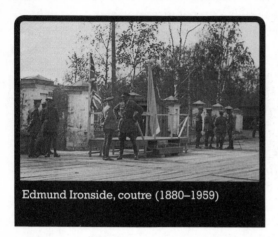

Edmund Ironside, coutre (1880–1959)

Concentration camps predated the Nazis. They were, in fact, a British invention, first used to subdue pesky locals during the 1899–1902 Boer War.

Southern Africa, then, wasn't a great place to be British in 1903. People tend to remember these things. A Scottish army officer named Edmund Ironside solved this problem by pretending to be a Boer instead. In a remarkable feat of espionage, the future field marshal accompanied a German military expedition across their southern colony in disguise as a local driver.

This wasn't his last dashing deed either. Eventually made 1st Baron Ironside by a grateful nation, this career soldier also managed to be tall and good looking, fluent in several languages, a wonderful sportsman and splendidly moustached.

You'd think these qualities would have made him generally disliked, but it seems that the Baron did have at least one fan. The novelist John Buchan (who also ended up a baron, as it happens, not to mention governor-general of Canada) used Ironside as the model for his archetypal adventure hero, Richard Hannay – another strong, silent, stiff-upper-lipped Scot who had done some cloak-and-dagger work during the Boer War.

The Thirty-Nine Steps, by John Buchan, was published in 1915

MUNICH'S AVNER

Yuval Aviv (b.1947)

If a spy's job is to keep people guessing, Yuval Aviv may be a master of the trade. In a world where a cover can be blown by an audible whisper – by an incorrect code word or a careless glance – Aviv has had a novel, a TV movie and a Steven Spielberg movie made about his time as an alleged Mossad agent, opened up a private intelligence firm, and appeared in the media as an espionage 'expert'. But a lot of people still say he's a cab driver.

All we really know for certain about this New York–based Israeli immigrant is that, in 1981, he was used as a source for a controversial book about Israel's Operation Wrath of God (upon which the Steven Spielberg movie *Munich* was based). It alleged that, after the massacre of its athletes at the Munich Olympics, a vengeful Israel dispatched a crack squad of assassins to do some massacring of their own.

So was Aviv the basis for Avner, the Mossad agent played by Eric Bana in *Munich*? According to Israeli and US officials, the answer is no. Aviv's a 'fabricator', a 'liar' and a 'con artist'. But they would say that, wouldn't they?

The man himself says he 'can't talk about it … It has become a popular thing lately for families of those who were killed to sue Israeli officials and ex-Mossad agents. Because of legal restrictions, one should not take responsibility for things. It's not smart.'

'On the record, I can only say that I'm familiar with those events.'

Munich premiered in 2005. Directed by Steven Spielberg, the movie starred Eric Bana

SYRIANA'S BOB BARNES

Robert Baer (b.1952)

The world is divided into two groups. There are people who understand *Syriana* – a brain-meltingly dense thriller in which a bunch of CIA agents, Arab princes, Hezbollah leaders, Lebanese assassins, Washington lawyers, Iranian arms dealers and Pakistani migrant workers all mutter unintelligibly and seem to have about 2492 hidden agendas each. And then there are the vast majority of us. Who don't.

The movie is 'confusing', admits Robert Baer. 'That's the whole point.' The world of geopolitical espionage really is the blind leading the blind through a dark maze filled with booby traps. 'They want you to ... walk away feeling the system's broken.'

A former CIA agent, who was 'disowned' by the agency after being (wrongly) accused of conspiring to murder Saddam Hussein, Baer wrote the largely autobiographical book on which *Syriana* is based. Flatteringly, for the character based on Baer (an agent falsely accused of going 'rogue'), the filmmakers cast George Clooney. Less flatteringly, it was on the proviso that the actor gained fifteen kilos and hid his face in a beard.

Syriana premiered in 2005. Based on a non-fiction book by Robert Baer, the movie starred George Clooney

IN THE LINE OF FIRE'S FRANK HORRIGAN

Clint Hill in action on JFK's car

Three US presidents needed to be assassinated before Congress decided it might be an idea to guard them – but that didn't stop there being a fourth. Interestingly, the Secret Service had wanted JFK to ride in an armoured limo that fateful day in Dallas, with agents trotting shield-like alongside. But that would have hidden his crowd-winning smile, so the behind-in-the-polls president said no.

Troubling for the agents, of course, but they nonetheless did their best. One of them even jumped on the car after the first shots were fired in an effort to 'take a bullet' for the chief. But just like *In the Line of Fire*'s Frank Horrigan (a Secret Service agent haunted by his failure to protect JFK), agent Clint Hill couldn't shake the feeling that he could have done more. 'It was my fault,' the hulking agent said in a famous TV interview, manly tear trickling down granite jaw. 'If I had reacted just a little bit quicker … and I could have I guess … I'll live with that to my grave.'

Despite being honoured for his 'extraordinary courage and heroic effort in the face of maximum danger', Hill retired traumatised at forty-three.

In the Line of Fire premiered in 1993. The movie starred Clint Eastwood and John Malkovich

GRAHAM GREENE'S QUIET AMERICAN

Ed Lansdale (1908–87)

The Quiet American was so damn quiet that we don't quite know who he was.

According to Graham Greene, his tale of Alden Pyle, a softly spoken intellectual who meddles in Vietnamese politics, was inspired by a naive aid worker the author met in 1951. Greene was so struck by the man's idealistic vision of a 'Third Force' in Vietnam – of a form of government in between communism and colonialism, propped up with American 'help' – that he wrote a novel attacking it.

Unfortunately, the success of *The Quiet American* didn't prevent the US from then attacking Vietnam. (The pen may be mightier than the sword, but it can't do much about bombs.)

Many people say that Greene's title character was also partially based on the architect of US involvement in the region, a former advertising agent turned CIA strategist called Ed Lansdale. His favourite strategy was generally 'more bombs'.

After the shining success of *that* war, Lansdale went on to head up Operation Mongoose, an attempt to overthrow Fidel Castro, because Cuba clearly needed a 'Third Force' too. His most constructive career move came in 1963. He retired.

The Quiet American, by Graham Greene, was published in 1955

SOMERSET MAUGHAM'S ASHENDEN

Somerset Maugham (1874–1965)

It's good to be yourself. Generally, though, it's better to be somebody else. Somerset Maugham, for example, *mostly* based his series of spy stories on his own cloak-and-dagger work during WWI. Like his fictional spy, Ashenden, the author really did get sent to Switzerland by the Secret Service, under the pretence of writing a play. And he too was subsequently dispatched to Russia, in a futile attempt to keep that country in the war.

Unlike Ashenden, however, Maugham was not a suave and dressy boulevardier, an urbane raconteur who could hold dinner parties spellbound with his lively anecdotes and polished bons mots.

Ironically, this short, shy author (a stutterer who found intelligence work 'monotonous') may have also helped inspire James Bond. Maugham's friend Ian Fleming certainly acknowledged the influence of the gentlemanly Ashenden, a spy who – just like Bond – has a chief known by a letter of the alphabet and orders a dry martini whenever he gets the chance.

And it was *Maugham*, by the by, who first said that a martini 'should always be stirred not shaken, so that the molecules lie sensuously one on top of the other'.

Ashenden: or The British Agent, by Somerset Maugham, was published in 1928

THE ENGLISH PATIENT

He may have been burnt by a plane crash, but the English patient's pain is more than skin deep. Emotional agony lurks beneath his mutilated surface thanks to an ill-fated love affair with his business partner's wife.

In real life, he would have been more interested in the business partner. And the real Lady Dorothy Clayton apparently despised the real-life English patient for being so obviously gay. 'She wouldn't even shake his hand in public,' says a biographer. While (like the character) he was a desert explorer who had a lover die prematurely, that lover was a Nazi soldier.

Other differences? He wasn't English – being born László Ede Almásy de Zsadány et Törökszentmiklós in Hungary. He was never a patient (at least, not until he died from dysentery). And he definitely *was* a Nazi spy, though he did do a bit of work for Britain as well.

The English Patient, by Michael Ondaatje, was published in 1992. The Academy Award–winning movie starring Ralph Fiennes and Kristin Scott Thomas premiered in 1996

THE RECRUIT'S WALTER BURKE

The 'Farm', the CIA's training school, isn't very nice to its livestock.

In *The Recruit*, Colin Farrell's character doesn't just have to pass various psychometric and psychological tests in order to become a spook. He has to put up with an absolute psycho. Deranged instructor Walter Burke begins the new recruit's training by making him jump through a window, then has him kidnapped, tortured and interrogated to see if he'll blurt out any fellow agents' names.

All quite inappropriate, really. Someone should have called HR. And what made it worse, it turns out, was that Burke himself was a blurter from way back. The movie is based on a real-life CIA instructor named Harold Nicholson, who gave the Russians the names of a few pupils in exchange for some serious bucks.

Nicholson is now well into a twenty-three-year prison sentence, but you can't keep a bad man down. In 2009, federal inmate no. 49535-083 was charged with selling America's enemies still more secrets from right inside his jail cell. Allegedly he'd been using coded letters and his son Nathaniel to perpetrate the leaks.

The Recruit premiered in 2003. The movie starred Al Pacino and Colin Farrell

Chapter 13
Shady businessmen

OLIVER TWIST'S FAGIN

Ikey Solomon (1785–1850)

Tune into talkback radio and you'll probably hear a pensioner complain about the youth of today. 'Kids don't do enough work,' they whine. 'Slack, slack, slack,' they say. But when one of those feckless youths *does* find a job – as a mugger, say, or a shoplifter – they generally have a gripe too. You just can't win.

Oliver Twist also suffered from this kind of unthinking prejudice. Gainfully employed by Fagin to pick the pockets of passers-by, that orphan was pretty much shunned by society until he was adopted by a kindly gentleman and put in a nice, clean suit.

Some say Oliver was based on Robert Blincoe, a six-year-old chimneysweep who later wrote a popular memoir about being down and out in Victorian London. Others say this is crap.

All agree about Fagin, however. It seems certain that Charles Dickens based *Oliver Twist*'s East End evildoer on Ikey Solomon, a real-life 'fence' who used a pawn shop to buy and sell stolen goods. Solomon became widely known after he got arrested in 1827 – and managed to escape before going to trial. Fleeing to Tasmania, he ran a 'tobacco store' until, after years of expensive legal wrangling, the British government finally found the authority to have him sent back.

Back in London, Solomon was put to trial and found guilty. His punishment? Exile to Tasmania. A phrase from *Oliver Twist* seems apposite: 'The law,' says one character, 'is an ass.'

Oliver Twist, by Charles Dickens, was published in 1838.
Roman Polanski directed a film version in 2005

SHYLOCK

Rodrigo López, right (1525–1594)

The Merchant of Venice may have been inspired by a doctor of London. In 1559, Rodrigo López fled Portugal, where Catholic inquisitors were torturing Jews, and went to England, where people merely loathed them. Declaring himself a Protestant, this highly skilled medical man soon came to the attention of the high and mighty. He was chosen to be Queen Elizabeth's personal physician, and through her accumulated some fabulous wealth.

That attention became less enjoyable in 1594, however. Lopez was accused of plotting to poison the queen. He insisted that he was innocent and evidence suggests he was telling the truth. But a wave of anti-Semitism had swept through the country, so the doctor was duly hanged.

Some say that *The Merchant of Venice*, created by Shakespeare shortly afterwards, was a cynical attempt on the part of the playwright to cash in on this sensational trial. What more topical villain could he have come up with than Shylock – a hook-nosed, sour-faced moneylender greedily yearning for his 'pound of flesh'?

A more charitable interpretation sees Shylock as a tragic hero – as a victim of prejudice, like López. And it's true that the play does contain a then–unusual plea for tolerance. 'Hath not a Jew eyes?' the much-abused loan shark cries. 'Hath not a Jew hands, organs, dimensions, senses, affections, passions? Fed with the same food, hurt with the same weapons, subject to the same diseases, healed by the same means, warmed and cooled by the same winter and summer, as a Christian is? If you prick us, do we not bleed?'

The Merchant of Venice, by William Shakespeare, was first performed around 1596

POWER WITHOUT GLORY'S JOHN WEST

John Wren (1871–1953)

The Chinese philosopher and military strategist Sun Tzu saw subtlety as a 'fine art'. Frank Hardy saw it as a waste of time. In *Power without Glory*, the 'novel' he wrote to expose corruption in Melbourne, influential archbishop Daniel Mannix became influential archbishop Daniel Malone. Cocky gangster Squizzy Taylor became cocky gangster Snoopy Tanner. Colourful politicians Frank Anstey and David Gaunson became colourful politicians Frank Ashton and Davey Garside. And Johnston Street, Collingwood became Jackson Street, Carringbush.

Most importantly, notorious Melbourne powerbroker John Wren became notorious Melbourne powerbroker John West. Born in the slums of Collingwood, Wren controlled an illegal gambling venue by his twenty-second birthday, then did his best to control everything else. Whether or not he bribed, blackmailed, rigged races and racketeered to the extent that *Power without Glory* implies, the wealthy businessman was much chummier with politicians and policemen than a good democrat would consider ideal.

Like so many crazy-busy career men, Wren was less chummy with his wife. In the novel, Nellie West has an extramarital affair that results in an illegitimate child. In real life, Ellie Wren's illegitimate child committed suicide a few years after the book was published. Perhaps subtlety would have been a better idea ...

Power Without Glory, by Frank Hardy, was published in 1950

EBENEZER SCROOGE

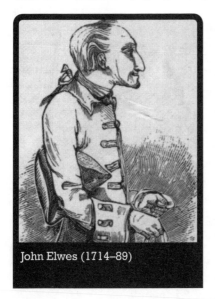

John Elwes (1714–89)

If you look after your pennies, your pounds will take care of themselves. If you look after your halfpennies, you could be a little nuts.

John Elwes was *very* nuts. Born John Meggot to a mother who died of starvation – apparently she was *that* stingy – this notorious miser adopted his grandfather's surname in order to get in his will.

He succeeded. Armed with about £40 million in today's money, Elwes somehow managed to spend less than £7000 of it a year. He wore the same ragged suit each day, and was frequently mistaken for a beggar. (Rather unfairly, given he happily made use of a tattered wig a beggar had thrown away onto a hedge.) Could he have been the inspiration for Ebenezer Scrooge?

Food was another economy. Not liking to throw anything away, Elwes would supposedly eat meat so full of maggots 'that it walked about his plate'. Another story has him chomping down a dead bird that had been pulled out of a river by a rat.

Elected MP for Berkshire (after investing 18 pence in his campaign), Elwes would travel to parliament on horseback, napping under hedgerows to save the cost of a bed. He spent his dotage in continual travel, having decided that it would be more economical to rent out all his houses, and stay in whichever one didn't have a tenant at the time. Riding, as he did, in the rain – and not liking to spend money on firewood – this practice eventually killed him. His doctor reported that he 'might have lived 20 years longer, but for his continual anxiety about money'.

A Christmas Carol, by Charles Dickens, was published in 1843

WALL STREET'S GORDON GEKKO

There's no-one quite like Gordon Gekko, the unscrupulous shyster of *Wall Street*. Sadly, there are at least four people.

Gekko's job description came from Carl Icahn – a corporate raider who lost at least $5 billion during the global financial crisis, but remains one of the richest men in the world.

The character's moral fibre came courtesy of Ivan Boesky, who racked up over $200 million in the 80s by betting on corporate takeovers. After winning a rather astonishing number of these bets, he was investigated for insider trading, and won a $100 million fine and two years in jail. ('Greed', by the way, didn't start out as 'good'. Boesky described it as 'right' in the speech upon which the famous line is based.)

For Gekko's style (braces, slicked-back hair, shoulder pads) *Wall Street*'s writer Stanley Weiner looked to Asher Edelman, a corporate-raider-turned-art-dealer. 'The sophisticated part of Gekko, his home and the auctions and that veneer of culture – I modelled all that on Edelman.'

And what about that belligerent charm? Amusingly enough, this aspect of the right-wing bogeyman was actually based on *Wall Street*'s left-wing director, Oliver Stone. 'Gekko's dialogue actually was inspired by Stone's own rants,' recalled Weiner. '[By] listening to Oliver's early morning cajoling and sarcastic phone calls … exhorting me to work: "Where the hell are you? Out having a gourmet breakfast, playing with the kids in the park?" … Other unpublishable barbs proved to be the precise varnish with which I needed to coat Gekko.'

Wall Street premiered in 1987. Created by Oliver Stone and Stanley Weiner, the movie starred Michael Douglas and Charlie Sheen

THE GREAT GATSBY

The Great Gatsby's title character is shrouded in mystery. So it's perhaps appropriate that the real Gatsby is too.

The wealthy 'jazz age' socialite Max von Gerlach 'would be an archetypal 1920s figure if we knew enough about him'. All we really know is that he was a millionaire neighbour of *Gatsby* author F Scott Fitzgerald in Long Island and that, like the character, he enjoyed spending money and calling everyone he met 'Old Sport'. There's a newspaper report of a failed suicide attempt in 1939 and a death certificate dated 1958. He 'seems to be one of those 20s figures who led the flamboyant lives and couldn't cope with the [depression of] the 1930s.'

And that's about all we know for certain. But like Gatsby – a mysterious millionaire who disguises his origins and throws big parties that he doesn't attend – von Gerlach attracted all manner of rumours. Some said that he was a German baron whose family fled their estate during WWI. Others thought that he was a retired-army-officer-turned-bootlegger (just like Gatsby, who also had his 'Oxford accent').

Some even say he had nothing to do with Gatsby. And that, we must admit, is quite possible too.

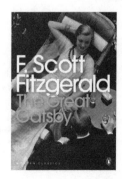

The Great Gatsby, by F Scott Fitzgerald, was published in 1925

THERE WILL BE BLOOD'S DANIEL PLAINVIEW

Edward Doheny, right
(1856–1935)

The character Daniel Plainview spends the first 20 minutes of *There Will Be Blood* painstakingly digging for oil. We see a lot of sweat, spit, dust and darkness – and hear not a single word. Yes, that's right: no dialogue whatsoever. Just one or two grunts and sighs, and a spade going *clink, clink, clink*.

The person Daniel was based on also committed a crime – though, in his case, it wasn't against moviegoers. Like the character, Edward Doheny was a rough-edged silver miner from Wisconsin who turned to oil at the turn of the century, initially doing all the shovel-work himself. He too built an international empire by old-fashioned hard work and even more old-fashioned graft.

Everything eventually came tumbling down in 1924, when Doheny was found to have bribed a senator to secure drilling rights on federal land. (The movie's famous final line – 'I drink your milkshake' – is taken from the senator's testimony before a Congressional committee.)

Though *unlike* the ruthless Plainview, we should probably note, Doheny never actually beat anyone to death with a bowling pin. His son *was* murdered in mysterious circumstances, however – and not long before he was due to testify. Did Doheny do it? We will never know.

There Will Be Blood premiered in 2007. The Academy Award–winning movie starred Daniel Day-Lewis

CATCH-22'S MILO MINDERBINDER

Two wrongs don't make a right. They can, however, make a profit. *Catch-22*'s Milo Minderbinder has done one or two things he isn't proud of – but he's also proud of doing some pretty terrible things.

Loyalty to the 'American way' of capitalism, for Milo, frequently means being disloyal to America itself. The entrepreneurial black marketeer even ends up bombing US army bases to help stimulate the free flow of trade: 'What's good for Milo Minderbinder is good for the country'.

There, however, he's wrong. It's actually 'what's good for *General Motors* is good for the country'. The character's famous quote came courtesy of Charles E Wilson – a former head of General Motors who in the 1950s became Secretary of Defense. 'I was writing the book in the post-war world, and I was dealing with much that was happening after the war,' said *Catch-22* author Joseph Heller. 'It wasn't about the army, it was about the birth of the multinational corporation.'

And what about the novel's narrator? Yossarian was named after Heller's fellow pilot Francis Yohannan but otherwise came out of Heller's head. 'He's not like me,' the author insisted. 'I had no complaints about my service in the army. What I did have was a lot of objections to people in authority in America, in military, in business, and especially in government – and a vivid, glowing sense of their moral corruption.'

Catch-22, by Joseph Heller, was published in 1961

GUYS AND DOLLS' NATHAN DETROIT

Arnold Rothstein (1882–1928)

Would you rather be known as 'Mr Big' or 'The Fixer'? 'The Man Uptown' or 'The Brain'? Arnold Rothstein got to be all four. The New York head of an elaborate crime organisation peopled by the likes of 'Lucky' Luciano, 'Legs' Diamond and 'Dutch' Shultz, Rothstein was the model for *Guys and Dolls'* Nathan Detroit (a gambling kingpin who sponsors floating craps games).

Rothstein was one of the first gangsters to realise that Prohibition represented a great business opportunity, but he was best known for his betting rings. A nobbler of favourites and fixer of dice, he was even thought to have fixed the 1919 World Series by paying the Chicago White Sox to throw a few games.

The mobster's luck finally ran out in 1928. He was shot dead after losing $320,000 on a poker game and declining to pay the debt.

Nathan Detroit first appeared in *The Idyll of Miss Sarah Brown*, the 1933 Damon Runyon short story upon which the 1950 stage musical, *Guys and Dolls*, is based

CHINATOWN'S HOLLIS MULWRAY AND NOAH CROSS

William Mulholland (1855–1935)

Here's a tip for any self-taught engineers out there. It's probably better that you get a degree.

The head of the LA's Water Department discovered this the hard way in 1928, after workers reported a leak on a dam. William Mulholland had built the dam himself, along with every other bit of the 233-mile-long aqueduct that had helped LA become one of the biggest cities in the world. He felt confident, therefore, that the minor leak would remain minor, and assured city authorities that all was well.

All wasn't. Just twelve hours later, the dam collapsed, spilling 12 trillion gallons and killing 500 people. 'Don't blame anyone else, you just fasten it on me,' Mulholland told reporters. They did.

The makers of *Chinatown* were also keen to fasten blame on the engineer (after whom Mulholland Drive, incidentally, is named). The movie, of course, focuses not on the collapse of LA's water system but on the shady dealings that built it up. Two of its characters owe a bit to Mulholland. One of them, Hollis Mulwray, is an engineer whose defective dam once killed hundreds. He represents Mulholland's well-meaning-but-inept side.

Noah Cross represents his deceit. Just like the *Chinatown* businessman, Mulholland's methods of obtaining water could sometimes seem a little shady. He misled farmers in Owens Valley into selling their water rights, for example, then drained their 260-kilometre lake dry. Admittedly, Mulholland said that he 'half-regretted the demise of so many of the valley's orchard trees'. But this was only because there were now 'no longer enough trees to hang all the troublemakers who live there.'

Chinatown premiered in 1974. The movie starred Jack Nicholson and John Huston

THE PIED PIPER

Was the pied piper a paedophile? One historian says yes. For William Manchester, there is something very sinister about the sprightly ratcatcher who lures away the children of Hamelin. The pied piper was 'horrible, a psychopath and pederast who … spirited away 130 children … and used them in unspeakable ways'.

Possible, but unlikely. In fact, he was probably more like a real-estate agent. In 1227, the German states won the Battle of Bornhöved, which meant that much of Eastern Europe was suddenly theirs. The area's new overlords were certainly anxious to colonise their new possessions, to prevent them being overrun by the Russians, so they dispatched some pied ('colourfully dressed') agents throughout Germany to encourage migration east.

One such overlord was Bruno von Schaumburg, the Bishop of Olmutz and a powerbroker in Hamelin. After the Battle of Bornhöved, he also gained control of what's now known as Beweringen in modern-day Poland.

Now Beweringen, as modern scholars have noticed, sounds very much like Beverungen, a village just south of Hamelin. Not a terribly exciting connection – until you look in a Polish telephone book. Living in Beweringen are numerous Hamels, Hamlers and Hamelnikows – all deeply un-Polish names that had to come from somewhere.

Did they come from Hamelin – thus taking away the flower of that town's youth? We will never know for sure.

The poem 'The Pied Piper of Hamelin' first appeared in Bells and Pomegranates No. 111, a book by Robert Browning

PG WODEHOUSE'S UKRIDGE

Some people will do anything for money, provided it doesn't involve work.

Ukridge is one of them. Constantly on the run from creditors, PG Wodehouse's mackintosh-wearing bounder is blessed with a never-ending supply of get-rich-quick schemes and a 'big, broad, flexible outlook'. He's the sort of shameless vulgarian you do your best to avoid but end up lending money to instead. A fellow very much like Herbert Westbrook.

The author met the 'self-centred, outrageous but likeable' Westbrook in 1903 and was talked into writing books and plays with him over the next ten years. 'One of those engaging inveterate hustlers who seem permanently trapped between his last disgraceful misdemeanour and his next grovelling apology', 'Westy' was a teacher at Emsworth House near Threepwood Cottage, where Wodehouse once spent a summer.

Brash, breezy and continually broke, Westy seems to have spent most of the friendship borrowing money and clothes. On one occasion (later immortalised in a Ukridge story), he 'borrowed' Wodehouse's banjo, then pawned it for some ready cash.

Wodehouse dedicated a short story to him ('To that Prince of Slackers, Herbert Westbrook'), then decided to take something in return – a novel.

Ukridge first appeared in *Love among the Chickens*, a 1906 novel by PG Wodehouse

CASINO'S 'ACE' ROTHSTEIN

Frank Rosenthal, left (1929–2008)

Talk-show hosts are generally terrible, but that doesn't mean they belong in jail. The exception to this rule was Frank Rosenthal, who hosted *The Frank Rosenthal Show* in the 1970s when he wasn't busy being a mobster, embezzler and thug. Frank spent twenty years managing the mob's Las Vegas casinos before city authorities finally kicked him out. Like *Casino*'s Ace Rothstein, his duties included embezzling profits, bribing judges and fixing sports events. *Unlike* Ace Rothstein, he also squeezed in cheery TV chats with the likes of Frank Sinatra and Bob Hope.

Frank's talks with Anthony 'the Ant' Spilotro, on the other hand, tended to be away from the public eye. This petite psychopath served as Frank's 'muscle', and he did his job rather well. Like the character Nicky Santoro in *Casino*, the Ant murdered at least twenty people – and squished at least one person's head in a vice. Naturally, he ended up getting killed himself. Most likely by a mob wielding baseball bats who thoughtfully buried him alive.

Another good way to get killed is via an overdose of valium, cocaine and Jack Daniels. Such was the method adopted by Geri McGee, a hustler and topless dancer who was married to Frank and presumably didn't enjoy it very much. She inspired Sharon Stone's character in *Casino*, Ginger McKenna.

Casino premiered in 1995. The film starred Robert De Niro, Joe Pesci and Sharon Stone

THE GODFATHER

Carlo Gambino (1902–76)

The Godfather was really a mum. When creating Don Corleone, the author Mario Puzo was partially inspired by an illiterate Neapolitan immigrant who had raised him and his eleven siblings singlehandedly amid the squalor of the New York slums. 'Whenever the Godfather opened his mouth, in my own mind I heard the voice of my mother … [She] was a wonderful, handsome woman, but a fairly ruthless person.'

Presiding over those slums was the Luciano/Genovese crime family. Like the Corleone clan of the movie, it steered clear of drugs, preferring protection rackets, bootlegging and casinos. Its head was Frank Costello, a gangster with a raspy voice much like the Don's. Like Corleone, he kept politicians and judges on his payroll, and often acted as a go-between between the government and the families.

Costello, however, lacked cunning, a quality one of his colleagues had in abundance. Like the ever-calculating Corleone, Carlo Gambino was softly spoken and seemingly humble, carefully avoiding all the trappings of wealth.

Corleone, then, was a composite – but *The Godfather*'s other characters are more straightforward. The character Moe Green ('the man who invented Las Vegas') was clearly Bugsy Siegel, while the real-life boss of the Jewish mob, Meyer Lansky, was simply renamed 'Hyman Roth'. Frank Sinatra, of course, was the character Johnny Fontane (a slightly seedy singer, who uses the Godfather to land a movie role). Ol' Blue Eyes later bumped into the author at a restaurant and angrily called him a 'pimp'.

The Godfather by Mario Puzo was published in 1969. The Academy Award–winning movie starring Marlon Brando and Al Pacino premiered in 1972

ROBBERY UNDER ARMS' CAPTAIN STARLIGHT

If you think no fate could be worse than death, go for a hike in the Australian outback. Vast, hot, dry and dusty, you can trudge 200 kilometres without seeing water – but there are always plenty of flies.

For three months in 1870, there were also plenty of cows. In one of the country's more remarkable crimes, an audacious cattleman named Harry Readford managed to steal about 1000 prime cattle in Queensland and sell them in South Australia – 1300 kilometres away.

'A bushman born and bred', who stood nearly two metres tall, Readford's feat became Captain Starlight's in the iconic colonial novel, *Robbery under Arms*.

Unlike that book's 'gentleman bushranger', however, Readford got off scot-free. Though caught by the police, the jury declared him 'not guilty' – those twelve good men being the first to appreciate good bushcraft, and to resent the huge cattle stations for their greed. Stunned, the judge said, 'I thank God that verdict is yours ... and not mine.'

Readford himself thanked the jury, shouting them drinks at the pub that night.

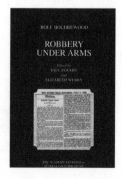

Robbery under Arms, by Rolf Boldrewood, was published in 1888

GOLDFINGER

Erno Goldfinger (1902–87)

The real 'Auric Goldfinger' didn't really love gold. Concrete was more his go. Ideally, great, big, ugly slabs of it, shoved somewhere that's otherwise nice.

Erno Goldfinger, as you have no doubt guessed, was a modern architect. In the 1950s, his war on taste saw him replace many a charming cottage with a great, big tower block. Ian Fleming was one of many Brits to object to this practice – but the only one to get his revenge. After the Bond author wrote *Goldfinger*, the architect's name became synonymous with supervillainy. He spent the rest of his life being pestered by prank calls – Sean Connery sound-alikes calling to say, 'Goldfinger? This is 007'.

The other model for the book might have welcomed a few prank calls. The businessman Charles Engelhard was so keen for people to notice the similarities between himself and the Bond villain that he once wore Goldfinger's signature sweatshirt and renamed a female staffer 'Pussy Galore'.

What were those similarities? Well, while he didn't use gold-painted prostitutes, eat gold food or drive a gold car, Engelhard *did* amass a large fortune in the substance – and, at the time Fleming knew him, was moulding it into all sorts of strange objects to avoid trade restrictions on bullion.

The novel's spiky martial arts expert Pussy Galore, by the bye, is said to be based on Blanche Blackwell, Fleming's neighbour in Jamaica and the love of his later life. Blackwell's son, a well-known music magnate, later 'discovered' Bob Marley and helped to make him a star.

Goldfinger, by Ian Fleming, was published in 1959. The movie starring Sean Connery premiered in 1964

SIX DEGREES OF SEPARATION'S PAUL

Personal space is hard to find. According to the 'Human Web' theory, if you are separated by one degree from all the people that you know, and by two degrees from all the people that *they* know, then you are at most six degrees of separation from every single person on earth. Damn.

In 1983, playwright John Guare was separated by two degrees from a smooth-talking shyster named David Hampton. After he managed to get into an exclusive nightclub by pretending to be Sidney Poitier's son, Hampton had taken the ruse and run with it – enjoying complimentary meals, large loans and free accommodation all over New York as the charming 'David Poitier'.

A friend of two of Hampton's hoodwinked hosts, Guare was inspired to write the play-turned-movie after the con man was finally found out. The result was that he and Hampton became separated by only one degree. The shyster issued death threats, gatecrashed a party and filed a lawsuit for $100 million.

Unable to con the judge, Hampton later raised money by pretending to be other people – a wealthy physician's son, a reporter for *Vogue* magazine, and so on. In and out of prison, he eventually died of AIDS.

Six Degrees of Separation, by John Guare, was first performed in 1990. The movie, starring Will Smith, premiered in 1993

FARGO'S JERRY LUNDEGAARD

Crime doesn't pay, if it's not done right. Attention to detail is everything. In *Fargo*, deep-in-debt car salesman Jerry Lundegaard learns this lesson the hard way after he hires two felons to kidnap his wife. Instead of pocketing the ransom paid by his father-in-law and living affluently ever after, his scheme goes violently wrong. A few bodies end up in a woodchipper, and Jerry ends up in jail.

In real life there was only one body, but the real Jerry did the murdering himself. Small-town airline pilot Richard Crafts was never what you'd call a great catch. He continually cheated on his wife, allegedly beat her, and collected enough hand grenades, machine guns, revolvers and rifles to fully arm fifty men. 'If something happens to me, don't think it was an accident,' his wife told her friends.

Smart woman. On 19 November 1986, for reasons no-one's ever really established, Crafts killed his wife, fed her into a woodchipper, and dumped the pieces in Newtown's Lake Zoar. You'll be pleased to know he was jailed for life.

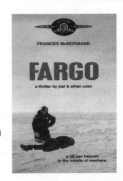

Fargo premiered in 1996. Created by the Coen brothers, the movie starred Frances McDormand and William H Macy

Chapter 14
Teachers

THE HEADMISTRESS OF ST TRINIAN'S

What would *Lord of the Flies* have looked like if the island had been governed by girls? Something like St Trinian's, you'd imagine. The subject of innumerable movies, this ostensibly respectable fictional boarding school is where the daughters of crims and bookies go to gamble, drink and smoke. The ink-stained younger girls also like chasing people with hockey sticks. Their short-skirted elders prefer to chase boys.

Presiding over the chaos is genial headmistress Miss Fritton – or Miss Lee, as she was known in real life. A 'radical' educationalist from Edinburgh, Catherine Lee founded St *Trinnean*'s school in 1922, with a well-publicised emphasis on self- rather than school-imposed discipline. In practice, all this really meant was that the students could organise their own homework schedules, a novel idea at the time. But as far as satirists were concerned, the genteel, middle-class St Trinnean's was the school 'where they do what they like'.

'There was a big rumpus when all [the cartoons and films] came out. We all felt they rather desecrated our school,' recalled one former student. 'Miss Lee stood up and told the school "After twenty years at St Trinnean's, I am broken-hearted."'

Ronald Searle's first St Trinian's cartoon appeared in 1942.
The first film, *The Belles of St Trinian's*, premiered in 1954

HARRY POTTER'S PROFESSOR SNAPE

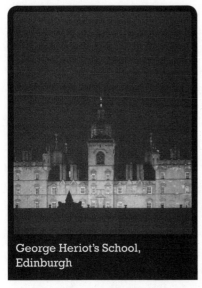

George Heriot's School, Edinburgh

Is it better to be famous for being a prat, or to never find fame at all?

Like anyone who's ever appeared on reality TV, John Nettleship picked fame. The black-haired chemistry teacher, who taught the young JK Rowling, now sells pamphlets claiming to have been her inspiration for her black-haired Professor Snape in the Harry Potter books. 'I knew I was a strict teacher but I didn't realise I was that bad.' The author herself admits that the sallow-faced sadist (named for the Suffolk village of Snape) was 'loosely based on a teacher I myself had', but she has never confirmed it was Nettleship.

Not that he's the only teacher wanting a slice of the spotlight. Rowling's history lecturer at university, Hugh Stubbs, has 'no doubt' that he was the model for the tedious Professor Binns, whose over-long lessons send students to sleep. 'I admit I could be a bit dopey first thing in the morning and I probably did give some pretty boring lectures.'

And how about Hogwarts, the magical castle where they teach? Scots like to believe it was based on George Heriot's School, an enormous Gothic edifice in Edinburgh, not far from Rowling's home.

As for Hogwarts's students, we know that the character Ron Weasley was based on Sean Harris, the author's long-time best friend. Ron 'isn't a living portrait of Sean,' says Rowling, 'but he really is very Sean-ish'. A major in the British Army and decorated veteran of Iraq, Sean owned a turquoise Ford Anglia in his schooldays, which inspired Ron's flying car.

Rowling herself is Hermione Granger, Ron's know-it-all, bookish girlfriend. 'She's a caricature of me when I was eleven, which I'm not particularly proud of.'

JK Rowling's first Harry Potter book, *Harry Potter and the Philosopher's Stone*, was published in 1997

DEAD POETS SOCIETY'S MR KEATING

Samuel F Pickering (b.1941)

If you'd like to get in touch with your sensitive side, but sometimes worry that you might not have one, just rent *Dead Poets Society*. Genghis Khan would shed a little tear at that 'O Captain! My Captain!' scene. Even Dick Cheney might wobble a lip.

Alternatively, you could visit the University of Connecticut. For there, in the English Department, you will find one Samuel Pickering, the model for Mr Keating himself. In between winning a Fulbright scholarship, authoring fifteen books and lecturing all over the world, Pickering once spent a year teaching English at Montgomery Bell Academy, whose well-to-do students included a future screenwriter.

'Our typical classes were a drag, taught by teachers who had been [at the school] forever, but the new Mr Pickering was great fun,' recalled one of those students. 'Each class was wrought with anticipation as to what he might say and do.' Prone to leaping onto his desk and proclaiming profundities with a raised fist, his 'antics and teaching style were such that you could not help but listen and think'.

In *Dead Poets Society*, Mr Keating is 'more restrained and a great deal more sensible than I was twenty-five years ago', Pickering admits. In retirement, however, he's less inclined to seize the day. *Carpe diem* 'would not do for me. I am too old to live anywhere near the fullest; and if I tried to seize but an hour, I would be swept up by a cardiovascular storm'.

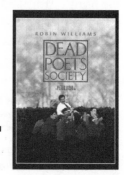

Dead Poets Society premiered in 1989. The movie starred Robin Williams

MY FAIR LADY'S HENRY HIGGINS

Henry Sweet (1845–1912)

If George Bernard Shaw had had his way, Julia Roberts would have ditched Richard Gere and married someone worthy and poor.

Pygmalion, the Shaw play upon which *My Fair Lady* and *Pretty Woman* are based, is a less-than-romantic affair. The abrasive, patronising Professor Henry Higgins doesn't so much fall in love with the Cockney guttersnipe Eliza Doolittle as threaten to wring her neck. She, in turn, thanks him for turning her into a soft-spoken society lady by storming off to marry someone else.

When it came to the real Henry Higgins, such scenes were all too common. Like the character, Shaw's good friend Henry Sweet was an abrasive amateur philologist who could enunciate seventy-two different vowel sounds. He too liked to send friends postcards in an unintelligible system of phonetic shorthand, and would sometimes break off a conversation in order to jot down notes about the other person's accent.

But despite penning such weighty works as *The Practical Study of Languages* and *A Primer of Spoken English*, Sweet never managed to get a professorship. This may be because he spent his life in a series of feuds. Lacking a certain 'sweetness of character', he would often show a 'boundless contempt for my stupidity', Shaw wrote, along with 'a Satanic contempt for [many] academic dignitaries and persons in general'. All in all, not really someone you could imagine wooing Julia Roberts.

Pygmalion, by George Bernard Shaw, was first performed in 1913. The musical based on the play, *My Fair Lady*, premiered in 1956

MISS JEAN BRODIE

Christina Kay, centre (1878–1951)

The prime of 'Miss Jean Brodie' didn't last very long.

Miss Christina Kay retired shortly after captivating the eleven-year-old Muriel Spark at an Edinburgh girls school, and passed away a decade later, long before Spark's novel *The Prime of Miss Jean Brodie* was published.

This may have been for the best. Unlike Miss Brodie, the character she inspired, Miss Kay was a respectable spinster, who kept busy caring for her sick mother when she wasn't moulding young minds. She never actually got fired, had sordid affairs or preached fascism (though a newspaper photo of Mussolini marching his troops *was* displayed on her classroom wall).

Like the character, however, she did pick favourites – taking Spark and Co. to plays, galleries and the ballet, and calling them her 'crème de la crème'. And, as in the novel, her classroom was filled with posters of Giotto, Leonardo and Botticelli – with talk of her travels in Europe, and the poetry of Blunden and Brooke.

'What filled our minds with wonder and made Christina Kay so memorable was the personal drama and poetry with which everything in her classroom happened,' wrote Spark. 'She was a character in search of an author.'

The Prime of Miss Jean Brodie, by Muriel Spark, was published in 1961

NICHOLAS NICKLEBY'S WACKFORD SQUEERS

Bowes Academy, Yorkshire

In *Nicholas Nickleby*, the golden days of childhood are more of a dark poo-brown. The novel starts with Nicholas enduring some picturesque suffering of his own (dead parents, sudden poverty, etc.). Then Charles Dickens makes him a teacher at the world's worst school, so we can all enjoy the suffering of others.

Filled with violence, vermin and 'pale, haggard' children, Dickens's Dotheboys Hall was a direct parody of Bowes Academy, a notorious school in the north of England that closed down after the book was published. Like the fictional principal, Wackford Squeers, Bowes's principal William Shaw had a patch over one eye, the initials WS and a slightly overdeveloped sense of economy. Bowes boasted two towels, five boys to a bed, and a conviction for 'gross neglect' (eight boys in its care went blind).

Wackford's favourite whipping boy, the weedy Smike, was inspired by a visit to the Bowes graveyard. Walking among the graves of thirty-odd students, Dickens came across the tomb of one George Ashton Taylor. He 'died suddenly at Mr William Shaw's Academy of this place, April 13th, 1822 aged 19 years', read the gravestone. 'Young reader, thou must die, but after this the judgment.'

'I think his ghost put Smike into my head, upon the spot,' said Dickens.

Nicholas Nickleby, by Charles Dickens, was first published in serial form from 1838 to 1839

MR CHIPS

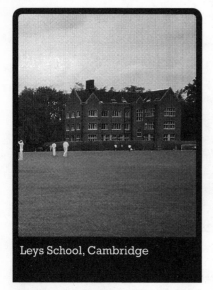

Leys School, Cambridge

The times, as Bob Dylan crooned, are a-changin'. These days, a teacher who treated an errant student to a pants-down 'six of the best' then invited him home for tea would be viewed with not a little concern. Parents would sue. Talk radio would buzz. Someone would write a strongly worded letter to the editor.

Eighty years ago, on the other hand, this kind of behaviour inspired admiring novels. William Henry Balgarnie was 'the chief model' for fiction's crustiest schoolmaster, the eccentric Mr Chips. 'When I read so many other stories about public school life, I am struck by the fact that I suffered no such purgatory as their authors apparently did, and much of this miracle was due to Balgarnie,' wrote his former student, the author James Hilton.

A Cambridge graduate who published translations of Sophocles, Euripides and Lysias, Mr Balgarnie spent fifty-one years at Leys School, and began roughly three million sentences with Mr Chips's catchphrase, 'I take it'.

The character's name came from one of his magnificently whiskered colleagues, who was naturally known to students as 'Mr Chops'.

Goodbye, Mr Chips, by James Hilton, was published in 1934

LUCKY JIM

Philip Larkin (1922–85)

The problem with 'keeping it real' is that, in reality, some people are crap.

As a part of the 'angry young man' movement (which later evolved into the 'grumpy old prick' movement), Kingsley Amis used his novel *Lucky Jim* to attack the supposed phoniness of Britain's cultural establishment. The novel's hard-drinking history lecturer Jim Dixon is beset on all sides by the effete, the pretentious and the highbrow. Eventually, this no-nonsense everyman escapes his university's 'home-made pottery', 'organic husbandry', 'recorder-playing' crowd and gets a non-academic job instead – thus becoming the 'lucky' Jim of the title.

The real Jim – the poet, Philip Larkin – was less lucky. He never escaped campus life. Larkin was an assistant librarian at University College, Leicester when he invited his old chum Kingsley Amis for a novel-inspiring drink in the common room. Then he worked as head librarian at the University of Hull.

In between, he produced poems about 'ordinary people doing ordinary things', drank a bit, swore a lot, scratched, burped and farted. Attacked for celebrating 'philistinism', the right-winger was also a 'casual, habitual racist and an easy misogynist'. Though this description wouldn't have bothered him, coming as it did from a female commentator. 'All women are stupid beings.'

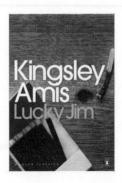

Lucky Jim, by Kingsley Amis, was published in 1954

DAVID LODGE'S PROFESSOR MORRIS ZAPP

In the 1970s (a time when $20,000 could still snare a nice house), America's most famous academic was asked why students should believe what he said. 'Because I'm Stanley Fish,' went the reply, 'and I teach at Johns Hopkins and I make $75,000 a year.'

Brash, flamboyant and relentlessly self-promoting, this Jaguar-driving English professor went on to chair Duke University's English Department with 'shameless – and in academe unheard of – entrepreneurial gusto'. Nowadays, you'll be glad to hear, he gets around $250,000 a year from the University of Illinois.

Fish never got any money out of David Lodge, however – which may perhaps be a little unfair. A lecturer at the University of Birmingham, Lodge's trilogy of campus novels famously satirised English and US academics by having two of them 'change places'. The trilogy's fictional English professor Philip Swallow is Lodge himself, of course: a stodgy, faintly anal conformist anxious to lead a quiet life.

And no prizes for guessing who was Lodge's model for Morris Zapp. A cigar-chomping, name-dropping, bed-hopping American, that character spends his time jetsetting between conferences and mentioning his salary to anyone who'll listen.

Morris Zapp first appeared in *Changing Places*, a 1975 novel by David Lodge

X-MEN'S PROFESSOR XAVIER

Martin Luther King (1929–68) (right) and Malcolm X (1925–65) (left)

It ain't easy being green. Or blue. Or purple. Created by *Batman* writer Stan Lee, the original X-Men had every eXtra power you could think of, except the ability to sell comics. Ignored by all right-thinking children, 'Angel', 'Beast' and the rest were quietly ditched in the 1970s and replaced by the excitable mutants adults try to ignore today.

Two of Lee's original creations survived the purge, however – which is more than can be said for the people they were based on. Professor Xavier, and his militant mutant rival, Magneto, are thought to have been inspired by two rival civil rights leaders: Martin Luther King (assassinated 1968) and Malcolm X (assassinated 1965).

Created during the civil rights struggles of the 60s, the mutants are victims of prejudice. They are often subject to Mississippi-style lynchings, and KKK-style hate groups. Like Malcolm X (a former criminal often accused of encouraging violence), Magneto's response to this persecution is aggressive – he basically wants to subdue mankind.

Professor Xavier, on the other hand, is more of a 'love your brother, however awful they may be' kind of guy. His quest for mutual tolerance is sometimes referred to as 'Xavier's dream' in the comics. Like Martin Luther King, he just wants people to 'judge [mutants] by the content of their character not the colour of their skin … Or the number of arms they have'.

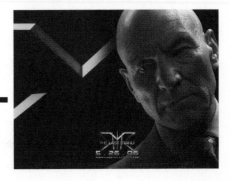

Professor Xavier first appeared in *X–Men #1*, a 1963 comic. The first of the films starring Patrick Stewart and Hugh Jackman premiered in 2000

SAUL BELLOW'S MOSES HERZOG

Saul Bellow
(1915–2005)

The outside world is all very well, but is there ever really a more interesting topic than oneself? Saul Bellow certainly didn't think so. Written while he was in the throes of a marital crisis, the Canadian-born, Chicago-raised, twice-divorced academic's most famous novel, *Herzog*, is all about one Moses Herzog – a Canadian-born, Chicago-raised, twice-divorced academic who is in the throes of a marital crisis.

Even Herzog's incessant letter-writing was semi-autobiographical: Bellow had spent the decade being 'inundated' with fan mail, and conscientiously answering it all. 'When a writer runs out of other people to write about there's no reason why he can't use himself,' he cheerfully admitted at the time.

The author also used his ex-wife Sondra and former friend, magazine editor Jack Ludwig. They appeared as Herzog's unfaithful wife Madeline and her duplicitous new lover, Valentine Gersbach.

Now considered one of the twentieth century's finest writers, Bellow emerged from his funk with flying colours, clocking up three National Book Awards, a Nobel Prize for Literature and a further three marriages.

Herzog, by Saul Bellow, was published in 1964

JURASSIC PARK'S DR ALAN GRANT

Jurassic Park wasn't really much of an acting gig. The cast's main role was to look awestruck or frightened, or awestruck *and* frightened, as computer-generated dinosaurs strutted about centre stage. Sam Neil's knowledgeable palaeontologist, Dr Alan Grant, probably came closest to having an actual personality (he got to talk about science when he wasn't looking awestruck/frightened) and for this he has a real palaeontologist to thank.

The discoverer of eight separate T-rex specimens, Dr Jack Horner served as a technical adviser on all three movies. He first came to public attention in the mid-70s, after finding the fossilised eggs and foetuses of a new species, the Maiasaura ('good mother lizard') – a feat attributed in *Jurassic Park* to Grant. This discovery gave us the disappointing intelligence that dinosaurs built nests and cared for their young.

And that's not the only blow for those of us who like our dinosaurs ruthless. Rather ironically, given what they get up to in *Jurassic Park*, Horner also maintains that T-rexes probably weren't the blood-splattered predators of popular imagination. With their spindly arms, poor eyesight and non-existent speed, they were more likely just lowly scavengers.

The novel *Jurassic Park*, by Michael Crichton, was published in 1990. The movie starring Sam Neil premiered in 1993

CHARLES DICKENS'S THOMAS GRADGRIND

James Mill (1773–1836)

'Now what I want is Facts. Teach these boys and girls nothing but Facts. Facts alone are wanted in life. Plant nothing else, and root out everything else … Stick to Facts, sir!'

Such was the educational philosophy of the novel *Hard Times*' headmaster, Thomas Gradgrind, a rigid, excessively 'rational' ideologue ever ready to 'weigh and measure any parcel of human nature and tell you exactly what it comes to'. Until, that is, his daughter has a mental breakdown and he discovers that emotions might be important too.

Here *Hard Times* was satirising utilitarianism – the idea that society can be scientifically 'rationalised' to better maximise social welfare. The utilitarian most directly in his sights seems to be James Mill, a philosopher famous for putting a Gradgrind-style theory into practice.

Mill started by separating his precious son John from all other children and teaching him Greek by the age of three. By eight, John had mastered Xenophon's *Anabasis* and the works of Herodotus, and begun learning Latin and algebra. He disposed of Plato and Demosthenes by ten, knocked over Aristotelian logic by twelve and started tackling political economy at thirteen.

At twenty, he had a nervous breakdown.

Hard Times, by Charles Dickens, was published in 1854

INDIANA JONES

Frederick Burnham (1861–1947)

Email Steven Spielberg or George Lucas to see who inspired Indiana Jones, and you'll get not a single reply. Trust me. I have researched this.

Google the matter, however, and you'll learn that their hyperactive academic was inspired by the heroes of the Republic Pictures – a matinee series they enjoyed as kids. If this is true (and how could it not be?), we find ourselves on firmer ground. For those charmingly low-budget matinees owed pretty much every plot line to Allan Quatermain, the hat-wearing hero of *King Solomon's Mines*. A friend to the 'natives' and foe to all evildoers, this quintessential Victorian gentleman spent most of his time in Africa, hunting big game, finding priceless treasures, discovering lost civilisations and battling Zulu warlords.

Dubbed 'watcher-by-night', Quatermain may seem like the stuff of fantasy, but he actually had a basis in fact. Frederick Burnham was a real-life small, dark and wiry explorer who Africans dubbed 'he-who-sees-in-the-dark'.

Born in the Wild West, Burnham had worked as a soldier, a cowboy, an army scout, a sheriff and a buffalo hunter by the age of seventeen. Tiring of the quiet life, the rugged outdoorsman moved to Africa to fight in the First Matabele War, then discovered the ancient civilisation of Great Zimbabwe, along with several stacks of gold. Luckily he returned just in time for the Second Matabele War, then did a little prospecting, served in the Boer War and popped over to London for dinner and medals with Queen Victoria.

In his declining years, Burnham slowed down a bit. Then he sped up again, discovering the Esperanza Stone, leading an expedition through the Upper Volta, and doing his bit during WWI.

Dr Indiana Jones first appeared in *Raiders of the Lost Ark*. Directed by Steven Spielberg and produced by George Lucas, the 1981 movie starred Harrison Ford

JANE EYRE

Charlotte Brontë (1816–55)

Haworth, a tiny village tucked away amid the Yorkshire moors, wasn't always such a lively place. While visitors these days can be entertained by a Brontë museum, and overhear American tourists to their heart's content, 150 years ago they could basically just walk down the High Street scratching their nose for a bit, then turn around and walk all the way back.

In such circumstances, even geniuses can be forgiven for a certain lack of imagination. *Jane Eyre* could be called *Charlotte Brontë*. Like her heroine, Charlotte was born in the dreary, desolate moors to a 'poor clergyman' father and a mother who died very young. She too had a grim-faced aunt step into the breach, providing plenty of rules but not much love. And she too was utterly miserable at school, thanks to a headmaster who saw suffering as part of becoming a 'responsible, God-fearing adult'.

Charlotte's life got a little less Jane-like in adulthood – but we are still left with a short, thin, quiet and 'not at all handsome' schoolteacher, just like Jane herself. Some speculate that the book's dark-eyed, raven-haired Mr Rochester (who 'most would have thought … an ugly man') was based on a Monsieur Heger, a 'little, black, ugly' teacher Charlotte fell in love with when working in Brussels. 'I think, however long I live, I shall not forget what the parting cost me,' the author wrote after returning to England.

Jane Eyre, by Charlotte Brontë, was published in 1847

IN & OUT'S HOWARD BRACKETT

There have been some memorable Oscars speeches over the years – think Gwyneth Paltrow blubbering like a two-year-old and James Cameron crowning himself 'king of the world'. But Tom Hanks's speech takes the cake.

Awarded the golden naked man for his turn as an HIV-positive victim of homophobia in *Philadelphia*, Hollywood's Mr Nice Guy was characteristically nice. Dutifully thanking the many good folk who had got him there, he made special note of one of 'the finest gay Americans that [he] had the good fortune to be associated with', his high-school drama teacher, Rawley Farnsworth.

Farnsworth's phone instantly started ringing, and didn't stop for a couple of days. Turns out he was still in the closet.

The screenwriter Scott Rudin was one of the two billion TV viewers who learned something new that day. The story of a closeted schoolteacher accidentally outed at the Oscars, *In & Out* pretty much wrote itself.

In & Out premiered in 1997. Written by Scott Rudin, the movie starred Kevin Klein

MR HOLLAND

Sometimes finding the inspiration for a fictional character can be a bit like an archaeological dig. To unearth the original 'Mr Holland' – the gruff yet loveable music teacher played so gruffly yet loveably by Richard Dreyfuss – we must first lay a spade on *Follow Me, Boys*, the 1966 Disney movie on which *Mr Holland's Opus* was based. (A feel-good family movie about a kindly scoutmaster and his rosy-cheeked troupe, *Follow Me, Boys* is also notable for having starred fifteen-year-old future action hero Kurt Russell as a wholesome boy scout.)

Pausing for a quiet vomit, we come to the novel that inspired *that* movie: *For God and My Country*, a paean to a man in charge of a scout troop, by Pulitzer Prize–winner MacKinlay Kantor.

A little more spadework and we uncover *his* scoutmaster – and the man to whom his novel was dedicated. The oddly named Murray McMurray founded Troop 17 in Webster City, Iowa, and awarded many a badge to young MacKinlay Kantor. And (apart from the fact that he was a banker who started a chicken hatchery) that's more or less all we know. Presumably he was gruff yet loveable.

Mr Holland's Opus premiered in 1995. The movie starred Richard Dreyfuss

Chapter 15
Teenagers

LITTLE WOMEN

Louisa May Alcott
(1832–88)

Little Women isn't really about life in the fast lane. Louisa May Alcott's chronicle of four young sisters is more like life in a car park. (A small one, that is. In a remote country town. Whose residents don't really drive.) Highlights of the first few hundred pages include a picnic and some amateur theatricals, plus a pulse-racing chapter where the girls neglect their housework.

But such, I suppose, was life for many women in the nineteenth century. Alcott based what she called her 'moral pap for the young' on her own experiences growing up with three sisters in the small town of Concord, Massachusetts. Just like the little women, the little Alcotts put on plays, gave away food, and endured an emotionally absent father. Like the fictional Meg March, Anna Alcott was drawn to the wealthy life, but ended up marrying for love. Like Amy March, May Alcott was an artistic type who married for love *and* wealth. And just like Beth March, Beth Alcott died young.

The author herself was of course Jo March – the 'masculine' writer who was forever scribbling away in a corner. A feminist abolitionist with bipolar depression, Alcott also wrote *racy* pap for the old. Some of her less well-known works include *A Long Fatal Love Chase* and *Pauline's Passion and Punishment*.

Little Women, by Louisa May Alcott, was published in 1868.
A film version staring Winona Ryder premiered in 1994

DIRTY DANCING'S BABY

If you don't get goosebumps from the sight of Patrick Swayze – crotch bulging, mullet quivering – declaring that 'nobody puts Baby in a corner', then you've probably got good taste. For the rest of us, however, this climactic scene from *Dirty Dancing* sadly remains a climactic scene in our lives.

Eleanor Bergstein, at least, can be forgiven for this. *Dirty Dancing* really was her life. 'It's based on a whole set of experiences in my youth,' says the screenwriter and former 'mambo queen', who really did have a doctor father who called her 'Baby'. 'I used to go to the Catskills with my family as a little girl and I would hang out at the dance studios.' The stories of one of the resort's instructors, Michael Terrace, helped give shape to Patrick Swayze's character, Johnny Castle – though sadly he and Baby never had an affair.

Disappointing fact number two: it was in the mean streets of Brooklyn, not a luxury resort in the Catskill Mountains, that Bergstein learned to 'dirty dance'.

'When I was making the film, I was going through the dance steps with the director and the choreographer and they said "Eleanor, maybe you should get some of your old partners to dance with you". I said, "My old partners are either in jail or out on parole". It was very rough neighbourhood.'

Dirty Dancing premiered in 1987. Written by Eleanor Bergstein, the movie starred Jennifer Grey and Patrick Swayze

SNOW WHITE

Philip II of Spain (1527–98)

Little girls who want to be princesses need to hear some cold, hard facts.

Quite apart from the day-to-day difficulties of medieval life (violence, disease, squalor, smelliness), there's the fact that women didn't really have rights. Margarete von Waldek, for example, didn't have much say in the matter when her hated stepmother sent her off to the Spanish court.

Once there, though, the sixteen-year-old countess cheered up a bit, having fallen in love with Prince Philip, the heir to the throne. Her stepmother disapproved of what would have been a politically inconvenient marriage – and, intriguingly, it never took place. The beautiful young countess died very suddenly – quite possibly due to poisoning.

Does she live on as Snow White? One German scholar says yes. Eckard Sander points out that yet another similarity to the fairytale can be found in Margarete's home town of Bad Wildungen, where her brother owned a mine. Unfettered by government regulations, this good capitalist naturally employed children to dig in it (kiddies being cheap and able to squeeze themselves down holes). Malnourished, overworked and barely seeing sunlight, these minor miners rarely grew very tall. Much like dwarves, in fact.

While Snow White's origins are uncertain, the medieval European fairytale was first written down in *Children's and Household Tales*, an 1857 compilation of German folklore from two philologists, the Brothers Grimm, and was later featured in a classic Disney movie

DAWSON'S CREEK'S DAWSON LEERY

Growing up in small-town America, there's not all that much to do. The men go huntin', shootin' and fishin'. The women go cookin', cleanin' and gossipin'. And the kids go and live in a city as soon as they possibly can.

Kevin Williamson went to Hollywood. After penning hits like *Scream* and *I Know What You Did Last Summer*, however, the writer's thoughts returned to his tiny North Carolina home town of Oriental, which really does have a Dawson Creek.

Dawson's Creek was the result. That series 'was so personal to me. That was my childhood and I got to do it'. The show's perennially optimistic, dreamily romantic would-be filmmaker, Dawson, was of course Williamson himself. Like the character, Williamson grew up obsessed with Steven Spielberg, and platonically shared a friend's bed.

It's unclear whether he also talked like Dawson ('Is the proposition of monogamy such a Jurassic notion?' was a typically pithy line). Let's hope not.

Dawson's Creek screened from 1998 until 2003. Created by Kevin Williamson, the TV series starred James Van Der Beek and Katie Holmes

TITANIC'S ROSE

Beatrice Wood with
Marcel Duchamp (1893–1998)

Adolescence didn't really exist before the 1950s. Until mods and teddy boys started rocking around the clock, teenagers were just underdeveloped adults, or children who had ceased to be cute.

Teenage urges *did* exist, however – and Rose DeWitt Bukater has them in spades. *Titanic*'s rebellious rich girl was partially modelled on Beatrice Wood, an American artist known as the 'mama of Dada'. Like Rose, Beatrice was the bohemian daughter of wealthy, disapproving East Coast parents – a free thinker who managed to live for over a century and pack in enough experiences to last a millennium. A well-travelled actor and sculptor, Beatrice danced with Nijinsky, meditated with Krishnamurti, and shagged that saucy Frenchman, Marcel Duchamp.

Unlike Rose, however, she never abandoned her fiancé for Leonardo DiCaprio. Nor did she let any of her lovers freeze to death in the Atlantic Ocean because she wouldn't make room on a raft.

Writer-director James Cameron read Beatrice's autobiography while writing *Titanic* and later presented her with a DVD of the movie. The 105-year-old never got to see it, however, passing away just a few days later.

Titanic premiered in 1997. The Academy Award–winning movie starred Kate Winslet and Leonardo DiCaprio

THE DAZED AND CONFUSED

Life, as they say, can be stranger than fiction. Generally, though, it's duller.

In real life, for example, the whacked-out party dudes who inspired *Dazed and Confused* very rarely chug down brewskies, and almost never thump out righteous beats. They're too busy suing the filmmaker, a former schoolmate, for having caused them so much 'mental anguish'.

Set in a Texas high school, the film sees star quarterback Randall 'Pink' Floyd contemplate not taking drugs during the football season, then suck down a few bongs instead. 'It's dreadful,' says the real Pink – a small-town car salesman named Rick Floyd whose sports career never quite took off. 'If I'm at a Chamber of Commerce meeting with my wife, who has a business here in town, and I'm asked about it, yes, it's going to cause me some embarrassment and some severe emotional distress.'

The real 'Wooderson' is even worse. In the movie, Matthew McConaughey's character graduated years ago, but still hangs around high school in a laudable attempt to pick up chicks. In real life, he is a computer systems engineer.

One final blow: Slater – the 'legalise marijuana' campaigner who spends the movie designing new bongs – is now in gainful employment. 'I was quite outspoken back then,' says Andy Slater, a building contractor. 'That's probably why [the filmmaker] might have chosen me as a character – because I disagreed with marijuana laws and I was vocal about that even in high school. But I was never walking around with a marijuana leaf on my shirt or handing out joints.'

And even if he was, the filmmaker wouldn't have got one. 'He never hung out [with us]. I never saw him … Maybe he was hiding in the bushes taking notes.'

Dazed and Confused premiered in 1993. Created by Richard Linklater, the film starred Matthew McConaughey

FOOTLOOSE'S REN MCCORMACK

Chocolate, wine, the music of Burt Bacharach … life is full of guilty pleasures. Chief among them, of course, is *Footloose*, the prize-winning camembert of cheesy movies. This 80s classic stars Kevin Bacon as Ren McCormack, a toe-tapping teenager stuck in a conservative small town whose elders won't permit a school dance.

Such non-grooviness, sad to say, can happen: *Footloose* was based on real events in an actual town. Located deep in the heart of Oklahoma, Elmore City is sometimes described as 'the buckle on America's Bible Belt'. Its 700 god-fearing citizens have seven different churches to fear God in – but not one single cinema or pub. In 1980, they also had a law outlawing the devil's pastime of dancing, which a local student named Rex Kennedy led a well-publicised campaign to change. 'We just wanted to do something different.'

Just like in *Footloose*, Kennedy's quest to hold a school prom was ultimately successful – but not before a few local nutters had said their piece. 'No good has ever come from a dance,' thundered the Reverend FR Johnson. 'If you have a dance somebody will crash it and they'll be looking for only two things – women and booze. When boys and girls hold each other, they get sexually aroused. You can believe what you want, but one thing leads to another.'

Footloose premiered in 1984. The movie starred Kevin Bacon

ARCHIE ANDREWS

Mickey Rooney (b.1920) as
Andy Hardy

Archie **comics were** designed to be about a completely average American boy. It was only by accident that they ended up a completely average comic.

In 1941, MJC Comics were failing to beat *Superman* comics at their own game (ever heard of 'Roy the Superboy'?), so the company thought up a game of its own. Instead of an extraordinary hero, they went for an extra *ordinary* hero, the polar opposite of the Man of Steel. The average all-American teenager they came up with, however, was very similar to another hapless redhead. For a prototype of Archie, check out Andy Hardy, the wholesome everyman played by Mickey Rooney in a then-popular series of movies.

If you want to meet the model for Jughead, try to track down Richard 'Skinny' Linehan, a former classmate of comic writer Bob Montana. Archie's slim, sexually ambiguous sidekick was apparently based on this man, who's now said to be married with children.

Pretty much the whole of Archie and Jughead's home town, in fact, was based on Montana's days in Haverhill, Massachusetts. Like Archie's Riverdale, it's a smallish river town with its very own Chocklit Shoppe. For 'Big Moose', 'Mr Lodge', 'Mr Weatherbee' and 'Miss Grundy', insert the names Arnold Daggett, Henry Cabot Lodge, Earl McLeod and Elisabeth Tuck.

Archie Andrews first appeared in *Pep Comics #22*, a 1941 comic by Vic Bloom and Bob Montana

HAPPY DAYS' RICHIE CUNNINGHAM

'The Fonz' was very nearly 'The Mash'. *Happy Days'* producer Garry Marshall wanted to give his family's original name of Masciarelli to the character that made it cool to hang out in toilets, but producers went with Fonzarelli instead.

'He's based on one of my high-school friends who had a motorcycle,' says Marshall of the shiny-haired babe magnet, 'a guy in a black leather jacket who stuck out his thumbs and said, "AAAYYY".'

Does that mean that Marshall himself is Richie Cunningham, Fonzie's aw-shucks, gee-whiz sidekick? The producer himself says yes ('I was certainly Richie in the layout') but so too does one of his co-producers, Tom Miller. 'Richie was me and Richie's mum was definitely my mum, Laverne,' insists Miller.

Who to believe? Well, Miller did grow up in Milwaukee (where *Happy Days* was set). And like Richie, he hung out in a diner ('the Milky Way') and wore the school colours of light blue and white. That producer's post–*Happy Days* career checks out too: he went on to produce corny sitcoms like *Family Matters* and *Full House*, shows it would be very easy to imagine the sappy, straight-laced Richie inventing.

But that said, Marshall has some pretty cheesy credentials too, having directed *The Princess Diaries* and *Runaway Bride*. Tough call.

Happy Days screened from 1974 until 1984. Produced by Garry Marshall and Tom Miller, the TV series starred Ron Howard and Henry Winkler

FERRIS BUELLER

'Geeks, sportos, motorheads, dweebs, dorks, sluts, buttheads … they all adore him. They think he's a righteous dude.'

But do they know he's a Republican? Ferris Bueller, a free-spirited high-school student known to enjoy a day off, was probably based on Edward McNally, a former senior counsel to George W Bush.

Now a well-known Washington lawyer, McNally grew up on the same Chicago street as *Ferris* creator John Hughes, and also attended the same high school. Like Ferris, however, he didn't attend it very often. One semester (during which he wagged twenty-seven times), McNally and his best friend Buehler even borrowed his dad's sports car for the day, just like the fun-loving Ferris. Afterwards the pair attempted to wipe 113 miles off the car's odometer by raising it on a pair of jacks and driving in reverse. And, just like Ferris, they failed.

These days, incidentally, kids would have every reason to wag that high school. Located on Chicago's Shermer Road, Glenbrook High appeared as Shermer High in *Ferris Bueller's Day Off*, *Weird Science* and *The Breakfast Club*. In 2003, it also appeared in many newspapers. Over thirty students were expelled for covering their juniors in paint, poo, pee and animal guts, then throwing in some punches for good measure.

Ferris Bueller's Day Off premiered in 1986. Created by John Hughes, the film starred Matthew Broderick

THE CATCHER IN THE RYE'S HOLDEN CAULFIELD

If you're a teenager keen to rebel, but are unsure how or against whom, try reading *The Catcher in the Rye*. JD Salinger's angst-riddled classic neatly catalogues your enemies (parents, phonies, authority figures), interests (alcohol, sex, brooding) and attitudes (angst, anger, more angst). It's even a good guide to your language, with six 'fucks', thirty-one 'Chrissakes', fifty-eight 'bastards' and over 200 'goddams'.

The reclusive author probably said 'fuck' a few more times after his novel was published. *Catcher* was so successful journalists used to pester Salinger endlessly: the goddam bastards were forever asking for interviews and being told 'For Chrissake, no!' But if you want to know more about the reclusive author, simply read the book again.

Like Holden Caulfield, Salinger was a misanthropic loner from Manhattan with a younger sister he liked and a younger brother who died. Like Holden, he lost his first great crush to an older man and was kicked out of a fancy Pennsylvania prep school for terrible grades.

'My boyhood was very much the same as that [of the boy] in the book,' Salinger said in a rare interview. 'It was a great relief telling people about it.'

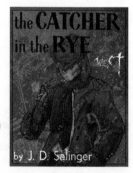

The Catcher in the Rye, by JD Salinger, was published in 1951

TWILIGHT'S BELLA SWAN

Stephenie Meyer (b.1973)

'I believe the children are our future,' sang Whitney Houston in 1986. Those children are now all reading *Twilight*, so the future looks pretty bleak.

The phenomenally successful Stephenie Meyer books are narrated by Bella, a timid, clumsy newcomer to a small-town high school who suddenly finds herself fending off the boys. Eventually she falls in love with the 'devastatingly, inhumanely beautiful' Edward – a century-old, vegetarian vampire in the body of a teenage super-hunk. They never shag (Meyer is a Mormon) but do spend many pages gazing at one another yearningly and having conversations best kept to themselves. ('I blinked the tears out of my eyes, torn. "Oh Edward!" … "Tell me Bella," he pleaded, eyes wild with worry at the pain in my voice.')

Hard to believe, I realise, but at least some of this guff is true. Physically, Bella is pretty much the author herself. Both Meyer and her character are pale-skinned, brown-haired and brown-eyed, with a 'wide forehead' and 'pointed chin'.

And some of their experiences match up too. 'I modelled Bella's move to [the small town] after my real-life move from high school to college,' says Meyer. 'In high school, I was a mousy, A-track wallflower. I had a lot of incredible girlfriends but I wasn't much sought after by the Y chromosomes … [Later, though] my stock went through the roof.'

Bella Swan first appeared in *Twilight*, a 2005 novel by Stephenie Meyer and was played on screen by Kristen Stewart

NAPOLEON DYNAMITE

Jared Hess (b.1979)

A lack of self-awareness can sometimes be a good thing. When Napoleon Dynamite, for example, looks in the mirror, he sees a groovemeister with 'illegal ninja moves'. A granite-jawed chunk of manpower who knows his way around a pair of nunchuckas. Other people, however, see a gangly super-geek. A wearer of moonboots and a drawer of unicorns.

Jared Hess see himself. *Napoleon Dynamite* was 'very autobiographical in nature', says the Mormon filmmaker, who 'felt like an outsider' during much of his childhood because his family was always moving around. 'It was me being able to look back on how awkward I was in high school and being able to laugh about it. I did wear moonboots and Hammer pants to school one time, which was pretty dorky ... [And] I had never seen a real true underdog drawing unicorns in class like I used to.'

Much of the film, Hess says, came from 'embarrassing family material'. He really did get a call from a brother wanting a chapstick. And a cow really did get shot in front of a school bus one day, upsetting quite a few of the kids.

Written and directed by Jared Hess, *Napoleon Dynamite* premiered in 2004

RIDGEMONT HIGH'S LINDA BARRETT

Fast Times at *Ridgemont High* involved many, many more scenes than just that one where Linda takes off her bikini top. It's just that no-one can remember what they were.

San Diego science writer Robin Weaver could probably remember, however. The character was partly based on her. As students at Clairemont High in 1979, Weaver and her classmates unwittingly provided material for a twenty-two-year-old writer named Cameron Crowe, who was spending the year posing as a student in order to research a book on teen life.

That book eventually became a screenplay. 'I looked at the movie [recently] and realised that we were young and stupid,' says Weaver. 'There is no way around it … It was the essence of adolescence.'

The class that inspired the movie recently met for a thirty-year reunion. San Diego's *Union-Tribune* reported that the sex-obsessed stoners had morphed into teachers and firefighters, businessmen and engineers – socially responsible suburbanites who probably don't even own a bong.

Sadder still is the real 'Spicoli'. Weaver's classmate Pat White was one of the models for *Ridgemont*'s long-haired surfer dude. Nowadays he's a balding tie-wearer, working in sales for a semiconductor company.

Fast Times at Ridgemont High premiered in 1982. Written by Cameron Crowe, the movie starred Phoebe Cates, Sean Penn and Jennifer Jason Leigh

JACK AND JILL

The Grand Old Duke of York
(1763–1827)

Jack and Jill may have gone up the hill, but it wasn't to fetch a pail of water.

If the residents of a small village in Somerset are to be believed (and, to be honest, they probably aren't), Jack and Jill were a young, unmarried couple in Kilmersdon who liked to shag about on the sly. The covert romance abruptly ended in 1697, however: Jack was killed on the hill, after being hit by a falling rock, and Jill died in childbirth a few days later.

Another famous hill in nursery rhymes is that marched up by the 'Grand Old Duke of York'. (As you may remember, he had 10,000 men. He marched them up to the top of the hill, then he marched them down again.) That conspicuously unsuccessful warrior might just be Prince Frederick, an unwarlike son of George III. The Duke of York and Albany, Fred led two deeply unsuccessful campaigns in the French Revolutionary Wars during the course of his deeply unsuccessful career. One of them involved an inglorious retreat down Mont Cassel, a hilltop town in Flanders.

Jack and Jill first appeared in *Mother Goose's Melody*, a 1791 book by John Newbery

BACK TO THE FUTURE'S MARTY MCFLY

Is there anything worse than imagining your parents having sex? Yes. It's imagining them *not* having sex and therefore never creating you. Such is the disastrous scenario facing Marty McFly in *Back to the Future* – one he resolves by performing 'Johnny B Goode' at a high-school prom, for complicated reasons I can't quite recall.

If the music of Chuck Berry had failed him, Marty would at least have lived on as Bob Gale, the filmmaker in whose image he was created. 'I was back in St Louis visiting my parents over the summer of 1980 … and I found my father's high school yearbook,' Gale later recalled. 'He'd been president of his graduating class. I thought about the president of my graduating class, who was someone I'd never have anything to do with, and I started thinking. When he was in high school, was my dad one of these rah-rah, school spirit kind of guys that I couldn't stand? And what would have happened if I'd gone to high school with my dad – would I have had anything to do with him or not? So that could be something that was a time-travel movie.'

'So when I got back to LA, I told [director Robert Zemekis] about this, and he was excited and he said "Yeah, I wonder if your mom was at the same high school" and it just started snowballing from there.'

Back to the Future premiered in 1985. Created by Bob Gale and Robert Zemekis, the film and its two sequels starred Michael J Fox

8 MILE'S RABBIT

If you move with the grooves and are hip to the jive – are fond of carving it up, then getting on down – then stay away from the mean streets of Detroit. Disaffected teenagers just don't talk like that anymore and they just might beat you up.

In *8 Mile*, on the other hand, our main character *does* know the language of the streets. (Apparently you just say 'beyatch' and 'foshizzle' a lot.) Jimmy 'B-Rabbit' Smith Jr is a young, white Detroit rapper growing up near a mostly African American ghetto. He's also basically just a renamed version of the man who plays him: young, white Detroit rapper Eminem.

Like Eminem, Rabbit has a troubled relationship with his mother, a Dr Dre–like mentor, and a wonderfully supportive posse. Though on the other hand, he has a whole range of enemy posses, with whom he likes to 'feud'.

8 Mile premiered in 2002. The movie starred Eminem

AMERICAN PIE'S JIM

Adam Herz (b.1972)

If you're on to a bad thing, stick to it.

Seven increasingly terrible movies about teenagers and their genitals, the *American Pie* franchise started out as one only slightly terrible movie: *American Pie*. That film of course sees four East Great Falls High students make a pact to lose their virginity. Happily, they succeed. But only after they swallow laxatives, masturbate into a pie, prematurely ejaculate on webcam, drink semen from a beer cup, and cause quite a few people to leave the cinema.

The characters 'were inspired by all my friends', says screenwriter Adam Herz. 'In the original draft I just named them so that I could keep the characters straight ... Everyone knows a Stifler, everyone went to high school with one, so I thought of a couple of jackasses that I went to high school with. And the characters are based on me too ... I tend to say [I am] "Jim", with all the insecurities.'

Quite a bit was changed from that original draft (for example, the line 'Play with my hairy balls' became 'Spank my hairy ass'). But you can still see traces of Herz's former high school, East Grand Rapids High in Michigan. *American Pie*'s East Great Falls High has a similar name, the same school colours, and a lacrosse team with a similar mascot (the 'Trailblazers' rather than the 'Pioneers'). Near the real school there's also a hotdog joint called 'Dog Years' – which is reproduced in the film's 'Yesterdog'.

American Pie premiered in 1999. Written by Adam Herz, the movie, and its first two sequels, starred Jason Biggs

WAYNE'S WORLD'S GARTH

At one point in *Wayne's World*, the co-host of Wayne's TV program is asked if he likes the new set for their show. 'It's like a new pair of underwear,' Garth replies. 'At first it's constrictive, but after a while it becomes a part of you.'

Another part of Garth was Brad Carvey. The actor and comedian Dana Carvey has performed a character based on his goofy brother since he first hit the stand-up circuit. For *Wayne's World*, he just made him a metalhead.

Brad is just a little brighter than the character, however. (The owner of two pubes named 'Fred' and 'Tony', Garth spends most of the movies saying 'sphincter', and wondering whether it's okay to find Bugs Bunny sexy in a dress.)

Instead of mooching off his parents, Brad has four rooms full of computers, including a few he designed in his teens.

A master of mysterious things like chroma keying, DSP Perception and Equilibrium DeBabelisers, Brad also owns an Emmy for 'Outstanding Achievement in Engineering'. He's actually quite famous in techie circles as a designer of animation software.

Garth Algar first appeared in a 1990 sketch on *Saturday Night Live*. The first *Wayne's World* movie, starring Mike Myers and Dana Carvey, premiered in 1992

JUNO

Diablo Cody (b.1978)

Diablo Cody used to be a stripper but in *Juno* she bares her soul.

Born Brook Busey-Hunt, this pole dancer-turned-blogger-turned-screenwriter never actually got pregnant as a teenager. That was 'a close friend'. She does, however, relate to her sharp-tongued title character Juno 'on a really deep, personal level'. 'I'm kind of an emotional scavenger because everything that I write about is drawn from life, it's drawn from experience that I actually had.'

On a less deep and personal level, Cody, like Juno, also grew up with a hamburger phone and profound affection for punk rock. She too had a heap of second-hand clothing and a boyfriend who was addicted to orange tic tacs.

Juno premiered in 2007. Written by Diablo Cody, the movie starred Ellen Page

THE GRADUATE

If you've ever wondered what Joe DiMaggio and the rest of it have to do with 'Mrs Robinson', here's your answer. Nothing. Simon and Garfunkel were writing a nostalgic song about America in times past when the director of *The Graduate* walked by. Needing more songs for the movie's soundtrack, he persuaded the pair to rename 'Mrs Roosevelt' – but the rest of the lyrics stayed pretty much the same.

A good financial decision, if nothing else, but Charles Webb would have disapproved. The author of *The Graduate* prefers bad financial decisions. During four poverty-stricken decades spent washing dishes, picking fruit and working at Kmart, Webb has declined an inheritance, given away four houses, and donated a Warhol print to charity. He now lives in a council house.

The otherworldly artist is, however, rich in spirit. Just like Benjamin Braddock, the gauchely rebellious teenager he based on himself, Webb found a freethinking girl who rejected wealth and convention, and married her in spite of their parents. She's now a nudist who calls herself 'Fred'.

So did Webb have an affair with Fred's mother-in-law, just like Benjamin in his book? Apparently not. But he did accidentally see the real-life Mrs Robinson stepping out of the shower one day, and suspects that his imagination, if nothing else, was aroused.

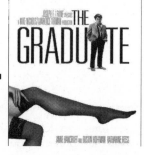

The Graduate, by Charles Webb, was published in 1963. Starring Dustin Hoffman and Anne Bancroft and with music from Simon and Garfunkel, the movie based on it premiered in 1967

Chapter 16
The long-suffering

BRIDESHEAD REVISITED'S SEBASTIAN

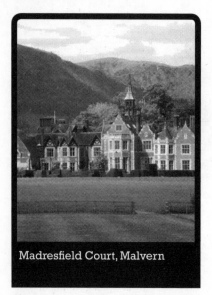

Madresfield Court, Malvern

There's no place like home, as the saying goes, but not all sayings are true. The owners of Madresfield Court, for example, might have found *Brideshead Revisited* faintly familiar. This is because it's on their home that the novel is based.

When he was an agnostic, middle-class Oxford student (much like *Brideshead*'s Charles), Evelyn Waugh befriended an aristocrat and spent several holidays at his stately home. Lord Hugh Lygon was a handsome, gay, Catholic, unhappy and ultimately doomed alcoholic who had a very happening pad. All he really needed to become 'Lord Sebastian Flyte' was a name change and a teddy bear.

Also in the book was Hugh's father, a former governor of New South Wales. Like *Brideshead*'s Lord Marchmain, he fled to Venice to avoid a scandal. Though in the real-life case, the illicit lover was a man.

Effectively orphaned, Hugh and his siblings Elmley, Maimie and Coote (the models for Bridey, Julia and Cordelia) enjoyed plenty of freedom at Madresfield – providing Waugh with some 'golden summers' and the beginnings of a damn good plot.

Brideshead Revisited, by Evelyn Waugh, was published in 1945

UNCLE TOM

Josiah Henson (1789–1883)

Forget bestseller lists and Booker Prizes, you know you've made it in literature when your book helps start a war. A tale of long-suffering slaves, *Uncle Tom's Cabin* was a hugely popular nineteenth-century novel that intensified hostility between America's North and the South. When the author met Abraham Lincoln at the start of the Civil War, Lincoln supposedly said, 'So this is the little lady who made this big war.'

A large man also helped. Being a teacher from Connecticut, the author had never actually set foot on a slave plantation, so for material she turned to *The Life of Josiah Henson*, the memoir of a slave who had. In the book, Uncle Tom's 'owner' Simon Legree is based on Henson's former 'owner' Isaac Riley – a brutal farmer who sold off Henson's brothers and sisters and cut off his father's ear.

Uncle Tom himself owed a bit to Henson, but that character's meek subservience was all his own. Henson himself escaped from Riley's 4000-acre tobacco plantation at age forty-one, founded a school in Canada, and became a businessman and Methodist preacher.

Uncle Tom's Cabin, by Harriet Beacher Stowe, was published in 1852

PORGY AND BESS

A good criminal in need of a getaway vehicle knows not to go in a goat cart.

Samuel Smalls was not a good criminal. When the disabled African American beggar (a familiar sight in the slums of Cabbage Row, Charleston) shot at one Maggie Barnes after an argument, the police found him easy to catch.

The minor crime made it into the newspaper, which was read by an insurance salesman the next day. 'Contemplation of Samuel's real and moving tragedy' inspired this white businessman to create Porgy – a disabled African American beggar with 'plenty o' nuttin', who drives a goat cart around Catfish Row.

Smalls, sad to say, never got to read the book – let alone see *Porgy and Bess*, the Gershwin musical it inspired. He died that same year, aged thirty-five, and was for a long time buried in an unmarked grave.

Porgy, by DuBose Heyward, was published in 1925. *Porgy and Bess*, the George Gershwin musical based on it, premiered in 1935

YES MINISTER'S JIM HACKER MP

Michael Howard (b.1941)

'Politicians are like children,' said *Yes Minister*'s sage Sir Humphrey. 'You can't just give them what they want. It only encourages them.'

Jim Hacker receives very little encouragement at the Ministry for Administrative Affairs. A typical episode would see that politician set out to do the right thing (if only for the publicity), fail hopelessly thanks to Civil Service stubbornness, then take solace in a pompous speech. As Humphrey so silkily put it, 'a career in politics is no preparation for government'.

Jonathan Lynn thought he'd give it a try anyway. While he was at Cambridge in the 1960s, this future TV writer wanted to be an MP. Then he attended a student union debate. 'All of the main debaters there, aged twenty, were the most pompous, self-satisfied, self-important bunch of clowns that I've ever clapped eyes on. They were all behaving as if they were on the government front bench, and twenty years later they all were ... I thought at that point that the only way that I could ever contribute to politics is by making fun of politicians.'

Unlike *Yes Minister*'s Hacker, however, none of Lynn's contemporaries in the Conservative Party's 'Cambridge mafia' ever managed to become prime minister. Michael Howard became a lock-em-up Home Secretary ('Prison works!'). John Gummer ended up Environment Secretary (and a 'shitbag' according to his Norwegian counterpart). Kenneth Clarke was a Health Secretary at one point ... and the chairman of a tobacco company after that.

YES, PRIME MINISTER
The Complete Series 1 & 2

Yes Minister and *Yes Prime Minister* screened from 1980 until 1988. Written by Anthony Jay and Jonathan Lynn, the TV series starred Paul Eddington and Sir Nigel Hawthorne

THE SCARLET LETTER'S HESTER PRYNNE

'Life is suffering,' said Buddha, who was never much fun at dinner parties. Puritans probably would have agreed. Fond of plain clothes, plain food and plain houses, America's first white settlers worked hard, prayed hard, went to church, then worked a little bit more.

In their leisure time, they discussed the Bible. In 1637, a Boston nurse named Anne Hutchinson attended one such discussion group, and aired a few silly ideas (like 'Native Americans are also God's children'; 'Being a woman is a blessing, not a curse'). Naturally, she was asked to leave.

Eventually banished for being a heretic, Hutchinson was declared 'a woman not fit for our society'. 'You have stepped out of your place,' thundered the magistrate. 'You have rather been a husband than a wife, a preacher than a hearer.'

All a bit unfortunate, unless you're a novelist in search of a plot. In *The Scarlet Letter*, Nathaniel Hawthorne's heroine Hester Prynne commits adultery rather than heresy but her punishment is much the same. Marginalised from the male-dominated society, Hester must wear the scarlet letter ('A') of shame.

The Scarlet Letter, by Nathaniel Hawthorne, was published in 1850

PHILADELPHIA'S ANDREW BECKETT

Hollywood doesn't often do irony, but some movies break the mould. Take *Philadelphia*, for example. This Academy Award–winning film sees a young, gay AIDS sufferer get fired from his law firm after purplish lesions appear on his face. He successfully sues, then dies. Nothing very ironic so far, of course: just Tom Hanks looking earnest and sad, and corporate lawyers being greedy and bad.

What's ironic is that the makers of this movie were later sued themselves. By the family of a young, gay AIDS sufferer. Who got fired from his law firm after purplish lesions appeared on his face. Successfully sued. Then died.

After three long years of litigation, *Philadelphia*'s lawyers finally admitted that the film 'was inspired in part' by the tragic saga of Geoffrey Bowers. They settled on an undisclosed sum out of court.

Philadelphia premiered in 1993. The movie starred
Tom Hanks

TESS OF THE D'URBERVILLES

Augusta Way, left (1870–1940)

In need of a morale boost? Then here, enjoy the story of Tess. A beautiful but dirt-poor dairymaid gets raped by her boss, abandoned by her husband and evicted from her home. Her child dies. Her father dies. She works a series of strenuous jobs. She lives in hopeless squalor. The happy ending sees Tess's husband come back only to abandon her again, which prompts her to kill the rapist and get hanged for murder. Good times.

The real Tess had an easier time of it. In 1888, the author Thomas Hardy would frequently visit a particular house in Dorset, 'as the lady who lived there thought he was clever and gave him great encouragement,' the 102-year-old daughter of Augusta Way recently told *The Times*. 'On his way, he would walk past a grey manor house … My grandfather ran a dairy there and my mother and her sisters would sit outside and milk the cows. It was before my mother married, when she was about eighteen years old … I don't believe Hardy ever spoke to my mother, as he was a very shy person … but she was a beautiful woman [and he later] said himself that the memory must have entered his mind when he was creating the character of Tess.'

Augusta Way went on to marry the local baker, racking up four kids and not a single conviction for murder.

Tess of the D'Urbervilles, by Thomas Hardy, was published in 1891

LITTLE DORRIT

Prostitutes were quite popular in Victorian Britain – and not just with the people who paid them. Prime Minister William Gladstone, for example, would often walk around London with a Bible in hand, trying to persuade 'fallen women' to change their ways.

Charles Dickens was a little more practical. With the help of a well-to-do heiress, the author set up Urania Cottage, a shelter where 'wayward' girls could eat, sleep and rebuild their future by training for a career in domestic service.

One such girl was Caroline Thompson. A 'pretty', 'gentle', 'small and young-looking' mother, she had been abandoned by her husband and turned to prostitution to support their child. 'There can never have been much evil in her,' Dickens reflected, 'apart from the early circumstances that directed her steps the wrong way ... I cannot get the picture of her out of my head.'

So he put it on a page. Little Dorrit – the meek, childlike defender of her family as it battles poverty and jail and worse – is easily recognisable as Thompson, whom the author later helped to emigrate to Canada.

Little Dorrit, by Charles Dickens, was originally published as a serial between 1855 and 1857

THE SHAWSHANK REDEMPTION'S ANDY DUFRESNE

Think your life's tough? Try coming home from a hard day at the bank only to see your wife dead in bed with a golf pro, go on trial for their murder, spend twenty years in jail with corrupt guards and pack rapists – and still have to do people's tax.

Such was the plight of Andy Dufresne in *The Shawshank Redemption* – one he accepts philosophically by immersing himself in literature and, less philosophically, digging an escape tunnel.

Stephen King, who wrote the 1982 novella upon which the Tim Robbins movie was based, didn't have to dig too deep for his plot. Now a controversial journalist, Britain's most notorious armed robber of the 1960s, John McVicar, famously tunnelled his way out of Durham Prison, covering his tracks with papier-mâché bricks. Recaptured soon afterwards, McVicar put his remaining years in jail to good use – reading widely, getting a degree and writing a bestselling autobiography.

'Rita Hayworth and the Shawshank Redemption', by Stephen King, was originally published in *Different Seasons* in 1982. The movie, starring Tim Robbins and Morgan Freeman, premiered in 1994

LES MISÉRABLES' JEAN VALJEAN

Eugene Vidocq (1775–1897)

Les Misérables has several translations – including *The Wretched Poor*, *The Miserable Ones* and *The Victims*. Whichever title Victor Hugo had in mind, his 1200-page saga of abused orphans and sickly prostitutes isn't exactly a mood-lifter.

Victim number one, of course, is Jean Valjean, a character Hugo based on a celebrity friend. Like the character, Eugene Vidocq started out as a petty thief, spent some time in jail, and adopted a fake identity upon his release. Both men were also muscle-bound do-gooders: the scene where Valjean lifts a cart to save someone crushed underneath was taken directly from Vidocq's life.

In that scene, Valjean's freakish strength reveals his identity to his watching nemesis, Inspector Javert. What's surprising is that it took so long. *Les Misérables'* policeman character, interestingly, was *also* based on Eugene Vidocq. Using his 'insider' knowledge, the former criminal spent the second half of his career as France's most famous policeman – a bona fide human bloodhound who pioneered the science of ballistics and was a private detective par excellence.

Les Misérables, by Victor Hugo, was published in 1862. The stage musical based on the book premiered in 1980

THE MAN IN THE IRON MASK

Pignerol Fortress, where the man in the velvet mask was jailed

To be 'on velvet' is a good thing. To be 'in velvet' probably isn't. Someone who could tell us for certain spent much of his time in Pignerol – a seventeenth-century fortress for prisoners Louis XIV liked to keep hidden from view. Something must have been *especially* embarrassing about this prisoner, however. No-one was told his name and his face was kept hidden by a black velvet mask. The island's governor fed him personally and burned all his possessions the day he died.

Over the centuries there have been many theories about the prisoner's identity but not much in the way of fact. In *The Three Musketeers*, of course, Alexandre Dumas gave him blue blood – underneath the 'iron' mask, our heroes find the king's twin brother and rival for the throne.

But in reality he probably had a blue collar. Surviving documents suggest that the man in the velvet mask was Eustace Dauger, the former valet of an executed traitor who knew a little too much for the king's (or indeed, his own) good.

Alexandre Dumas dealt with the man in the iron mask in the third instalment of his Three Musketeers saga, 1847's *Vicomte of Bragelonne*

THE FUGITIVE

In law, you are innocent until proven guilty. The beauty of life, on the other hand, is that you can be innocent *and* proven guilty.

In the movie *The Fugitive*, Dr Richard Kimble gets the double – after seeing his wife getting murdered by a 'one-armed man', he finds himself accused of the crime. Over the course of the next ninety minutes, the character gets sentenced to death, escapes from prison, dives off a cliff and uncovers the real killer – and still finds time for a shave.

The real Richard spent even less time as a fugitive. Ohio osteopath Sam Sheppard meekly allowed police to arrest him after he saw his wife get murdered by a 'bushy-haired intruder', and spent a passive ten years in jail. Since he hadn't been blessed with the most impartial of judges ('Well he's as guilty as hell. There's no doubt about it,' remarked His Honour on day one), a mistrial was eventually declared.

The doctor went on to become a wrestler, oddly enough, before dying of alcohol abuse at forty-seven, his twenty-year-old second wife by his side.

The Fugitive screened from 1963 until 1967. The Harrison Ford movie based on the TV series premiered in 1993

DEATH OF A SALESMAN'S WILLY LOMAN

After WWII the US was meant to be wonderful – a prosperous utopia of white-picket families digesting the fruits of the American dream. Happiness, for Dad, was a successful career – or a new house or new fridge or new car.

In reality, of course, it could be a nightmare. All that go-getting and can-doing – that kicking of goals so as to keep up with the Joneses – doth not a rich life make. Arthur Miller's classic play reflects this. In *Death of a Salesman*, a fiercely competitive travelling salesman, Willy Loman, reflects on his decades travelling and selling and sees … disappointingly little. The character's existential angst is compounded by the latest failure of his son – a once-promising sportsman who's become a hopeless bum.

Miller wrote the play after bumping into his uncle Manny Newman – a long-time travelling salesman, and 'competitor at all times'. Despite it being their first meeting in over a decade, his uncle had immediately started boasting about his offspring. He saw 'my brother and I running neck and neck with his two sons in some horse race [for success] that never stopped in his mind'.

His uncle's household, wrote Miller, was one in which you 'dared not lose hope'. 'I would later think of it as a perfection of America for that reason … It was a house trembling with resolution and shouts of victories that had not yet taken place but surely would tomorrow.'

The shouts ended eventually. Like the character, Manny committed suicide.

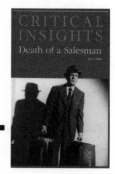

Death of a Salesman, by Arthur Miller, was first performed in 1949

THE HITCHHIKER'S GUIDE TO THE GALAXY'S ARTHUR DENT

The Hitchhiker's Guide to *the Galaxy*, you may be surprised to learn, was very much a work of fiction. No Englishman has ever bumbled around space in his dressing gown, lurching haplessly from crisis to crisis.

An Englishman has, however, lost a house thanks to bureaucracy gone entirely mad. *Hitchhiker* begins with our dressing-gowned hero learning that his local council plans to knock down his house and build a big road in its place. The character Arthur Dent does not, however, discover this by the process of opening his mail. Instead, the council notification is 'on display in the bottom of a locked filing cabinet stuck in a disused lavatory with a sign on the door saying "Beware of the Leopard".' He could have stopped the demolition nine months earlier, says the council, if he'd only lodged an objection at the time.

Here, art was imitating life. In the 1950s, a milkman named Edward Pilgrim became a cause célèbre, when Romford Council did some similar manoeuvring, eventually confiscating his house for just £65. The scandal led to a revision of the *Town and Country Planning Act*, but for Pilgrim, it came too late. He had hanged himself in his tool shed.

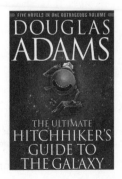

Douglas Adams's *The Hitchhiker's Guide to the Galaxy* was first performed as a radio play in 1978

SEINFELD'S GEORGE COSTANZA

Seinfeld should have been called *David*. Jerry might have come up with the shtick of 'a show about nothing' but his neurotic co-creator Larry David gave the series its bite.

He also gave us George. *Seinfeld*'s 'short, stocky, slow-witted, bald man' is David to a tee. Like George, he began balding in his early thirties – not long after moving back in with his parents. Both men worked as bra salesmen. Both tried to steal an answering machine from a girlfriend's apartment, so she couldn't hear the angry message they had left. Both entered a contest to see who could avoid masturbating the longest. And both quit their job in a fit of rage – only to slink back the next day hoping nobody noticed.

Only Larry, however, lived across the hall from Kramer. Cosmo Kramer, Seinfeld's neighbour in the show, is based on Kenny Kramer, David's neighbour in real life. An ideas man like his alter ego, Kenny has had a long and unsuccessful career as a stand-up comedian, and two short and unsuccessful stints managing karate fighters and a reggae band. He has also tried his hand at politics, running for New York mayor on the Libertarian Party ticket with a promise to 'cut the red tape for other entrepreneurs who want to live their own American dream'. Voters didn't share the dream, giving him 0.18 per cent of the vote.

The evidence is a little less definitive when it comes to the identity of the real Elaine. Probably the best bet is Carol Leifer, a feisty stand-up comic who once dated Seinfeld and also wrote a bit for the show.

Seinfeld screened from 1989 until 1998

ANNA KARENINA

Every year, around 40,000 Russians die from drinking bad vodka. Others hurl themselves under trains. Such, of course, was the fate of Tolstoy's fictional heroine, Anna Karenina, after her scandalous relationship turns sour.

Anna Stepanova would have sympathised – but she'd been run over by a train as well. The mistress of one of Tolstoy's neighbours ('Tut!' cried society; 'Shame!'), Stepanova was horrified when her hunky boyfriend, Bibikov the snipe hunter, declared he was leaving her to marry someone else. 'You are my murderer,' said her suicide note. 'Be happy, if an assassin can be happy. If you like, you can see my corpse on the rails at Yasenki.'

Tolstoy *did* like. The author attended Stepanova's autopsy the next day. 'How shameless, he thought, and yet how chaste,' wrote Henri Troyat, a biographer who could apparently read minds. 'A dreadful lesson was brought home to [Tolstoy] by that white, naked flesh, those dead breasts, those inert thighs that had felt and given pleasure. He tried to imagine the existence of this poor woman who had given all for love, only to meet with such a trite, ugly death.'

Yes. Well. Anyway. *Anna Karenina* was what he imagined.

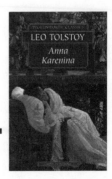

Anna Karenina, by Leo Tolstoy, was published in serial form between 1873 and 1877, and in book form in 1878

HUMPTY DUMPTY

Richard III (1452–85)

Who or what Humpty Dumpty was will probably never be known. But that doesn't prevent people having a guess. The most popular theory says that the wall-dwelling egg was Richard III, the malevolent old hunchback immortalised by Shakespeare (who actually didn't have any deformities and died at just thirty-two).

That death, of course, came during the Battle of Bosworth Field. (He was fighting against an ancestor of Shakespeare's king, which perhaps explains why the playwright was so keen to demonise him.) After having 'a great fall' off his horse – which some folklorists insist was nicknamed 'the wall' – King Richard was hacked into several pieces. Sadly, all the king's horses and all the king's men couldn't put him back together again.

Does that make him Humpty Dumpty? We don't know. What we do know is that the much-maligned monarch's last words weren't the ones supplied by Shakespeare. In place of 'A horse, a horse, my kingdom for a horse', put the rather less ringing 'Treason! Treason! Treason! Treason! Treason!'

The first written reference to Humpty Dumpty occurs in
Mother Goose's Melody, published in 1803

JUDE THE OBSCURE

Thomas Hardy (1840–1928)

Jude the Obscure was far from obscure. When the Bishop of Wakefield burned the scandalously sex-filled novel, it had a wonderful effect on sales.

Jude *was*, however, unhappy. (As you would be if you were deserted by your wife and then your mistress. Then saw one of your children kill the other two. Then fell ill. Then died.)

Jude was also Thomas Hardy. Just like the character he created, Hardy was a self-taught working-class man from Dorset whose dream of going to university was denied. He too studied Greek and architecture, and toyed with the idea of becoming a parson. And he too had a crush on his cousin, and a partner who grew increasingly religious as he grew less so.

Above all else, both men had deeply unhappy marriages. Hardy's became rather more so after he wrote about it in *Jude the Obscure*.

Jude the Obscure, by Thomas Hardy, was published in 1895

DR ZHIVAGO'S LARA

Olga Ivinskaya (1912–95)

Being Russian is hard work. Historically, at least, it sometimes seems like if you weren't a serf toiling in the field, you were a soldier lining up to be slaughtered or a factory worker starving to death.

Another option was to waste away in prison. Such was the fate of Olga Ivinskaya, the woman who inspired *Dr Zhivago*'s brave, bright, bookish Lara Guishar. A translator and editor (who, in true Russian fashion had already lost one husband to suicide and another to disease), Olga met the book's future author Boris Pasternak at a literary function, and began an affair with him soon afterwards. Talking to him, she told a friend, was like 'talking to God'.

Three years later, Stalinist authorities started objecting to the apparent subversiveness of God's work – so asked Olga to denounce him as a spy.

Her refusal didn't go down so well. Sent without trial to the Moldovan Republic, she endured a miscarriage and some long stints in solitary confinement. After that came hard labour in Siberia.

Dr Zhivago, by Boris Pasternak, was published in 1957. The movie starring Julie Christie and Omar Sharif premiered in 1965

THE PORTRAIT OF A LADY'S ISABEL ARCHER

Isabel Gardner (1840–1924)

The Portrait of a Lady is actually a portrait of Isabella Gardner. A typical Henry James novel (insofar as it involves wealthy Americans getting the hell out of America, so they can be all refined in Europe), the 'lady' of the title is Isabel Archer. Blessed with money, taste and style, she is stifled by a loveless marriage and the social conventions of her time.

Like the character, Gardner was a New York-born Bostonian who discovered she couldn't have children, so did her best to take solace in art. She too was well known for her eccentricity ('eccentricity' in the nineteenth century being defined as 'a woman with a mind of her own'). A freethinking friend of actors and artists, academics and aesthetes (as well as writers like Henry James), Gardner smoked cigarettes, wore a baseball cap to concerts and travelled the world doing what she pleased.

Her most lasting legacy is the Gardner Museum in Boston. Modelled on a Venetian palazzo, it contains more than 2500 objects from her collection. Visit it to see some rare books, old masters and precious textiles from ancient Rome, Renaissance Italy and the East.

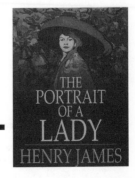

Portrait of a Lady, by Henry James, was published in serial form between 1880 and 1881, and as a book in 1881

NINTENDO'S MARIO BROS

Ultimately, death comes to us all. But if you're a video game character, it comes all the time. The perennial plaything of pimply teenagers, Mario spends his life plunging off ledges, getting murdered by monsters, and fleeing from evil frog kings.

In real life, his only worry is bad tenants. A landlord and real-estate developer in Washington state, Mario Segale stepped into video game history in 1981, when he visited Nintendo's American office to complain that the company was late with its rent. A heated argument ensued in front of the staff, who were busy developing 'Mr Video', a new character for the Donkey Kong arcade game.

Mr Video, needless to say, became Signore Mario: a pudgy Italian plumber with blue overalls and an almighty moustache.

Segale is said to be less than impressed. The avid duck hunter and Democrat is 'still waiting for my royalty checks', he once told the *Seattle Times*.

Mario first appeared in *Donkey Kong*, a 1981 video game by Nintendo

Chapter 17
Writers and journalists

THE SHINING'S JACK TORRANCE

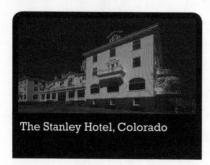

The Stanley Hotel, Colorado

Having a family is a wonderful thing. Spending time with them frequently isn't. In *The Shining*, Jack Torrance is deeply aware of this distinction. Based on a Stephen King novel, the film opens with him snarling impatiently as wife and child chatter in the car. It ends with him trying to gut them with a butcher's knife.

Good stuff. About the only person who didn't enjoy it was Stephen King himself. The character, you see, was at least partly autobiographical: an alcoholic, thirtyish writer who struggles with moments of unprovoked rage. 'I was able to invest a lot of my unhappy, aggressive impulses in Jack Torrance,' said King, who came up with the plot after a rather fraught family holiday at the Stanley Hotel, a supposedly haunted mansion tucked away in the Rocky Mountains.

They were only ever impulses, however. In the novel, Jack is a genial, inherently good man who's had to grow up with an inherently shit dad. The demon of alcoholism leads him astray as much as any actual demons – but he never actually kills anyone and ultimately lets his family go.

The Shining, by Stephen King, was published in 1977. Starring Jack Nicholson, the Stanley Kubrick movie based on it premiered in 1980

CLARK KENT

Harold Lloyd, centre (1893–1971)

Reporters don't tend to be 'mild mannered' (the job calls for a certain pushiness), but there are exceptions to every rule. The Man of Steel's alter ego, of course, was one such exception. Put on a pair of glasses and Superman became Superdork: an awkward, klutzy weakling bullied by editors, mocked by office boys and in-no-way-lusted-after by Lois Lane.

Co-creator Joe Shuster knew just how Clark Kent felt. A former newspaper boy at Toronto's *Daily Star* (the model for the *Daily Planet*), Superman's co-creator was also a shy spectacle wearer who didn't exactly fight off the chicks. While the movie stars of the day also contributed to the character – he was named after Clark Gable and Kent Taylor, and stole some traits from another accident-prone glasses wearer, the comic actor, Harold Lloyd – Clark Kent's main model was the writer himself.

'Joe believed in lifting weights and making himself strong, but ... he looked like the stereotypical, ninety-pound weakling getting sand kicked in his face,' said Shuster's cousin Frank. 'And it later occurred to me that he was Clark Kent – the sort of nebbish in glasses that everyone wanted to kick around but underneath was the Man of Steel.'

Clark Kent first appeared in *Action Comics #1*. The 1938 comic was created by Joe Shuster and Jerry Siegel

BORAT

Mahir Çagri (b.1962)

Only an unusual person would want to be considered the model for Borat, the mankini-wearing, Jew-hunting son of Boltok the town rapist.

Mahir Çagri is an unusual person. The world first came to realise this in the late 1990s, when the eccentric journalist created a (very) amateur website urging women to visit his Turkish home. Rated one of *PC World*'s '25 worst websites', it featured photos of Çagri playing ping-pong and wearing tight red shorts alongside catchphrases like 'I like sex'. 'My tall 1.84 cm. My weight 78 kg. My eyes green. I live alone!'

This homemade homepage was naturally a hit. Çagri became one of the first ever internet celebrities, and was soon showcasing his bad suits and broken English on TV. (His future wife must 'keep the house nice for me', he told one interviewer, and 'be very clean and always wash before and after sex'.)

Was Borat's creator watching? Sacha Baron Cohen claims the character was inspired by an unintentionally hilarious doctor he met in southern Russia and early versions (like 'Kristo the Albanian') do appear to pre-date Çagri's website.

Still, the similarities are striking. Just like Çagri, Borat enjoys ping-pong, tight red shorts, big moustaches and bad suits. He too is a journalist (though he has also worked as a gypsy catcher and animal sperm producer). And, in case you have forgotten, he too 'like sex'.

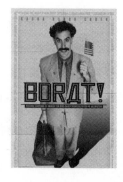

Borat Sagdiyev first appeared in *Da Ali G Show*. Created by and starring Sacha Baron Cohen, the movie *Borat: Cultural Learnings of America for Make Benefit Glorious Nation of Kazakhstan* premiered in 2006

SEX AND THE CITY'S CARRIE BRADSHAW

Candace Bushnell (b.1958)

'**Sex and the** City' didn't actually have that much sex. The newspaper column that inspired the show certainly had the overpriced shoes, oversized flats and overbearing people. But for the zipless fucks and 'cock' talk, we must thank the show's writers and no-one else.

'In the TV series they go out and meet a different guy every week. That just doesn't happen to most women,' says that columnist Candace Bushnell, a thin chain-smoker with implausibly blonde hair. 'I have some girl friends who'd go to a party and they'd met a footballer or something and they'd have sex with him in a closet, and I was always, "Oh my God! How could you do that?" ... That's so not me. I actually couldn't do that ... I'm very conservative.'

Born in waspy Connecticut to a family that came over on the *Mayflower*, Bushnell spent most of her twenties sipping cocktails, dating venture capitalists, and making sure her toenails were looking tiptop. 'We were glamorous,' she modestly admits.

Approached to write a column, she naturally chose to write about herself. Candace Bushnell became Carrie Bradshaw (note the initials). Hot-shot *Vogue* publisher Ron Galloti became hot-shot businessman Mr Big. *Sex and the City*'s warm and supportive sisterhood, Samantha, Charlotte and Miranda, are said to be a composite of Bushnell's blonde brigade. Though one observer has said that the real-life friends are actually more 'like cats in a sack, constantly trying to scratch each other's eyes out'.

SEX AND CITY
Essentials

Candace Bushnell's *New York Observer* column, 'Sex and the City', ran from 1994 until 1997. The TV series starring Sarah Jessica Parker screened from 1998 until 2004, and spawned two movies

DAVID COPPERFIELD

Charles Dickens (1812–70)

Charles Dickens never wrote an autobiography – so *David Copperfield* will have to do. Interested in the author's upbringing? Then read about David's father being imprisoned for debt, which forced the twelve-year-old to leave school and slave in a sweatshop. The same thing happened to Dickens.

Curious about his career? Then read about David's time as a legal clerk turned parliamentary reporter, who finally manages to become a novelist. Dickens's career path, precisely.

Or would you rather learn about his love life? It's a pretty safe bet that Dora – David's sweet but empty-headed 'child-wife' – reflected Dickens's dissatisfaction with Catherine, the somewhat dull first spouse from whom he separated after a few years. Even David Copperfield's initials are the same as Charles Dickens's – just reversed.

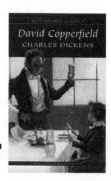

David Copperfield, by Charles Dickens, was published in 1850

STEPHEN COLBERT

'George W Bush: a great president or the *greatest* president?'

Such are the hard-hitting issues tackled on *The Colbert Report* (when its egomaniacal host isn't spruiking his latest autobiography or competitively priced jars of man seed). Distrusting books ('all facts, no heart') – as well as liberals, feminists and the French – the 'well-intentioned, poorly informed, high-status idiot' Stephen Colbert is a parody of pretty much every shock jock who's ever hosted a show on the Fox network.

First among them is the host of *The O'Reilly Factor*, author of *Culture Warrior* and *The No Spin Zone*, and owner of an ego almost as big as his salary. Right-wing political pundit Bill O'Reilly spends most of his time talking about right-wing political pundit Bill O'Reilly. About his clear-sightedness. His plain-spokenness. His decency. His common sense. To be attacked by Bill O'Reilly is to be reassured you're doing something right.

The Colbert Report airs at the same time as *The O'Reilly Factor* and parodies some of its segments. 'The Word', 'Inbox', 'Balls for Kidz' and 'That's the Craziest F#?king Thing I've Ever Heard' are a direct send-up of O'Reilly's 'Talking Points Memo', 'Factor Mail', 'Children at Risk' and 'Most Ridiculous Item of the Day'.

'If it wasn't for you,' Colbert once cheerfully told O'Reilly, 'this show wouldn't exist.'

Sir Dr Stephen T Colbert first appeared as a correspondent on *The Daily Show* in 1997. *The Colbert Report* premiered in 2005

TINTIN

Robert Sexe (1890–1986)

'Tintin' started out as 'Totor', a boy scout in charge of the 'Cockchafer Patrol'. (Yes, this also troubled me at first. Apparently it's a species of beetle.) A chubby insect enthusiast and doer of good deeds, this early version of the character appeared in *Le Boy-Scout Belge* magazine in the mid-1920s – and was mostly met with a series of yawns.

Rather more read about at the time was a real-life, boyish-looking outdoorsman – the French photojournalist Robert Sexe. He was all over the news after travelling through Russia, the Belgian Congo and the US on his motorbike, and being generally rather dashing and blond.

Tintin debuted shortly afterwards. He too is a roving reporter, with blond hair and a passion for motorbikes. His best friend, Snowy the dog, is called 'Milou' in French; Sexe's best friend was one René Milhoux. Furthermore, Tintin's first three adventures took place in Moscow, the Belgian Congo and the US – and some of the drawings in those comics resemble photos by Sexe.

So, yes, along with Hercule Poirot, Tintin has long been pretty much Belgium's only famous person. But the sad fact is he's French.

Tintin first appeared in *Tintin in the Land of the Soviets*, a 1929 comic by Hergé

ALI G

Quick quiz. What sort of person struts about with baggy pants and a thick Jamaican accent saying things like 'Dat's a lot of flava!' and 'Wassup?'

If you answered a middle-aged, middle-class son of a bishop, then you got dat straight. For reasons no-one's ever quite managed to establish, DJ Tim Westwood has managed to become the pasty white face of British hip-hop over the years. With signature catchphrases like 'We out!' and 'Drop the bomb!', he has his own radio show and production company, hosts *Pimp My Ride* on MTV, and knows all sorts of complicated handshakes.

You'll be glad to know that the former private schoolboy gets 'tremendous love out there, man, tremendous love'. But life can of course be tough on the streets and Westwood admits that some cats 'be hating on me'. The DJ has been beaten up at a party, and shot at by a passing motorist.

Comedian Sacha Baron Cohen has fired a few shots as well. 'We used to go to these hip-hop happenings and even then [Westwood] was kind of laughable. Once I found out that he was actually the son of a bishop, it became even more absurd.' Cohen's Ali G character may be da baggy-panted voice of da yoof but he also lives with his grandma in an irredeemably middle-class part of town.

Created and performed by Sacha Baron Cohen, Ali G first appeared on *The Eleven O'Clock Show* in 1998

TOMORROW NEVER DIES' ELLIOT CARVER

The real villain in Pierce Brosnan's third James Bond outing was, of course, the producer. The first film to be funded entirely by product placements, *Tomorrow Never Dies* was basically 90 minutes of 007 drinking Smirnoff Red Label vodka, driving a BMW Z8 and checking the time on his Omega watch.

Occasionally, we also got to see him battle Elliot Carver, a media mogul prepared to create all manner of chaos so that his newspapers can cover it the next day.

Screenwriter Bruce Feirstein says he modelled the bespectacled evildoer (who uses an Ericsson mobile phone) on Robert Maxwell – a UK press baron known for cozying up to Eastern European dictators, and being fairly ruthless with everyone else. Maxwell's mysterious death aboard a luxury yacht (was it suicide? murder?) led to revelations of shady business dealings and allegations of links with Mossad.

Carver's (apparent) death aboard a luxury yacht probably led James Bond to drink another Smirnoff.

Tomorrow Never Dies premiered in 1999. The movie starred Pierce Brosnan, Teri Hatcher and Jonathan Pryce

THE DEVIL WEARS PRADA'S MIRANDA PRIESTLY

Anna Wintour (b.1949)

It's possible to see *Vogue* editor Anna Wintour as a worthwhile human being. First, however, you would need to overlook her personality. Nicknamed 'Nuclear Wintour' by her colleagues (and 'cold-hearted shrew' by me), the scary-thin fashionista loves fur and hates fat. ('Most of the *Vogue* girls are so thin, tremendously thin, because Miss Anna don't like fat people,' said one of her employees). Working-class people aren't much liked either. ('We once had a piece about breast cancer which started with an airline stewardess, but she wouldn't have a stewardess in the magazine so we had to go and look for a high-flying businesswoman who'd had cancer.')

'You definitely did not ride the elevator with her,' says a former assistant of the notoriously haughty editor. 'She doesn't do small talk. She is never going to be friends with her assistant.' One later-jailed former employee of Wintour's even wrote a journal entry about wanting to kill her.

Another one wrote a book. Lauren Weisberger spent ten months making coffee for Wintour at *Vogue*, then wrote about it in *The Devil Wears Prada*. Like Wintour, her novel's icy magazine editor is a London-born, size-zero-thin trustee of the Met. Both editors also have a Texan partner, two children by a previous husband, and an inability to remember their assistant's names.

The Devil Wears Prada, by Lauren Weisberger, was published in 2003. The movie starring Meryl Streep premiered in 2006

FEAR AND LOATHING IN LAS VEGAS'S RAOUL DUKE

Hunter S Thompson (1937–2005)

Mathematics can be fun. Take Hunter S Thompson, for example, and add alcohol, marijuana and coke. Multiply the result by mescaline and you get … a slightly woozy Hunter S Thompson. Keep adding acid, however, then throw in some amyl nitrate and adrenochrome, and at some point he becomes 'Raoul Duke', the free-wheeling narrator of *Fear and Loathing in Las Vegas* and a dozen other articles and books.

Even Thompson was never quite sure where his alter ego began or ended. 'I am living a normal life but beside me is this myth, growing larger and getting more and more warped … I'm never sure which one people want me to be and sometimes they conflict.'

Fear and Loathing was certainly inspired by real events. Like Duke, Thompson took a few trips to Las Vegas in 1971 in the company of 'a 300-pound Samoan', and they certainly had a good time. (The real 'Dr Gonzo', a portly lawyer/activist named Oscar Zeta Acosta, was another big amphetamines fan. He disappeared three years later while travelling in Mexico.)

But Thompson seems to have spent most of his time 'feverishly writing' in his hotel room, rather than feverishly trashing it like the Duke.

Fear and Loathing in Las Vegas, by Hunter S Thompson, was published in 1972. The movie based on the book, starring Johnny Depp and Benicio del Toro, premiered in 1998

SCOOP'S WILLIAM BOOT

The writer Evelyn Waugh, says William Deedes, was 'a natural shit'. 'A fantastic snob' and 'a pig', with a 'deep inner contempt for everyone'.

He certainly had contempt for Deedes. That former journalist and politician almost certainly helped inspire the naive nature columnist in Waugh's novel *Scoop*. Prone to ornate sentences like 'feather-footed through the plashy fen passes the questing vole', William Boot is mistakenly sent to cover a war in Africa. Despite never quite working out precisely who is fighting who, or why, he somehow stumbles onto the 'scoop' of the title.

Waugh wrote *Scoop* in 1938, while covering Mussolini's invasion of Abyssinia for the *Daily Mail*. Among his fellow foreign correspondents was the dandyish, Harrow-educated Deedes, who had arrived at the train station with nearly half a ton of luggage, a scene parodied in the novel. 'My inexperience and naivety as a reporter in Africa might have contributed a few bricks to the building of Boot,' Deedes cheerfully admitted. 'I was young, I was unmarried, I could be insured at a very low rate ... Most of the office thought they'd probably never see me again, and at twenty-two ... I was dispensable.'

He became less dispensable over time. Later known as Lord William Deedes KBE, MC, PC, DL, he was the only Brit in history to work both as cabinet minister (under Harold Macmillan) and as the editor of a major newspaper (the *Daily Telegraph*).

In fairness to Waugh, by the way, we should point out that he didn't have a 'deep inner contempt for *everyone*'. Much less successful than *Scoop* (and quietly removed from circulation during WWII) was a companion non-fiction book expressing support for Mussolini in his efforts to 'remedy a savage black country'.

Scoop, by Evelyn Waugh, was published in 1938

ANCHORMAN

Jessica Savitch (1947–83)

America's conservatives think men and women belong together – but only recently has this applied to the news desk. In the 1970s, Philadelphia's KYW-TV became the first ever TV station to have a man-and-woman news team, rather to the man's chagrin. 'Change is always difficult,' former newsreader Mort Crim admits these days. 'There was [an] initial resistance to an upheaval of the newsroom culture.'

In a 1990s documentary, however, he admitted a little more. 'He still talked like this,' recalled *Anchorman*'s creator Will Ferrell, adopting an ever-so-solemn TV anchor voice. 'And he was saying, "Back then, I was a real male chauvinist pig." It just made me laugh … I called up my friend … and said, "We should write a comedy that takes place in the early to mid-70s … and they have to work with a woman for the first time. And they're just scotch-drinking, cigarette-smoking chauvinists who have to deal with this very capable female journalist, and they don't know what to do".'

In *Anchorman*, the male newsreader ends up marrying that very capable journalist. In real life, he spoke at her funeral. The life of America's first anchorwoman was far more drama than comedy. Drug abuse plagued Jessica Savitch's career, and an abusive relationship and two failed marriages (one to a closet homosexual who committed suicide) didn't help.

On 3 October 1983, Savitch made national headlines with a slurring, disoriented performance on *NBC News Digest*. Later that month, she and another man drove their car into the Delaware River, sank into the mud and died.

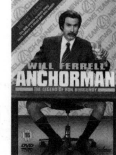

Anchorman: The Legend of Ron Burgundy premiered in 2004. The movie starred Will Ferrell and Christina Applegate

BRIDGET JONES

Helen Fielding (b. 1958)

Success can have its drawbacks. When perpetually single journalist Helen Fielding was asked to write a regular column about being perpetually single, her sense of dignity meant the answer was no. 'The idea of writing about myself in that way seemed hopelessly embarrassing and revealing.'

Being 'rather short of cash', however, she eventually came up with a compromise. Fielding would submit *anonymous* articles about an 'exaggerated, comic' character – 'Bridget Jones', a binge-drinking, chain-smoking, calorie-counting collector of self-help books and fuckwits. 'I assumed no-one would read it, and it would be dropped after six weeks for being too silly.'

Instead, as we now know, several million people read it. And saw the films. And are now looking forward to the stage play. When we think Helen Fielding, we may admire her weighty work on the *Sunday Times* and the *Telegraph*. We may note with interest that she has made documentaries in Africa, dated *Blackadder* writer Richard Curtis, and had two children with a producer of *The Simpsons*. But we're really just thinking that she's Bridget Jones.

Bridget Jones first appeared in 'Bridget Jones's Diary', a 1995 newspaper column by Helen Fielding. The movie starring Renée Zellweger, Hugh Grant and Colin Firth premiered in 2001

ALMOST FAMOUS'S WILLIAM MILLER

Kids these days get their ears pierced at ten and start loathing their parents at twelve. By sixteen, they're pretty much done with rebellion and studying hard to get into law.

In the 70s, things took a little longer. In *Almost Famous*, the baby-faced teenage journalist William Miller starts out as a stranger to the sex-and-drugs side of rock and roll. But then *Rolling Stone* sends him on tour with hard-living rock gods Stillwater – during which he falls in love with a groupie, falls out of virginity, and gets to know the whole teen rebellion thing reasonably well.

'Tis all true. Screenwriter Cameron Crowe was a youthful prodigy just like William, producing precociously brilliant music reviews when he wasn't skipping grades at school. Still *Rolling Stone*'s all-time youngest contributor, he went on tour at sixteen with the Allman Brothers Band. 'He charmed a lot of people,' *Rolling Stone*'s editor once commented. 'He was the "Aw, shucks" guy, [continually saying] "I'm glad to be backstage. I love this band".'

Penny Lane, the film's somewhat needy groupie, is partly based on Pennie Trumble, a saucy 70s 'band aid' who led a group of fans known as the Flying Garter Girls. (Her colleagues included Marvellous Meg, Sexy Sandy, Caroline Can-Can and The Real Camille.)

That character also got a few qualities from Bebe Buell. A former *Playboy* centrefold, and the mother of Liv Tyler, Buell is said to have slept with Iggy Pop, Mick Jagger, Jimmy Page, Rod Stewart, Elvis Costello, Jack Nicholson and Steve Tyler – and possibly even a few non-famous people too.

Almost Famous premiered in 2000. Written by Cameron Crowe, the movie starred Patrick Fugit and Kate Hudson

BARTON FINK

Selling out can come at a cost. When the character Barton Fink, a high-minded chronicler of 'the common man', abandons playwriting to pen a Hollywood wrestling flick, that cost involves waking up beside a mutilated corpse, sharing a hotel with a notorious serial killer, then watching his bedroom get engulfed in flames.

The real Barton watched his credibility turn to ash instead. A long-time left-winger, Clifford Odets made his name writing grim, bleak, political plays – the sort of tracts in which hardworking proles wake up amid squalor and decay, toil beneath the yoke of a capitalist oppressor, then trudge home for some stale bread and angst.

Things got a little more up-beat when he moved out west. 'Odets, where is thy sting,' wondered a fellow playwright, after yet another work about moderately happy people on a living wage. The criticism got rather more marked in 1952, however, when Odets appeared before the House of Un-American Activities Committee, denied any communist leanings, and avoided the blacklist by 'naming names'.

He died eleven years later, reportedly tortured with guilt and revulsion.

Barton Fink premiered in 1991. Created by the Coen brothers, the movie starred John Turturro and John Goodman

THE END OF THE AFFAIR'S MAURICE BENDRIX

Graham Greene (1909–91)

Not all popes spend their time praying. Paul II, for example, died of a heart attack while in bed with a pageboy. Benedict IX 'feasted on immorality' (particularly enjoying bestiality and orgies), while John XII snacked on incest, and turned the Basilica di San Giovanni into a brothel.

All of which may have been reassuring to Graham Greene, another Catholic with a soft spot for sin. The relentlessly devout writer was already busy with a wife, a mistress and 'a prostitute friend' when he met a housewife, and fellow Catholic, named Catherine Walston. She herself was seeing an American general, an IRA activist and a Labour MP. So naturally they started shagging right away.

In between taking her to brothels, Greene wrote to his 'dark-eyed', 'highly sexed' lover that he loved her 'wildly, crazily, hopelessly'. 'It was a hell of an affair', noted *The Independent*. 'Glossy, amoral, perverse, sexy, guilt-ridden, triumphant, selfish and self-absorbed; as dramatic and puzzling as a good novel.'

No-one's clear quite why the couple broke up but Greene at least got a good novel out of it. Dedicated to 'C', *The End of the Affair* blames a pact with God for the split. 'Sarah' promises to end the sin after 'Maurice' is injured by a German bomb, provided He lets the writer live.

And it's true that Catherine *did* sort of take to religion after Greene. She 'ended her life an alcoholic who enjoyed all-night drinking binges with live-in Jesuits and Dominican theologians'. Apparently she particularly enjoyed 'flirting with priests'.

GRAHAM GREENE
The End of the Affair

The End of the Affair, by Graham Greene, was published in 1951

CITIZEN KANE

A good way to make people notice something is to go out of your way to hide it. The world doesn't believe Citizen Charles Foster Kane was based on Citizen William Randolph Hearst because the filmmaker told us so. 'You know, the real story of Hearst is quite different from Kane's,' was Orson Welles's comment on the subject.

The world believes it because the media mogul went out of his way to suppress the movie, banning all discussion of it in his newspapers and doing his best to destroy the prints.

There's certainly a bit of Hearst in Kane. Their CVs are very similar – think ownership of thirty-plus newspapers and magazines, and one or two forays into politics. And *Citizen Kane*'s ludicrously ornate mansion, Xanadu, is a clear parody of Hearst Castle. But, unlike Kane, the real-life press baron was born wealthy, was not an orphan, and didn't spend much time feeling bitter and alone. Thrown out of Harvard for a prank, Hearst was actually a pretty chirpy character.

Citizen Kane's co-writer was also a pretty chirpy character – though he did carry a scar from his past. As a child growing up in Pennsylvania, Herman Mankiewicz treasured a bicycle he'd been given for Christmas. One day, sadly, it was stolen. For Herman, that lost bicycle forever represented the innocent delights of childhood – the happiest time of his life.

Its name? Rosebud.

Created by Orson Welles and Herman Mankiewicz, *Citizen Kane* premiered in 1941

Index

Picture credits

Bonarde Ucci, Caroline: p216
BrokenSphere, Wikimedia Commons: p191
Cadman, Steve: p150
Chris73, Wikimedia Commons: p195
Corbis Images: p2; p214; p235; p258; p260; p265;
    p309; p336
Getty Images: p69; p178; p183; p236; p238; p243;
    p244
Great Ormond Street Hospital Children's Charity: p36
Hausken, Randi: p48
Holland, M: p315
MDC archives: p344
Shankbone, David: p179
Richter, Franz: p183 (left)
Wad, Harry: p219
Van Pelt, Ted: p6
Wangtopgun: p202